The author is Professor of Government, Harvard University

D0982888

CAMBRIDGE STUDIES IN THE HISTORY
AND THEORY OF POLITICS

EDITORS:

Maurice Cowling, G. R. Elton, E. Kedourie, J. G. A. Pocock
J. R. Pole and Walter Ullmann

FREEDOM AND INDEPENDENCE
A STUDY OF THE POLITICAL IDEAS OF HEGEL'S
PHENOMENOLOGY OF MIND

Freedom and Independence

A STUDY OF THE POLITICAL IDEAS OF HEGEL'S
PHENOMENOLOGY OF MIND

JUDITH N. SHKLAR

HARVARD UNIVERSITY

CAMBRIDGE UNIVERSITY PRESS

CAMBRIDGE

LONDON · NEW YORK · MELBOURNE

Published by the Syndics of the Cambridge University Press
The Pitt Building, Trumpington Street, Cambridge CB2 1RP
Bentley House, 200 Euston Road, London NW1 2DB
32 East 57th Street, New York, NY 10022, USA
296 Beaconsfield Parade, Middle Park, Melbourne 3206, Australia

Library of Congress catalogue card number: 75-26273

ISBN: 0 521 21025 9

First published 1976

Printed in the United States of America by
Vail-Ballou Press, Inc., Binghamton, NY

Library of Congress Cataloging in Publication Data

Shklar, Judith N
    Freedom and Independence.

    (Cambridge Studies in the History and Theory of
Politics)
    Includes bibliographical references and index.
    1. Hegel, Georg Wilhelm Friedrich, 1770–1831.
Phaenomenologie des Geistes. I. Title.
B2929.S48   320.5'092'4   75-26273
ISBN 0-521-21025-9

CONTENTS

ACKNOWLEDGMENTS

Sections of chapter two appeared originally in 'Hegel's Phenomenology: An Elegy for Hellas' in *Hegel's Political Philosophy* edited by Z. A. Pelczynski (Cambridge University Press, 1971), sections of chapter three in 'Hegel's Phenomenology: The Moral Failures of Asocial Men' in *Political Theory*, vol. I, no. 3, August 1973 (Sage Publications Inc.), sections of chapter four in 'Hegel's Phenomenology: Paths to Revolution' in *Theory and Practice* edited by Klaus von Beyme (Martinus Nijhoff, 1971), sections of chapter five in 'Hegel's Phenomenology: Beyond Morality' in *The Western Political Quarterly*, vol. XXVIII, no. 4, December 1974. They are here reprinted with the permission of their respective publishers.

I have been fortunate in receiving much help in preparing the manuscript from many people who read and corrected it at various stages of its preparation. I would like particularly to thank Barbara Herman, Stanley Hoffmann, Arthur Jacobson, Harvey C. Mansfield, Jr, Patrick Riley, Nancy Rosenblum, Susan Shell, Dennis Thompson and Michael Walzer for their advice and assistance. Mrs Marian Adams and Miss Sally Cox helped me to transform a messy script into a readable typescript and I am grateful to both. For many years I have enjoyed talking and arguing about Hegel with two dear friends, George A. Kelly and John Rawls. I wish for their sake, as much as for my own, that this were a better book.

PREFACE

This book is both modest and ambitious. It is modest because it is only a commentary on another book, and indeed on only a part of the latter. It has been written specifically for students of political theory, both undergraduate and graduate, who have found Hegel's *Phenomenology of Mind* incomprehensible and who might, with the help of a guidebook such as this, manage to understand it more readily. It can never be easy. That is why even an interpretation that strives for simplicity, and therefore not for vulgarity, must be an ambitious undertaking. Hegel's work is genuinely difficult. Its subject matter is stated quite accurately in the title. It really is an account of the phenomena of the human spirit, a formal re-structuring of Europe's intellectual development. It is an historical psychology of the conscious mind, and also a justification of such a science. The subject is of such obvious importance and Hegel's execution of his project so instructive that even the casual reader knows that it deserves his close attention. Nevertheless he may feel defeated. In order to be of some help to him this commentary is written in plain American English and in as unpretentious a style as possible. It is devoted to only those chapters that deal with moral and political ideas. These, however, are of capital importance to the whole and, in fact, make up more than half of its contents.

In presenting Hegel's ideas I have generally followed the sequence of the chapters as they appear and have indicated in the footnotes the exact pages that are being discussed. I have departed from this procedure only in the first two chapters. The first one of these is an overview of the *Phenomenology*

as a whole. It is meant to give the reader an idea of the organization of the entire book and the trend of the general
argument. As indicated in the footnotes this chapter deals
only briefly with those sections that are taken up at length
later on. The second chapter, which begins the investigation
of political ideas, gathers together all the sections dealing
with ancient Greece. These actually appear at the beginning
of several of the later parts of the book, and are briefly mentioned again when these sections are considered. However,
the immense importance of the memory of Hellas to Hegel's
political thought could not be brought out by following his
organization. He has several introductions. By turning these
into a single one it is easier to grasp the structure of argument as a whole. The three subsequent chapters follow the
arrangements of the book very closely. I have, in these, been
more repetitious than one might like. In this I have followed
Hegel who began each section with at least one brief outline
of what was to come. Sometimes he did so more than once.
The reason for this is not difficult to guess. Hegel assumed
that the reader had to be prepared for the novel ideas which
he was going to face. This decision seems to me to have been
a very wise one, and I have taken my cue from Hegel. In
chapters three and four especially I have gone over many passages twice.

From time to time I have drawn the reader's attention to
Hegel's other works. This was done invariably to illuminate
or illustrate some point that Hegel discussed elsewhere perhaps more clearly or elaborately. I hope that these references
will be used and serve as an inducement to read Hegel's other
writings. *The Lectures on the History of Philosophy* covers
many of the same topics as the *Phenomenology,* often less ob-
scurely. The 'Introduction' to the former is a fine preface to
Hegel's philosophy in general and the study of Socrates is a
small masterpiece that no student of political theory can afford to ignore. *The Philosophy of Fine Arts,* especially those
of its sections that deal with literature, are an extension of
the pages devoted to the drama in the *Phenomenology.* Again
the *Philosophy of Right* cannot be fully understood without
a knowledge of the earlier work, as the many references Hegel
gave to the *Phenomenology* make evident. Where there is a

restatement of ideas, as is often the case here, I have noted it. Moreover, the discussion of hypocrisy is a simple continuation of the *Phenomenology* and I have, therefore, included it here as part of that work.

I have not considered the place of the *Phenomenology* in Hegel's work as a whole. My aim has been to elucidate a single work as a discrete entity. That is why references to his other books play such a very minor part in this commentary. Anyone interested in the logical bearings of the *Phenomenology*, especially its relation to the *Science of Logic,* should consult Stanley Rosen's *G. W. F. Hegel,* which in many ways complements the present volume.[1] I have in fact not added a bibliography because I would simply be duplicating Professor Rosen's. Anyone who thinks that he should read some general book about Hegel, before concentrating on any one of his works, might well try G. R. G. Mure's *The Philosophy of Hegel,* which is as reliable as it is brief and clear.[2] I have mentioned very few of the authors who have written about the *Phenomenology* and engaged in no debates with any of them. That is not because I have no respect for their work or because I have learned little from others. In fact, I owe a great debt to most of them. However, my hope is that the readers of this commentary will immediately turn to the *Phenomenology* itself and then be in a position to cope with the outstanding disputes and various readings directly.[3]

Again with my specific audience in mind I have used English translations whenever possible and referred to the most available edition of any work, whether by Hegel or any other author. These are not always the best scholarly editions, but they are the ones that most readers can actually find and use. I have no solution to the extremely trying difficulties of translation, especially from the German. The only translation of the *Phenomenology* that is now in print is far from perfect. Having tried to do better and failed, I no longer am so ready to heap scorn on the translator. I have used J. B. Baillie's translation throughout, quoted it when it seemed useful, para-

---

1. New Haven, 1974.   2. London, 1965.
3. H. B. Nisbet's transl. of Hegel's *Lectures on the Philosophy of World History* (Cambridge, 1975) with an introd. by Ducan Forbes arrived too late for me to use.

phrased when that seemed better. For those who have any German at all page references to the best German edition have been supplied in the footnotes. Some of the shortcomings of the translation are unavoidable. *Das Allgemeine* means the universal, the general, the common and the public. It is probably the most important single word in the vocabulary of the *Phenomenology* and Hegel used it in all possible ways. To translate it always as the universal is not the best solution, but it may be the most obvious one. This merely shows the scope of the difficulties confronting a translator. In two important cases, however, Baillie made unfortunate errors of judgment. *Gleich* means both equal and like and Baillie used the former too often. It should generally have been the latter, occasionally both. The reader should therefore try out 'like' and 'unlike' whenever he finds 'equal' and 'unequal' in the English text. Secondly, Baillie erred when he translated *Volk* as nation. It should read people. Hegel uses the word nation only once in the *Phenomenology*, in referring to the pan-Hellenic Pantheon. This is the only occasion when the various Greek peoples united to celebrate a common set of gods in a shared language. He chose, at that point, to emphasize that these polities were not states and that their nationality manifested itself only very occasionally as in the Olympic games. With these exceptions and a few other ones to be noted in the text Baillie will have to do. He is obtainable and not misleading in general, even if a superior translation can well be achieved. I remain grateful to him, in any case.

The real complexity of the *Phenomenology* is not the fault of the translator. It may not even be a fault at all, since it is simply inherent in Hegel's design. Hegel relied partly on the traditional vocabulary of philosophy. However, since his aim was to go beyond the latter, he also devised a new terminology to serve his purposes. Secondly, the book is written on two levels, one descriptive, the other allusive. The first is an account of the dynamics of the development of consciousness, from the most simple stage of sense certainty to the fullness of self-knowledge. Hegel regretted that the natural, direct philosophizing of the founders of philosophy, the Greeks, was no longer possible. They had been able to create philosophy naturally out of experience. Latecomers are of necessity educated by an already established structure of thought. Thus philosophy is now the creating and recreating of the history of philosophy. The *Phenomenology* offers an account of what such philosophizing implies. It is a model of the process by which we come to know what we have become. That is its structure. The content of that history consists, of course, of the great works of literature. Hegel assumed that his readers would have been educated as he had been. They would be perfectly familiar with the literature of Europe, at home with Sophocles and Shakespeare, Aristophanes and Molière, the Bible and Luther, Pascal and Voltaire. A total familiarity with French and German literature was simply taken for granted, as was a complete knowledge of philosophy, ancient and modern. To point to specific works would seem pedantic, perhaps even insulting, in writing for such an audience. So Hegel merely alludes to them.

No such readers exist now. I have done my best to draw the attention of students to the most important and necessary of the works to which Hegel refers so casually, but I may have missed some. I have not offered summaries of the works that come up. I did not wish to give a crude and false impression of their real character. I can therefore do no more than entreat my readers to hasten to acquaint themselves with the Bible, the classics of dramatic literature and the writings of the philosophers.

At the outset of the *Phenomenology* Hegel firmly reminds us that philosophy should not be edifying. It is not and should not offer spiritual uplift or gratify the demand for high-minded sentiments. The task of philosophy is to dispel illusion and correct incomplete and incoherent ways of reasoning. Hegel certainly took to this work with energy, and the *Phenomenology* is certainly not edifying. Its tone is angry and often sarcastic and the style polemical to a degree. Hegel could not have avoided that even if his contempt for the pious had been less explosive. The deepest underlying current in the history of thought is the struggle between reason's quest for truth and the mind's equally intense need for certainty. This perpetual war within the human soul can admit no compromise, and Hegel certainly suggested none. The central political theme of the *Phenomenology*, which gives

the present study its title, reinforced Hegel's polemical style
of thought and expression. The core of Hegel's argument is
that freedom is the identity of the personal goals of individual
citizens and the public ends of the polity as a whole. This is
a dynamic process in which the laws are created by each and
all, and are in turn expressed and realized in the minds and
actions of every member of the society. Such was Periclean
Athens in which a naive trust bound the citizens to their city.
The restless demands of reason were bound to break this
spontaneous state of confidence and to assert the destructive
force of individual autonomy. Since Socrates asserted the
claims of independent reason amid the ruins of the beautiful
city, the spirit of independence has dominated Europe's spiritual life, bringing it all its intellectual glory and little social
harmony. Indeed, the demands of independence outrun reason itself, for at their most extreme they dictate a flight from
the earthly world. Politically they culminate in the French
Revolution and its philosophical aftermath. Since most of
Hegel's contemporaries continued to oscillate between independence and dependence, each one perfectly satisfied with
his ideological certainties, Hegel saw many occasions for dis-
pute. He neglected none of these. I have tried to indicate
who some of his opponents were, and again I hope that
readers will take the trouble to read them.

No commentary can claim to be wholly impersonal. This is
an interpretation after all, not a textbook summary. I have
discussed Hegel as the successor of Rousseau and Kant rather
than as the precursor of Marx and Nietzsche, although he was
certainly both. I think it more illuminating to see how he
moulded the thinking of the past to his own purposes than to
reflect upon his influence on later philosophers, although
that also may help one to read him. The *Phenomenology* like
any great work of literature is written for us and we ought to
allow ourselves to be enlightened by it directly. 'Explaining'
it by seeking the 'causes' that may or may not have moved
Hegel to write it does not in fact tell us what he said. These
'causes' whether general and social or specific and personal
may help us to integrate what was said into a pattern of historical or psychological discourse, but they do not help us to
follow an argument or to think about it critically. Hegel tried

to teach us how to think and we have much to learn from that lesson. That he has been dead for some years does not seem to me to matter one way or the other. It is important only if one feels compelled to assess his guilt for crimes committed by some of his readers in our own century. I have not forgotten them, but I cannot see that anyone is guilty except those who performed these acts. There is no reason why Hegel should be discussed in terms of events in which he did not participate. The history of philosophy should not be a grading system in which we distribute good and bad marks to our predecessors. We learn by criticizing and rethinking, their and our own words and thoughts, not by placing them on a scale and assigning them their weight once and for all.

NOTE

B stands for *The Phenomenology of Mind,* translated and edited by J. B. Baillie (London, 1949), and H for *Phänom-enologie des Geistes,* edited by Johannes Hoffmeister (Hamburg, 1952).

I should like to emphasize that in the following pages 'autonomy,' 'independence,' 'liberty,' and 'self-sufficiency' are used interchangeably and carry the same meaning.

CHAPTER ONE

A TOPOGRAPHY OF
THE PHENOMENOLOGY OF MIND

What do we know? That is the great question of philosophy, ancient and modern. In his *Phenomenology of Mind* Hegel set out to answer that very question. In that respect it is a perfectly conventional philosophical treatise, but its resemblance to any other such work also ends with that. It is unlike anything else. For all his debts to his predecessors, Hegel wrote a totally original book, and it remains unique in our literature. That is largely due to its daring. Hegel undertook to explore in a single work every conceivable human experience that could be thought of as knowledge. Moreover, he did not limit himself to the forms and content of the various kinds of knowledge, but also considered their relationships to each other and to the transforming processes of learning to know. He thus combined a critique of knowledge with a psychology of the knowing mind. In the course of this fantastic project Hegel moved from an account of Everyman's simple awareness of knowing something to his realization that he must know himself if he is to know what knowledge is. From seeking this self-knowledge the individual is ineluctably driven to seek knowledge of what man generally, what humanity, is. That knowledge eludes him. Hegel then followed all the religious, ideological, theoretical, moral, cultural and historical dispositions of the mind that prevent it from reaching its end. Yet these failures are intellectually creative and instructive and in reviewing them we are led step by step to the door of truth.

Hegel's way

Ever since Socrates began asking his questions in Athens it has been the task of philosophers to show us that all our certainties are built on intellectual sand. Philosophers have generally been the enemies of spiritual peace and comfort. Hegel was very much a part of this tradition when he set out in the *Phenomenology* to reveal that 'mere certainty vanishes in favor of truth.' [1] Mere certainty is indeed the greatest obstacle in the way to knowledge, which for Hegel is synonymous with truth. That is a conviction that has united the most diverse philosophers through the ages. However great their differences, all can agree with Locke that those who 'are sure because they are sure' do not think well.[2] Whether it be myth, enthusiasm, piety, conventional belief or social habit that makes the 'sure' so certain, philosophers are determined to shake them out of it. To analyze an idea, even if inadequately, is bound to 'do away with its character of familiarity' and that is what counts. For, as Hegel went on to scoff, 'whatever is familiarly known is not properly known, just for the reason that it is familiar.' [3] The war between the emotional need for certainty and the intellectual demand for truth is the most constant theme of this book.

The 'sure' or 'familiar' are just general states of mind. Each philosopher tends to be aroused by some specific manifestation of unthinking habit. Official religion and inherited social beliefs had aroused the critical fury of Hegel's immediate predecessors, the men of the Enlightenment. To him it appeared that 'sound common sense' was the temple in which the dogmas of 'the familiar' were now enshrined.[4] That is not surprising, since, as he well knew, Hegel lived in a new world which was both secular and individualistic to a degree. The content of conventional thinking had altered, but not its laziness. In order to carry on the traditional mission of

1. B218; H133.
2. *An Essay Concerning Human Understanding*, Book IV, ch. 19, s. 8.
3. B92; H28.
4. B127–8, 176–8; H56–7, 100–2. Herbert Marcuse has particularly drawn attention to the way in which Hegel's philosophy 'destroys the experiences of daily life' in a radical way. *Reason and Revolution* (New York, 1941), 103–20.

philosophy Hegel had to concentrate on very novel targets of attack. He was determined to write a deeply upsetting book, and in this he certainly succeeded.

Personal independence was ever the delusion of Europe and since the French Revolution to the point of lunacy. Each individual was taken to be a self-reliant proprietor of the truth, or at least capable of becoming one. Common sense reigned supreme. Hegel thought this belief to be mistaken in every way, though he certainly did not regret the passing of the submissive attitudes of earlier ages. It was 'more to follow one's convictions' than to 'hand oneself over to authority.' [5] Unfortunately that change often only meant converting opinions once held on authority into personal convictions. In either case, opinion is merely opinion and dogmatism remains. Truth does not replace error just because clerical authority has been replaced by personal opinion. If there has been any gain, it is in the rise of scepticism which these changes encourage. Scepticism at least does 'make mind, for the first time, qualified to test what truth is.' [6] Scepticism, however, induces spiritual despair and paralysis, mental distraction and disintegration. The prevalent cult of individual conviction and of sentimental subjectivity thus stood unchallenged. Yet as Hegel was to say many years later: what is more obvious than the statement, 'This is what *I* think'? It is a pleonasm. Who, after all, can do your thinking for you? [7] If anything, it only proves that such thinking, because it is treated as a personal possession, is only an opinion. He illustrated the point with one of his awful puns. *Mein* (mine) has the same sound as *meinen* (to opine) in German and Hegel made much of that.[8] Nevertheless, he knew well enough that for anything to be true it 'must fall within experience and be felt to be true.' [9] There is no point in drumming the truth into a man's head. The past achievements of independence were not in question, but its limitations had to be demonstrated. For it was still only belief, not knowledge. Even if the old obstacles to intellectual self-realization had been overcome only yesterday, the time for criticizing the new dispen-

5. B136; H68.   6. B136–7; H68–9.
7. *Lectures on the History of Philosophy*, trans. by E. S. Haldane and F. H. Simson (London, 1968), I, 60.
8. E.g., B153–4, 279; H82–3, 180–1.   9. B800; H558.

sation had come. The French Revolution had pushed over a false religion and a decadent regime but it was also a hope lost. His own age was in Hegel's eyes only a time of transition.[10] However, because the changes that had occurred already were so immense, a wholly novel critique was required to deal with the new illusions. That it was needed was clear, for the truth was still unknown. Hegel, in short, had to be highly inventive if he was to perform the traditional functions of a philosopher.

The familiarity of good sound common sense views was not their only failing. The received ideas of the age, Hegel complained, were mostly empty generalities which referred to no experience whatever. Like Vico before him, Hegel saw Descartes at the roots of modern education which taught young people to deploy general formulae which they could not and did not relate to anything concrete or particular.[11] While the education of the ancients had gradually drawn pupils from natural to contemplative thinking, the moderns just stuffed their minds with ideas that existed in a wordy vacuum. Genuine experiences seemed to have been forgotten. If there was to be any spiritual vitality again, 'positive immediate existence' would have to become a part of philosophy, which now ignored it. The ancients had given natural experiences a philosophical meaning; the moderns must bring them back into their devitalized thinking.[12] It was for Hegel not just analytical geometry, as Vico had thought, but the whole tendency to use big words such as 'necessity' and 'essence' without even remembering what they implied in any specific context.

To break up these habits and to remind his readers that philosophy deals with the experiences of living beings, Hegel found that he had to employ a new vocabulary. He was neither the first nor the last philosopher to do so. Indeed Descartes had been able to celebrate natural reason only in a language new to philosophy: the simple language of daily life. Having mockingly dismissed his own education, and

10. B75; H15.
11. G. B. Vico, *Oeuvres Choisies*, trans. and ed. by Jules Michelet (Paris, 1855), I, 131–70, 221–35. All of Hegel's Descartes critiques, in fact, strongly resemble Vico's, especially in their concern for the anti-historical bias of Cartesian thought.   12. B94–5, 176–8; H30–1, 100–2.

with it past philosophy, Descartes sat down by his stove and began to ruminate in the most natural manner. At least that is how he presented himself in the act of thinking everything over anew. Hegel, now in revolt against the results of Descartes' reflections, which seemed to be as clear and distinct as they were empty, turned in reaction to another style of speech, to the language of intense emotion. Thinking was now an activity charged with feeling. It reveals, as such changes usually do, a revolutionary temper. Hegel's indifference to the classical distinction between passion and reason emerges at once in his choice of words. A great part of the novelty of the *Phenomenology* is due to his use of the language of the emotions to discuss the work of reason.

The 'science of the experience of consciousness,' which Hegel proposed to develop, was not concerned with some isolated faculty of ratiocination.[13] It was Hegel's peculiar gift to be able to show that we feel intensely when we think, that our whole being can be involved in this activity. To do this he had to write about it in passionate terms. Truth is a 'bacchanalia,' the 'instinct of reason' drives us on, even though consciousness 'suffers . . . violence at its own hands' as it 'destroys its own limited satisfactions,' The 'fear of the truth' cannot deter the conscious mind for long, for it cannot endure 'indolence,' nor will the 'gloating' of self-satisfaction stop it.[14] That is only a random sample of Hegel's style. Scepticism is suicidal, Christianity an 'unhappy consciousness,' sentimental morality ends in frenzy, and hedonism in baffled despair. The *Phenomenology* treats the conscious, thinking mind as it had never been discussed before. The cost of such novelty was high. There are as many interpretations of the book as there are readers. Even the calmest reader joins in the action to bring his own personality to bear upon its meaning. The book is both enormously readable and yet utterly obscure. One can only quote Josiah Royce's remark about it with utmost sympathy: '[Such] writers and their works must be treated with the same freedom they themselves exemplify . . . In the presence of the wayward, I too may be free to judge in my own individual way.' [15]

13. B144–5; H74–5.   14. B105, 138; H39, 69.
15. *Lectures on Modern Idealism* (New Haven, 1919), 141.

Conventional thought was to be shaken emotionally, but that was not all. The self-satisfied individualism of the day had also to be disturbed. In its self-reliance, its confidence in its self-made ideas, common sense showed a total ignorance of the part that culture plays in the development of thought. As Descartes had rejected historical knowledge, so everyone now took himself to be the sole creator of his own knowledge, unaware of his debt to his inheritance and to his education. Yet without these the individual mind is incomplete. No one can understand the process of knowing unless he is aware of his own place in the cultural whole and of all that the past has contributed to the present. Those who forget the past are not only doomed to repeat old errors, they willfully deny their own character. It was not the least of Hegel's ambitions to expose the folly of such privatization and delusions of intellectual self-sufficiency. Indeed the better part of the *Phenomenology* is devoted to reminding philosophers of the importance of culture and of social interactions in structuring all thinking.[16] Independent thought is not enough.

Clearly Hegel was a very angry man when he wrote the *Phenomenology*. His 'Preface' especially reads like an outburst of philosophical rage. It would have helped if he had possessed some of Voltaire's wit. To be sure, his determination to take philosophy into uncharted territory made it necessary for him to treat others critically, but Hegel was abusive and polemical to an unusual degree. That cannot be attributed only to his state of mind or temperament. Hegel in fact believed that the dynamics of intellectual change always involved intense conflict, and he meant to show that clearly. There is no change in the human mind unless there is some compelling motive for it, a shudder in the soul. People do not adopt new opinions unless they become convinced of the inadequacy of their previous ones. The most important experiences of consciousness occur when a thinker is driven to the abandonment of an accepted intellectual position because it has revealed its inherent limitations to him. He then resorts to more satisfactory ideas that do not suffer from the deficiencies that had destroyed the earlier ones, but this is not a lasting impression. Presently a different, but just as serious

16. B88–92, 274–5; H26–8, 177.

set of faults becomes evident. These successive failures all have something in common. Each one involves the discovery that its certainties no longer meet its own criterion for certain knowledge. Such self-realization is not a painless or calm change. Conflict is at the very heart of such development. The great experiences of consciousness are transformations, and they are violent as is all history, even spiritual history. It is an epic and heroes end badly, as do philosophers and their great deeds. Failure then was Hegel's topic and that greatly enhances the generally negative tenor of this whole work.

The experiences of consciousness though marked by failure at every turn are tragic, not futile. Its contests are between states of mind that are all valuable in some way. Although all go down in defeat, each one plays a necessary part in the development of the drama as a whole. Each one contributes something that is necessary for the mind's growth. Death is followed by reincarnation and disintegration leaves matter for reconstruction. The struggle for true knowledge is neither aimless nor shapeless. It is more like a voyage homeward, than one of interminably added discoveries.[17] The men who seek truth have a sense of where they must end. That is fixed: the mind's insight into what knowing is.[18] There is no stopping until that goal is reached and however indistinct, the travellers do have an intimation of where their Ithaca is. What they cannot foresee is what they will have to live through before they reach their destination. Nevertheless, the end to be reached is before them and it shapes and guides every choice made along the way. For this is not only a journey, but also a development, a process of maturing which ends with an understanding of the purpose and significance of the voyage. The development of human thought is an unfolding of our potentialities (what we are *in* ourselves, inherently) which we are spiritually self-driven to realize (to be *for* ourselves, to create ourselves actively).[19] The truth is no sudden revelation or accident. It is a 'morphogenetic process,' a gradual ascent that presupposes its end from the very beginning.[20] The 'know yourself' with which philosophy begins is also its aim and end, true 'self-consciousness' which we

17. B90; H27.   18. B137–8; H69.   19. B86, 140–2; H24, 71–3.
20. B90, 80–1; H27, 20.

reach only at the moment of fulfillment. Only *we*, who look back on the entire movement, however, can know that.

The *Phenomenology* is the science of these experiences. It is an account of consciousness' unfolding as a lesson in self-recollection.[21] The question that confronts the reader now is 'Whose recollections of whose experiences?' What mind is Hegel talking about? This psyche needs an identity. Certainly the sequences of intellectual experiences paraded before us do not mirror Hegel's personal development. Some are obviously wholly alien to him and are presented so as to reveal their full idiocy. Their importance is in their hold on the minds of others. Here Hegel is clearly a spectator, but only partly so. He is never a passive observer. He has arranged the order in which philosophies and ideologies appear and tells us what they mean. Even when the order is chronological (from Stoicism to Christianity) or when characters out of literature (*Antigone* or *Rameau's Nephew*) speak their messages to us, we are always aware of Hegel's organizing hand. The thinkers of the past are his raw materials, to be structured and placed. These experiences as such were all there, but Hegel has obviously altered them in a creative act of remembering. That after all is *his* contribution to philosophy. The episodes are therefore rarely given their original and usual titles and Hegel very rarely names an author in order to attribute any conceptions to him. He thus avoids the charge of distorting the outlook of any specific thinker. What he has done is to create models of minds. These are not pictures of his own mind, but they are his mental creations, structures he built out of pieces of other men's ideas. Only the whole is *his* philosophy. It is also the history of philosophy as a whole.

Thinking is, in this view, not a mental event, nothing that happens *to* us, but an activity, something we *do*. Ideas are human creations, not inflictions. The work of philosophy is to organize, clarify and extend specific spiritual experiences into increasingly comprehensive conceptions.[22] This is neither a sequential history not a judgment visited upon past ways of thought, but their intelligible re-ordering. The principles of ordering differ. One, the movement from sense per-

21. B76, 105–6; H16, 39.   22. B118–19, 143–4; H49–50, 73–4.

ception to self-consciousness, is borrowed from Kant. Sometimes Hegel depended on chronology. And occasionally, when he discussed moral attitudes, the pattern is psychological. In every case, however, Hegel has invented the links that tie his models of thought together. It is history as art, but since he does not defend his decisions they do seem arbitrary, though not random. The ordering is always made to seem plausible, even though there is no evidence to prove its necessity or advantages over other possibilities. To a degree this method of discourse is due to Hegel's determination to avoid certainty, to prevent his readers from taking any model and perhaps even his arrangements for granted. Philosophy has to keep moving. It does not, like religion, invent images to stimulate belief.[23] It does not, like morality, mathematics or common sense, simply declare propositions to be right or wrong, proven or unproven, true or false.[24] Only when a philosopher has completed his task, to show what knowing is, can he ask for acceptance. By that time he should have transformed rather than just convinced his readers. Certainly by the end of the *Phenomenology* one does realize, at the very least, that one has been forced into a wholly new manner of thinking.

Hegel's models of intellectual activity can best be called outlooks, points of view, philosophical attitudes or forms of consciousness. They are ensembles, occasionally caricatures, of historically known theories. We are thus not faced by Plato, Descartes or Kant, but by platonism, cartesianism, and the 'moral point of view.' Moreover, these composites have been so artfully put together by Hegel that their self-destruction and place in a sequence has been built into their very character. Change from one model to the next is thus made to appear as both a rational and emotional necessity. The science of the experiences of consciousness is thus a psychology of learning. It is not an empirical or descriptive enterprise. It is attributive. Hegel's models have the impulses and feelings necessary to give them intellectual mobility. Even in the case of recognizable historical forms of thought, he has added emotions and perplexities of his own invention to give them life and death. The past is not just there for us to pick it up like an object. It is a creation, a composition in

23. B72–6; H12–16.   24. B98–101; H33–5.

which the remains left to us are put into a symmetrical and self-educative whole. Hegel chose to make the past into a self-correcting process which does lead to truth in the present, or, at the very least, to enhanced self-knowledge. This is not just a dredging up of all that rests in our collective unconsciousness. It is a re-membering, a selective rebirth of deposits buried in us all, to be used in the creation of a new state of being.[25] Like birth it can come only in its own time.

Hegel's model in creating his characters out of the known past and arranging them with a view to a known final end was the classical drama.[26] The author and his readers, 'we,' are assigned the dual role of audience and chorus, participating observers, lamenting and warning as the spectacle unfolds. That the end and indeed all the events are known has always been a part of the experience of tragic drama. It is reliving the true, not a childish expectation of surprise and novelty. Nor is Hegel's, or any dramatist's, version of a tragedy the only possible one. The fates of Orestes and Oedipus can be redramatized in many ways. Hector has not died for the last time. Even comedy can be redone. Jean Giraudoux claimed that his was the thirty-eighth telling of Amphitryon's cuckoldry. 'We' who always know more than the heroes on the stage are still compelled to relive their experience and suffer with them as they meet their doom. We also move from a condition of 'both knowing and not knowing' to one of clear knowledge with Oedipus.[27] Indeed Hegel's drama of human consciousness bears a more than superficial resemblance to that of Oedipus the Tyrant. He is the man who having solved the riddle of the Sphinx has within him all possible knowledge. However, not until the end at Colonus may he know what he is and what his place in the cosmic order is, and even that remains enigmatic.[28] 'We' also, who have traversed the tragedy of the European spirit to the point of the French and Kantian Revolutions, stand at the door of some

25. B88–90; H26–7.
26. There are some illuminating remarks on these matters in K. R. Dove's 'Hegel's Phenomenological Method,' in W. E. Steinkraus, *New Studies in Hegel's Philosophy* (New York, 1971), 34–56.   27. B740; H513.
28. For an extended and marvelous interpretation of Oedipus along these lines, see Jean-Pierre Vernant and Pierre Vidal-Naquet, *Mythe et tragédie en Grèce ancienne* (Paris, 1973), 71–131.

final possible answer, which may also be the hour of death, of ending. We may know what knowing is.

The *dramatis personae* that Hegel puts before us appear in five discrete sequences or cycles. Before looking at them in any detail, an enumeration and quick review of these cycles may be convenient. There are five in all, called consciousness, self-consciousness, reason, spirit and religion, respectively. The first is natural mind, certain of the knowledge given to it by sense impressions. It moves on to describing and finally to explaining or understanding the evidence of the senses. These meet their doom in Kant's critique. Aware that knowledge depends on conceptions devised by its own self, the mind turns inward to seek self-knowledge. It is now self-consciousness. That ends in a state of utter subjectivity. This first and basic cycle, the cycle of consciousness, is the primary and fundamental cycle of the human mind in search of certainty. It is the course which individual minds confronted by an impenetrable world, by 'things' that are just 'there,' follows over and over again. The second model is the cycle of self-consciousness, of the mind's effort to arrive at self-knowledge. The account of this experience is essentially a psychological and social one. It is again a tale of woe, for no real self-knowledge, no answer to the question, 'What is mankind?' is found. This is also a repetitive cycle, but with variations, for self-consciousness is usually structured by social experiences, mostly painful duels. It begins when the ego recognizes itself as desire for both self-sufficiency and communion with others, as it seeks knowledge. The ego can remain integrated even though it be complex, but the possibility of a split between its two aims is always there. A series of historical experiences shows us how that division of the self in fact occurs and why independent, asocial men cannot end it. It begins with the separation of men into masters and servants and with the pursuit of self-sufficiency by the stoical and then sceptical consciousness. The rift becomes a gaping abyss in the isolated Christian 'unhappy consciousness,' which vainly seeks to find a community away from this vale of tears in some distant 'beyond.'

In due course, a part of that unhappy mind, 'reason,' liberates itself from this faith and in a third cycle returns home to earth to seek its truth there. The wounds inflicted by the splitting of the ego, however, persist. The projects of 'reason,' both in its theoretical and practical phases, are all defective. They traverse the same path as the natural mind, repeating the primary cycle, and end in subjectivity, isolation and aimlessness. The failures of reason are particularly afflicting because reason goes on, from observing nature, physical and organic, to looking at man as if he also were a 'thing.' The lowest point the human mind ever reaches is that of pseudoscience, of phrenology, one of the rages of the last century. From there, as Hegel saw it, a mind can only go up. He just turned from it to a new series. For there are two kinds of reason, theoretical and practical, scientific and moral. In Hegel's account there is no obvious connecting link between these two, but there is a similarity: both forms of reason are dissociated and subjective. Both come to dead-ends. In turning to models of morality Hegel began a new chapter, in effect a new cycle of reason. Again the basic cycle of consciousness sets the path, but only vaguely. It is actually altogether novel. Here the models still proceed to their own disintegration, but it is an entirely new, emotional experience. It occurs when these moral minds find that they neither can nor wish to actualize their standards. Subjectivism is too self-centered for success. Its social capacity is limited to withdrawal or overt hostility. From this point on the various models are held together only by Hegel's undeviating effort to expose subjectivity in all its deforming manifestations. That becomes a guiding thread of the *Phenomenology*.

There is now also a new tone. In the parade of types of subjective morality the models do not just reveal their character as they come and go. They are confronted at the very outset by a model opposed to them. Perhaps in order to show that subjectivity was not an unavoidable limitation of human nature, Hegel at once put in the contrasting picture of a free people in a harmonious community. It had once existed in Athens, where 'I' and 'we' were spontaneously at one. That 'happy state' may never be consciously achieved, but it is a beacon. It hovers as a memory over this cycle as it moves from the hedonistic man to the Kantian, autonomous self-legislator. Freedom and independence, ethics and autonomy,

community and self-sufficiency confront each other throughout. This contrast between freedom and independence is
also with us as we go to Europe's public values since the end
of the polis. The development of this social mentality is the
fourth cycle, that of culture. Its typical forms all find their
culmination in the French Revolution, in Kantian moralism
and in a world still incapable of reaching an ethical consciousness comparable to that of Antigone and her people.
Hegel's classicism was neither that of radical republican political theorists, nor that of the aesthetic romantics. The former
had hoped to revive the civic spirit of antiquity here and
now. That hope had turned into a bad joke in the mouths
of the Jacobins. Hegel did not believe in a return to the
past, and he did not admire the military–pagan civic ideal of
modern republicans. The spontaneous harmony of Periclean
Athens was his utopia. However, political education remained
his concern, not the aesthetic, asocial romantic yearning for
an age of beauty. He was far from blind to Greek art (the
polis is, among other things, a city of beauty), but for the
present Athens had to serve as a reminder of a political
possibility, not an aesthetic one. It is made to stand in
contrast to the present disarray of public life.[29]

The fifth and last cycle is that of religious belief. It is brief
and serves only to prove that religion has been replaced by
philosophy which has realized self-knowledge, that is, knowledge of mankind as it has created itself in time. This knowledge is mind's final homecoming and there can be no doubt
that it is a return from the exile created by Christian other-
worldliness. Philosophy is the heir of the Christian sense of
the unity of mankind, but it knows that unity to exist in
time, here and now, as history. Collective self-knowledge has
now been achieved, and the intellectual defects of subjectivity have been overcome. The isolated mind knew neither
its own cultural character, nor its own past. It cut itself off
from communication with others past and present, and be-

29. The unromantic and anti-Christian quality of Hegel's Hellenism has
been explained particularly well recently by Walter Kaufman in his
Hegel (New York, 1965), 41–60, 102–7, 273–8. This may also be an appropriate place to mention my debt to his annotated translation of the
preface to the *Phenomenology*. To see the entire context, Henry Hat-
field, *Aesthetic Paganism in German Literature* (Cambridge, Mass., 1964).

cause it did not think of itself as 'we' could not attain the truth of retrospective knowledge. Hegel, in remembering, reunited us with the spiritual past which defines both what we are and what we know.

With this end before us, the structure and passage of Hegel's models become intelligible and coherent, even though it is not a self-evidently necessary arrangement. Hegel offers no argument for or against any of his selections, choices and imputations. We can take or leave his account of the experiences of consciousness. The expectation appears to be that we will be altered by it. That, to be sure, is the impact one expects from a drama. However, we need not be dominated by Hegel. He leaves us at what he took to be the end of an era. However, the actualization of knowledge, the creation of unity in social action, was still in the future of the 'world-spirit.' Behavior had not yet caught up with knowledge. It evidently has not done so yet. The mind's journey has not been completed then or now. We can therefore still join Hegel in his voyage or try a different route. At least he has left us some notion of the aim of such an enterprise. History is not one damn idea after another, but self-knowledge. It is not a mindless recital, but the imposition of present, self-generated concepts and purposes upon a chosen past. If it were just 'there' it would be a mere chaos. To make it intelligible is to create the past. That certainly holds a threat of arbitrariness. We are, however, saved from that danger by the communal character of both the recollected past and the activity of remembering it. It is this that makes it possible for us to recognize at all the difference between knowing and not knowing ourselves. The philosopher as hero measures himself against those whom he joins, his fellow-strivers, past and present, and intellectual history becomes a spiritual community and a philosophical ascent.

The search for certainty (consciousness)

If the *Phenomenology* is a journey that is not wholly complete then it is the path traversed rather than its end that matters most to us. We can now begin to follow Hegel more carefully. How did he begin to think about the experiences of the spirit in search of knowledge? The first, most primitive question put by the mind is 'What am I sure of?' [30] That is all the 'natural' mind asks. That question is its only thought. Descartes had already investigated the mind to find what one could be sure of and had found that only the consciousness of thinking remained. That is all that natural reason can claim as its one certainty. Hegel also thought that it was possible to reach an irreducible minimum point in the psyche's reflective experience, and one even more 'natural' in its certainty than Descartes'. This mind has its certainty not in the self-awareness of thinking but in pure sense experience. It is sure as sure can be of what it sees and touches. 'The bare fact of certainty is there,' and that is all. Such a mind is indeed pre-linguistic as Descartes' isolated thinker is not. We really have nothing but felt certainty here – a pointing to this, here, now. As soon as this mind is made to prove its certainty, it must act like a human being and speak. Language, however, is its undoing. For language is more realistic. It is inherently conceptual and reveals that without 'hereness' (space), 'nowness' (time), 'thisness' (matter), and 'I-ness' (man) there is no way of communicating particular sense experiences. Language moves us instantly from the specific to the general. Language is, moreover, not only communication, though that is its primary aim. It is also creative. Words have symbolic significance as well. We may endow things with any meaning we wish. Language uses things as symbols. Indeed even animals know that things are not just here now, but are useable. They eat them. We have other uses for bread and wine. They can stand for Ceres and Bacchus, for the fertility of the earth and the ecstasy of wine. Their symbolic function in the Christian Mass need only be evoked.[31] Language then reveals what man really is, communicating and creative.

30. There are several very fine discussions of the 'Consciousness' section available now. The most remarkable is Hans-Georg Gadamer's 'Die verkehrte Welt' reprinted along with several other useful studies in H. F. Fulda and Dieter Henrich, eds., *Materialien zu Hegel's 'Phänomenologie des Geistes'* (Frankfurt am Main, 1973). Of all living writers on Hegel, Gadamer seems to me by far the clearest, the most learned and the most illuminating. Another helpful essay is Charles Taylor's 'The Opening Arguments of the *Phenomenology'* in Alisdair MacIntyre, ed., *Hegel* (New York, 1972), 151–87. There are several other helpful articles in this collection of essays also.   31. B149–60; H79–89.

The end of our quest is implicit at its very beginning, but that is only something *we* who are well beyond bare sensation can even suspect.

Even as pure sense-being, man is driven by an 'instinct of reason.' It manifests itself in mythology, in art, but above all in the creation of knowledge.[32] It is a basic drive that keeps us moving. If this is what separates us immediately from other animals, it is speech however that reveals this to us. What is mere fodder to an animal is god to a speaking, creative being. Our very capacity to think is displayed only in language and it is only there that we store our thoughts so that there is a continuity in thinking.[33] It is only in speaking that we become aware of thinking as an activity that orders and categorizes mere impressions. Language which is inherently universalizing forces the mind from the particular to the general. Consciousness cannot escape that movement. The natural, bare mind that lives in primitive certainty of sense-knowledge is thus a fiction. Anyone who thinks that this is a model of the human mind will discover his mistake as soon as he gives it a tongue. It is therefore inaccurate to say 'I feel, or I think, therefore I am.' It is rather 'I speak therefore I am.' [34]

⟋ The next model of the mind is more modest in its claim to certainty. It is the model of common sense that is ready to settle for things as it finds them and to 'grasp' them. It attributes a very high degree of probable certainty to that knowledge. It is still sense evidence but with due concessions made to language.[35] It tries to overcome the mute perplexity of pure sensation when it is forced to speak, without abandoning sense-certainty altogether. It no longer looks upon itself as a mere receptacle of sensations. It does something and that is quite an advance. It takes truth to be there to be perceived, but it accepts the possibility of inaccuracy. However it can hold on to enough of what it sees and touches by describing it thoroughly. It 'grasps' the properties of things by cataloguing them. Of these it is at least sure. The language of description, however, proves surprisingly complex. It can-

32. *Lectures on the History of Philosophy,* I, 82.
33. *Science of Logic,* trans. by A. V. Miller (London, 1969), 31–2.
34. B660–1, 716–17; H458–9, 496.   35. B163–78; H90–102.

not rest with simply adding up qualities (hard, white, sweet = sugar). It must for the sake of accuracy account for the relationships between the qualities of particular objects. Then it must distinguish between different objects (hard, white, sweet = poison). It must also cope with alteration in both cases. To do so it must employ such terms as identity, likeness, difference, unlikeness, cause, and effect. None of these are properties of any object whatever. Above all the need for explanation imposes itself. Why is one set of qualities' make-up sugar and why does it vanish in water? Description is self-destructive. It forces the mind to go beyond. Common sense finds itself divorced from the objects it tried to grasp by describing their properties. It is merely a healthy instinct of reason expressing its need for order and classification, but it remains crippled by its demand for mere certainty, rather than for truth.[36]

Common sense, so ready to accept the 'given,' the data of describable objects, has now been badly shaken out of its certainty. Its claim to find certainty flounders when it finds itself trapped by conceptual thought, by causality, contradiction, identity and their like. It has fallen short of its own criterion of validity. 'Grasping' is no better than was mere pointing. The mind in search of that satisfying feeling of certainty turns to analysis and to explanation, to 'the understanding' of chemistry and physics. This is still a belief in knowledge as consciousness of objects lying outside us, but not as mere sense evidence. That is an immense leap because the primitive hyper-empiricism of the natural mind and of common sense has been given up. Not only are the natural sciences an offense to common sense, they evoke modes of thought wholly remote from it. Idealism is a necessary response to the scientific approach to nature. The 'understanding' embraces both. Here Hegel was on solid historical ground. Whether we think of Plato, Descartes, Berkeley or Kant, idealism is inseparable from the context of the natural sciences of its time. The understanding is thus a volatile ensemble including the natural sciences and idealism.[37]

To understand nature is to go inside, beneath and behind the observed objects. One must stabilize the experience of their constant change. Chemistry, for instance, looks into sub-

36. B285–8; H186–9.   37. B180–1; H103–4.

stances to find the 'forces,' the actions and reactions of their component parts to account for all that cannot be adequately ascertained by mere description of externals. These 'forces' are now understood to be the real, although invisible, being of all matter. To be sure these forces are known only indirectly, as they manifest themselves in physical change. Strictly speaking there is only the idea of 'force.' To understand an object is thus a perpetual shifting from its invisible 'inner' forces to its external appearances. The changes observed in the 'data' are thus understood by referring them back to the 'play of forces.' The 'data,' however, are regarded as mere appearances of this underlying reality. To some people this scientific understanding means that all appearances are just illusions. The world of things loses all its credibility for them, since it only reflects something unperceived. Because they cannot absorb that 'beyond,' it is for them a void. It has no place in their consciousness. These are the prisoners of Plato's cave, aware of its uncertainties, but unable to leave it. The man of science is not among them. He tries to penetrate the 'beyond,' to find explanations for physical order. The play of forces must be understood in terms of something outside it. Since these interactions are an endless flux of causes and effects the understanding seeks stability by measuring and defining the forces at play. That is the function of explaining.[38]

To explain the experience of flux is the task of physics, the science that establishes the laws of matter and motion. It imposes rules upon the unstable, chemical, 'inner' structure of things. Initially these are part of theistic assumptions. A lawgiver regulates the physical world, and is, as it were, in charge of the flux of forces which is now subsumed under laws emanating from a 'beyond.' That view does not last. The laws, whatever their ultimate source, must explain the natural world directly. To cover all the plays of forces requires a multiplicity of laws to embrace all the relationships and distinctions between forces. As more of these are noted more laws must be devised to fit all regularities into the universal order of laws. Not only must causality, interaction, velocity, time and space in general be legalized, but ever more specific

38. B182–93; H105–13.

plays of forces must be fitted into the pattern of rules. With this multiplication of laws the specter of an endless process again arises. Moreover this process of explanation is tautological. These laws are not imperatives, orders issued by God, nature or any other agency, but descriptions of observed recurrences. A law is a generalization about repeated instances of a sequence of events; it does not command it. Any new instance is 'explained' as falling under the rule, the describing norm thus set. The laws of electricity are generalizations drawn from the observation of numerous cases of lightning. Any new occurrence of lightning is then explained by referring it to the law of electricity. It is circular. Moreover, the basic laws of nature, especially the law of causality, do not really stand above the flux of forces. Causality merely registers its manifestations. The human mind remains aware only of the flow of change. It has come to no resting point; it cannot yield the stability that explanation seeks.[39]

The political overtones of these remarks are not made explicit, but surely they are present. Hegel knew very well that the age of science was not far advanced in either Athens or in modern Europe before there were sophists to notice that law apart from force is nonsense. Above all the laws of society like those of nature are not decreed by any deity or by nature. Laws reflect the interaction of forces in nature, and the display of power in society. The world of nature is one of unstable flux, of changing and interacting forces. Thus also is society an arrangement of power between men of force. Yet Hegel no more than Protagoras or Hobbes was inclined to slander law. It is the truth of the understanding. This idea of law is the understanding's immense advance and an enduring contribution to human thought. The modern state is the political truth of the age of science. It expresses our most immediate sense of reality. For Hegel, unlike Protagoras and Hobbes, there was more to be known, but what consciousness has now achieved is scarcely negligible.[40]

There are discernible echoes of Berkeley's critique of Newton's metaphysics in these pages.[41] Idealism had known

39. B200–1; H118–20.   40. B193–203; H113–21.
41. Berkeley, *A Treatise Concerning the Principles of Human Knowledge*, ss. 101–33, and *Of Motion*. Hegel was as unfair to Berkeley as Kant had

for some time that the sciences that establish predictable probabilities cannot directly yield laws of causality. Hegel went on from there. Not only were many so-called laws of nature tautological, but that explanation itself is a process of endless regression. That emerges from the law of 'forces.' To explain the play of forces a law of attraction and repulsion is posited. The interplay of forces must, it is said, involve a positive and a negative force. However, every negative force acts as a positive force and vice versa. It is a distinction that is no distinction. Again every cause is the effect of some other cause and so the difference between cause and effect is merely verbal. The law of causality mirrors only an unending succession of 'whys' and 'becauses.' Like and unlike simply keep changing places in the process of explaining which is just 'an ebb and flow of change.' [42] To establish a stable understanding of the world of flux a new set of laws will have to be devised in order not only to register flux but intellectually contain it. To gain certainty about change one must skip from flux to a non-fluctuating mental world, that is, a supersensible order that is the complete opposite of the world of appearances. This is the inverted world of Platonic 'ideas' and also of mathematics. These are not generalizations about occurrences, but static statements of the pure intellect.[43]

If one were to be literal about the inverted world, white would be black and sweet would be bitter there. No one has ever said such a silly thing, of course, and Hegel knew that perfectly well. The only 'inverted' world ever invented was not the reverse of the flux of nature, but of 'another sphere of experience,' politics. The turn to the social aspects of any shape of consciousness was, for Hegel, the decisive moment. All defects become evident at this point. He was to return to this crucial juncture again and again. For though the specific experiences are different in each case, the illuminating power of social phenomena is recurrent.

The inverted world is a utopia. It is the nowhere that is

been, but he did not accuse him of reducing experience to illusion, but of failing to integrate experience and conceptual thought. He therefore simply left the former to empiricism. Kant, *Critique of Pure Reason*, trans. by N. K. Smith (London, 1961), and Hegel, *Lectures on the History of Philosophy*, III, 364–9.

42. B201–2; H119–20.   43. B203–4; H121–2.

the exact opposite of the here and now. Plato's *Republic* is indeed the archetype of all future utopias. It is the 'idea' of a city, a 'true' city, seen by the pure intellect which makes it possible to establish the standing of all the false, ephemeral cities. In the latter revenge is thought to be the appropriate response to injury. Socrates, however, argues for the very inversion of this belief. It is better to be injured than to inflict injury. The man who injures another really harms his own soul and he may even suffer in the next world thanks to his self-inflicted deformity.[44] The injured party has really benefited. Is punishment a disgrace in the actual city? It is an honor in the inverted one. A crime may seem very evil in the former world, but if it has a good intention, which is what counts in the inverted city, it is really a good deed. We have now, not unexpectedly, moved from Plato to Kant. For Kant, who in many ways was critical of Plato's theory of ideas, fully appreciated and admired their social import. The *Republic*, he noted, was the model of what we must strive for as moral men, a city in which wisdom has replaced punishment as the source of order. Here Plato's ideas are not pseudo-explanations, but objects of aspiration. The purpose of utopia is to move us upward and onward toward justice.[45] Hegel deliberately began by ridiculing the upside-down world because he did not share Plato's or Kant's obsession with justice. Only in the sphere of politics will men take a nonsensical upside-down world seriously. No scientist needs a world where hydrogen is oxygen, but political philosophers seem to find it quite reasonable to invent laws that are the antithesis of actual laws. They do it because they do not really wish to know what culture is. A crime is not wrong because of the criminal's intentions, but because it is an unlawful deed. It merely activates the law which by punishing the offender wipes out the irregularity and returns to its quiet and normal authority. The conflict between the individual and the community has been overcome, and the law having asserted its primacy, remains in undisturbed supremacy. Only the criminal is the 'inverter' of reality, for the law is real, it is the expression of the spirit of a culture, of a world. The law 'is.'

44. That is the chief burden of Socrates' outburst against Callicles in the *Gorgias*.   45. *Critique of Pure Reason*, 310–13.

The criminal, even the greatest and best, Socrates, is merely an individual who 'inverts,' or refuses to abide by, the public law, the only one there is, made by men collectively.[46]

The inverted world and its laws that are no laws, but a rebellion against law, collapses because it also has no basis apart from the experience of flux. It also is fluctuating, for it defines itself as the opposite of the actual world and so has no existence apart from the latter. It is dependent upon its changing antithesis. There is nothing 'above' appearances, just as the criminal (the inverter) is defined by and a part of the actual law he breaks. The upside-down world is the fluctuating world challenged, not another world at all. It also is a distinction that is no distinction. The recognition of the unity, the singleness, of the flux and its opposite is, however, a novel experience for consciousness. The self-contradictions of the inverted world bring a new thought to the mind: infinitude. The consciousness of distinctions that collapse and of opposites that coincide raises the notion of infinity, even without the experience of the inverted world. The interminable regression of causality is enough to force us to 'think flux,' to think contradiction and paradox.[47] The mind as a whole clearly contains all these, as well as the idea of infinity as part of the process of explanation.[48] This is the infinity which is merely an interminable repetition of some single self-contradiction, a paradox from which the mind recoils.[49] With this, as with Kant's antinomies, the human mind is at the limits of understanding and forced back upon itself. It becomes self-conscious as it begins to examine itself.

Throughout these adventures of the understanding, *we,* who have read Kant, are reminded that this mind still does not know that the objects it seeks are not out there, but are its own artifacts. It is the mind itself that imposes distinctions such as space, time and motion, laws of nature and 'ideas' upon itself in order to know phenomena. The reason why explanations are so pleasing is really that the mind always meets itself in them. It is a form of self-recognition. When the

46. B204–6; H122–4.   47. B206–7; H124–5.   48. B204–10; H126–7.
49. Hegel held Zeno in high esteem and insisted that his paradoxes, especially those of the infinite divisibility of units and of motion, remained insoluble. He is clearly offering his own version of these paradoxes here. *Lectures on the History of Philosophy,* I, 208–9.

upside-down world collapses the mind is finally brought face to face with its own activities. When it sees itself unable to rise above the flux of cause and effect it discovers the idea of infinity. That also can be mathematically understood, but infinite regression is a terrible shock to a mind that still wants certainty. The mathematical world view has become a threat not only to common sense, but to the understanding itself. A wholly new outlook must be found. The cycle of consciousness, which now is completed, is the primordial, the basic, the primary pattern of the mind which is repeated over and over again, whenever the mind has to find immediate certainty. It recurs in the career of modern rationalism and in religion and many other occasions. It is the treadmill of incomplete knowledge.

While Hegel never mentioned Kant's *Critique of Pure Reason* he presupposed that his readers knew it all along. Moreover, the sequence of experiences attributed to 'consciousness' is wholly modelled on Kant's examination of these theories of knowledge. The difference is also clear, for Hegel did not argue with other philosophers. He showed why their views were psychologically intolerable to a mind in pursuit of certainty. That is especially clear in the reactions he attributes to the understanding when it finds itself doomed to knowing only the infinity of repetitions. The final stage of the cycle of consciousness is now at hand. Here he leaves Kant as we move on to self-consciousness. It is the mind aware that it generates the categories of thought required for knowledge itself. It knows that it is self-structuring and self-determining. The veil is gone and mind has found itself behind it. The self must now confront itself. The ego is now what it was unconsciously all along: the object of its own knowledge. It has found itself behind all appearances.[50] The quest for certainty has become a search for self-knowledge. The question 'What do I know?' has ineluctably been changed into the question 'What am I?' At last mere certainty vanishes in favor of the search for truth.[51] With self-consciousness, as Hegel called this state of mind, we have reached 'the native land of truth,' its home.[52]

At first the self is aware of itself only as thinking, or as

50. B212–13; H218–19.　51. B218; H133.　52. B219; H134.

Fichte put it, the ego divides itself into ego and non-ego so the first can make the second the object of its thought. This non-ego is what the understanding externalized as something to be explained. Now the self is alone with itself. It is left with the bare tautology, ego = ego, and it experiences itself as pure desire, desire for self-knowledge. Self-consciousness is its own dynamic project, 'for itself,' and it has a long journey ahead.[53] *We*, who look back upon the first steps of that process, know that the mind as thinking has an unending life, as the process of continuous creation and recreation. Life is the whole that divides itself into individual forms which have an independent being, but which perish to be absorbed in the process of new creation. Every member of a species dies, but in reproducing itself, creating a new self, perpetuates the life of the species. Each genus, as part of the whole, goes through the same process of development. Only life itself is permanently itself. As it goes through the process of articulation and absorption of forms it is self-creative. Life is not that aimless infinity of flux, that 'away and away, for ever and ever,' but a morphogenetic process of self-projection, self-absorption and growth.[54] As a whole life is more than the sum of its parts. It is these as well as the process of creating and destroying them, in which it merely preserves itself.[55] The active ego is a form of life, that is why there must be desire. For as Aristotle had noted long ago without desire there is no human activity. Desire is not a part of the soul as Plato had thought, least of all a low part thereof. It is present throughout the psyche. It is the soul's motion. When all else has been stripped from it, the ego knows only itself and only as pure desire.[56] It must find an object to know. Desire as unmixed self-awareness can only be a manifestation of life. I am aware of myself as living. Life is experienced as a psyche-in-

53. B220–1; H134–5.
54. B80–1; H20–1. *The Logic of Hegel*, trans. by William Wallace (Oxford, 1892), s. 28.   55. B221–4; H135–8.
56. B219–20; H135. Hegel's debt to Aristotle from this point on is immense. It is one of the few that he was always gratefully ready to acknowledge. His admiration for *De Anima* especially was unlimited. He thought it the best, indeed the *only* book on the subject. *Hegel's Philosophy of Nature*, trans. by A. V. Miller (Oxford, 1970), ss. 378, 389; *Lectures on the History of Philosophy*, II, 180–206. For Aristotle's remarks on desire, see *De Anima*, 415b, 432b–433b, *Nicomachean Ethics*, 1139a–b.

motion, as desire. Death as immobility is its only possible alternative. Desire is the psychological sign of life, as bodily movement is its physical mark. Life for Hegel was much like Aristotle's unmoved mover, the origin as well as the end of all striving. It spread itself in a process of self-division into genera and species. Every living thing can be known by its place in this general pattern of life. As a rose can be known only as a plant, so man can only know himself as a member of the human species. The human mind which is the highest form of life is itself self-moving and as such generates genera and species in thinking. It creates the categories of thought and as such is active living and indeed the highest point of its perfection. For life is entelechy.[57] At some point self-creation will cease. All this is immanent in the ego's awareness of itself as desire, but it is not knowledge for the ego. The process of its development toward self-realization has not even begun. Desire as such is not thought even. It is rather the most primitive point from which knowledge can and will emerge. It is the active beginning of truth, as the 'natural' mind that begins with certainty was not. It is the germ of the true model of the mind. The rest of the *Phenomenology* is concerned with recollecting the voyage of the desiring ego as it painfully works its way toward knowledge.

Having come to the end of the experiences of mere consciousness we are now ready to move on to the next cycle of the mind: self-consciousness. At this point we can already discern the enormity of Hegel's task: to create a dynamic psychology of the thinking mind as it suffers defeat and renewal through the ages. The implications of a philosophic discourse that imitates the drama, rather than mathematics, are also becoming clearer now. The difficulties are great. There are no justifications for any positions here. Just a presentation. Hegel scarcely advances any reasons for imputing these particular experiences to consciousness. This is no Socratic effort to reveal confusion and bring others to see their own deficiencies. Neither is there a defense of various propositions by logical proof or illustrations or examples, or evidence of any sort. These, finally, are not meant to be hypothetical models

57. B220–7; H135–40. *Lectures on the History of Philosophy*, II, 156–63, for Hegel's dependence on Aristotle's *Physics*.

awaiting substantiation. These are true portraits of our experiences and if we fail to recognize them as such that is due to intellectual immaturity or faulty development. The unconvinced stand accused of 'false consciousness' and an inability to recognize the path their own minds took or ought to have followed. Anyone who sees strengths and advantages in the superseded stages is self-condemned. For he has been confronted by the necessary and real movement of the human mind. This is not like the difference between truth and error. For this history of consciousness is not something external to us. It claims to represent our spiritual history. An inability to identify oneself with that is thus a special sort of deficiency: 'false consciousness,' spiritual self-denial, and self-illusion. We have come to know its penalties. Hegel, to be sure, had a defense. He goes on in the *Phenomenology* to show the disadvantages of every other picture of the human mind.

What are we? (*self-consciousness*)

The second stage of the human mind is inherently social. To know itself the ego must generalize itself, get to know itself as part of a species. The set-backs and disasters that the ego experiences in its ascent to truth are rooted in its very structure. The desires of animals are limited to self-preservation. They are, as Aristotle put it, nutritive. Creativity and reason are no part of their desiring. The desiring ego is also in part self-maintaining. It turns inward to preserve itself. Here is the source of all our selfishness and greed. Hunger is the obvious physical analogue of this spiritual desire. This is the solipsistic, self-imprisoning desire of the ego that cannot go beyond the knowledge that ego = ego. It is doomed to traverse the cycle of natural consciousness over and over again. It can never go through the door to knowledge. Nevertheless this desire is not just a futile activity of the ego. It is also the source of individuality, of the absolute difference between each human being and every other. It is thus a necessary force within the ego, required to keep each psyche in that state of tension which is its enduring character. For calm self-absorption is only part of the ego's desires. The ego is also erotic and creative. As life is both passive endurance and active stirring, so is the desire of the spirit. Sexuality is the physical analogue of the erotic ego. This erotic ego desires to project itself, to externalize itself, to reproduce itself and so to escape from the confines of the given. It is not content merely to consume, it desires to recreate itself. It seeks another self-consciousness, in order to become 'we,' even as both remain egos. The erotic ego enters into communication and interaction with a projection of its own self, with another self-conscious being. To know itself the ego cannot stop with pure solipsism. For real self-knowledge each ego must confront itself as another, external self. It must face another human being in mutual recognition and communion. As the passive ego looks for the security of certainty, so this erotic ego dares to aspire to truth. Each is an inherent part of the human psyche desiring knowledge.

The desiring ego, because it has different possibilities open to it, is always in danger of self-division or inner disruption. Survival and reproduction, consumption and creation, selfhood and otherhood are not inherently incompatible, but they certainly can diverge. And that is what has occurred. The rest of the *Phenomenology* tells of the experiences of the divided self. If Hegel has so far offered us a psychology of the conscious mind in its search for certainty, we now get a psychology of its efforts to reach truth. Since this is the erotic activity of the ego Hegel is much more explicitly historical now. The figures we meet are constructed directly out of the known historical past of human thinking, from Homer to Christianity. For history is the realm of erotic expansion and the recollection of these efforts. In seeing a divided self as the psychic root of history, Hegel was not unlike Rousseau. The latter had also found a passive, purely self-loving ego in nature which is overcome by its own driving self-perfecting powers. The latter transforms man into a being dependent on others, not only for survival, but for his very sense of his own identity.[58] This erotic self, though it is the source of all culture and morality, is also competitive and restless, and Rousseau was mainly concerned to find ways to contain its destructive powers. Hegel attributed a very similar structure

58. For an account of the importance of Rousseau for Hegel, see G. A. Kelly, *Idealism, Politics and History* (Cambridge, 1969), 29, 336, 340–2.

to the ego, but he saw erotic energy as an ascent. In this respect more akin to Plato than to any other thinker, Hegel
pictured the possibility of erotic love as arising from immediate satisfaction to fraternity, to political activity and ultimately to philosophical thought. He had learned from the
Greeks that all culture is erotic. Eros brings nature and custom together. The desire for knowledge of self and then of
another become also the desire for the good and for harmony
in a polity.[59] That is the road open to the erotic ego. Its
actuality is less exalted. History is the scene of its failure to
reach its destiny.

The first move of the erotic ego is to impose its awareness
of its own other self upon another ego. It projects the passive
side of the self upon the other. The active ego only sees an
object to be consumed or used in order to ensure its own
existence. The other confronted ego has exactly the same
attitude. Each looks upon the other as a threat to his own survival and imitates it. That means a battle to the death of one
or the other. This is a struggle of pure self-assertion, the duel
between epic heroes. In the course of this battle, however,
each one must realize what he and the other are. Each is a
free agent. For only a free being could choose to risk his life,
rather than to submit to another. The duel alters the self-
consciousness of each combatant and each must now project a
new self upon the other. They now mutually recognize each
other not only as persons, but as men. This is the moment of
truth when men know each other for what they are: alike and
individual in their freedom. It is a fleeting moment, since this
recognition occurs in the course of mortal combat. If one
hero kills the other the battle must be repeated, since the
other has been reduced to a thing. This is the treadmill of
history. More significantly the defeated hero may be enslaved.
Again, he is made into a thing, but a continuing relationship
is established with profound implications. We now have
masters and servants, and with it the view that only some
men are free. Between the free and the bound there is no
erotic relationship, no recognition. The possibility of a single
humanity of 'we,' of communion, is lost. Out of the struggle

59. Again for Hegel's debt to Aristotle, see *Lectures on the History of Philo-
    sophy*, II, 145–50, 202–5.

of master and servant a new self-consciousness is eventually born, that contains both of these discordant elements. It is the self that thinks of itself as both free and unfree, and which culminates in the 'unhappy consciousness' of Christianity.[60] It passes through Stoicism and Scepticism to a state in which the believer is free in the 'beyond' but unfree in this world. He is at home in neither one.

The Christian consciousness is an extreme state of self-division. One half of the ego experiences itself as pure nothingness, as utterly worthless. The true self and home of the erotic ego is in a 'beyond' where all men will eventually be one. The life below is but a pilgrimage. Since the 'beyond' is unreachable, this self is always 'unhappy' and dissatisfied, and only aware of itself as a soul lost. It is a mind that does not really think at all. Lost in piety and devotion, it senses the spirit as something out there and yearns for it. Whatever may be of value in work or enjoyment down here is attributed to God and is received gratefully as a gift. However, even in giving thanks for grace the self remains aware of its own existence as a mind that thinks and cannot, for all its longing, lose itself wholly in God. This is such a terrible threat to the unhappy consciousness that it attributes its continuing selfhood to the work of the devil. The self is now a battleground between the god-fearing self and the devilish self. Asceticism and self-deprecation seem to be of no help. The best cure is to give up all one's own powers of willing and deciding altogether to another agency: to the Church. The ego is thus stripped of self-consciousness and reduced to a thing. As long as the 'unhappy consciousness' still thanked God directly for grace it retained some measure of independence as a conscious self. When it gives itself up to the Catholic Church its spiritual life is reduced to 'meaningless ideas and phrases.' However, life is not that easily destroyed. Where there is consciousness there is some spark of reason. The spirit reserves a place for reason, even though the 'instinct of reason' and faith are at war with each other. Reason finally turns its back upon 'the beyond' and the two live utterly apart.[61]

In this contempt for Catholicism, which never abated

60. B229–51; H143–58. Since this section is treated at length in the next chapter, it is mentioned only briefly here.   61. B251–67; H158–71.

throughout his life, Hegel showed himself a man of the Enlightenment. He was nineteen years old when the French
Revolution broke out and he had absorbed some of the attitudes of the eighteenth century in all their original intensity.
If he became more tactful in his words about Christianity in
general in later life, his dislike of the Church and the medieval age remained undiminished. Unlike the pre-Revolution-
ary atheists, however, Hegel had a very deep sense of the
enduring wounds that the 'unhappy consciousness' had inflicted on the European spirit. Even when it had been liberated from the shackles of Catholicism, the end of the religious
spirit was far off. The goal of the erotic ego had been put out
of reach for ages to come and it was not yet home.

The search for objective knowledge (reason)

The difficulty of freeing the mind from the burdens of the
Christian legacy are best appreciated when one examines the
thought of just those men who strove most valiantly to establish the rule of reason. Even they cannot reintegrate the
ego sundered so radically between an erotic striving for the
'beyond' and the passive ego left to cope here below. Cartesian philosophy and modern natural science certainly think
of themselves as indifferent if not hostile to traditional religion, yet they are its legatees in one respect at least. They
think of the human self as a 'thing,' an object of thought and
eventually of observation. To be sure, they do not despise or
reject the natural world. The new consciousness discovers the
world as its own new and real world which in its permanence
possesses an interest for it.[62] We have returned to our earthly
home at last. However, this has been achieved at great cost
to the spirit. The new third cycle of consciousness is not only
'objectifying,' it is also wholly isolated. Reason appropriates
the world for itself in total forgetfulness of the path it has already traversed. It exists in a historical and psychological
vacuum. This is the epitome of independence. Having
wrenched itself free from the 'beyond,' reason also turns its
back upon its past, upon history, upon culture and indeed
the very idea of development.[63] It clings to the one and only

62. B273; H176.   63. B274–5; H176–7.

intuitive certainty that can escape the devastating doubt by which it achieved its liberation. The self knows that it is, that 'I am I' or that 'I am because I think.' I observe myself thinking and so I am a thinking thing, the object of my own cognition. Others stand next to me conscious only of their own thoughts. No one realizes that this state of mind is a cultural manifestation, a stage in 'the world spirit,' or of our history, and that it will, in due course, be overcome. Not to know this is, in fact, the very core of Cartesian idealism.[64] The scars left by the 'unhappy consciousness' are evidently deep. The rationalist eye is still averted from much of its real home.

The new rationalism with its one pure intuitive certainty is initially an extreme idealism. It has no direct link to things at all, and indeed finds considerable difficulty in accounting for the relation between mind and body. It produces only different formulations of its one category: thought. It is pure idea, and only one idea at that. 'Things' are at most postulates. Yet rationalism quickly turns into its own opposite, simple empiricism. Hegel clearly used Kant's distinction between 'understanding' and 'reason,' his present topic, for purposes all of his own, but he agreed with him about Descartes. Kant had already observed that to know that 'I think' is to make thought dependent on some external stimulus, since one always thinks of something.[65] Hegel made the same point psychologically. The 'thinking I,' which is all that is known, has appropriated external impressions and these are accepted since they are its very own. It is back again to *'mein'* (own) and *'meinen'* (opining).[66] The path of mere consciousness is to be retraced, for this rationalism is still only the instinct of reason, not reason fully developed. It is not like the instinct of animals which 'ends with self-feeling.' The instinct of reason is reflective, but it is still the drive of the uncommunicative, consuming ego, even if it be aware of itself. Its knowing is an appropriation and it knows itself as knowing only things external to itself. The rationalist has absorbed, or possessed, mere 'things' out there.[67] It is the best mind can do all by itself, as an intellectual entrepreneur.

64. B275–6; H177–8.   65. *Critique of Pure Reason*, 337, 378n.
66. B276–80; H178–82.   67. B297–8; H196.

'We,' who have already followed the cycle of consciousness, know where this empiricism must end, but rationalism out to 'repossess' the natural world does not. It observes things joyfully. It does not know that these observations will have to become abstracted conceptions and that eventually these will lead back to the conscious self. Reason resists this implication and it does not, in fact, leave off observing. The ego absorbed in things continues to prevail and the moment of true self-consciousness is postponed.[68] Instead the instinct of reason, following the cycle of consciousness, comes back over and over to the solipsistic dead-end of 'ego = ego' from which it simply turns away by taking up a new field of observation, by discovering a new science. And this can go on and on.

The instinct of reason begins its observations with description and classification. Linnaeus comes to mind. Classification requires some analysis of the 'data' to be so ordered. With that the observer must move on to explanations of their properties and their relationships to each other, that is to causality.[69] Laws expressing the observed causal regularities are then framed, and these are understood for what they are. They are not mistaken now for 'oughts.' What is effective is valid and that suffices. There is no inherent need to defend it, if probability of recurrence is all that is demanded. Probability is not truth, but it is enough for observing reason. Experiments can be and are repeated and that is all that the laws of cause and effect need.[70] There is no loss of certainty here, as in the case of the understanding. What does happen is that the instinct of reason by expressing its findings in mathematical terms and by turning to such concerns as electricity and velocity loses touch with sense-observation. '[The] testing of the law in every sense-particular cancels the merely sensuous existence of the law,' and it universalizes them so that they 'express' a non-sensuous element of sense. The notion of 'pure law' emerges from the process of experimentation.[71] The instinct of reason does not, however, stop to worry about the philosophical implications of this aspect of its work. It simply turns to another field of observation: to biology.

Hegel offers no proof for this psychological change in sci-

68. B281–3; H183–5.   69. B283–8; H185–8.   70. B288–92; H188–92.
71. B292–3; H192–3.

entific orientation. There is no historical or psychological evidence to suggest that the abstractness of physics drives experimental science to biology. There is, to be sure, nothing wrong with thinking of scientific curiosity as an insatiable appetite that takes in whatever can be observed. Hegel could just have left it at that, but that would not have satisfied his model of the dynamics of human consciousness. The mind must move toward the self, that is its given end. And so the limits of physics must be made the occasion for turning the mind, clinging to its thinghood, toward biology. This must be the next step in the sequence that leads on to the final dénouement of 'objectifying' reason. Moreover, Kant had turned from the critique of physical science to consider our knowledge of organic nature, and this progress may well have structured Hegel's thinking. For he also meant to establish a relation between natural and human purpose. What follows might therefore best be read as a dissection of Kant's *Critique of Judgement* rather than as a critique of biology.

Every organic being is an indivisible living whole. All its component parts have a function in maintaining this whole. The description of any organism must therefore be teleological. As Kant had noted, not even the organization of a blade of grass can be adequately understood in purely causal terms. Even this modest organism must be considered teleologically to account for the part that each of its features plays in the structure of the whole. Since, however, we cannot on the basis of any knowledge available to us impute purposes to nature as a whole, the prevalence of purpose in each organism must remain a puzzle to us.[72] Causality will serve to explain the relationships between organisms and between any organism and its environment, but not the organization of the organism itself. We are therefore simply forced to accept the limitations of human reason here. Nature remains inaccessible to us in some degree. The best we can do is to attribute an 'inner' and an 'outer' existence to organisms. The 'inner' is to be treated teleologically and the 'outer' as subject to the determinations of cause and effect and measurement. The consequences of this separation in Hegel's view

72. *Critique of Judgement*, trans. by J. H. Bernard (New York, 1951), 222–4, 236, 248.

led observing reason to treat the 'outer' character of organisms as expressions of the 'inner.' Describable properties, such as sensibility, instability, and reproductivity are first presented as responses to external stimuli. They are subject to causal explanation and measurement. However, these properties are said to have a bearing on the 'inner' structure of an organism and on its self maintenance, but this cannot be observed. To cope with this unobservable nexus, reason invents a bridge. It simply takes the 'outer' to be the manifestation of the 'inner.' The latter can thus be ignored, the organism be treated as a mechanism and the two aspects kept apart, as Kant had said one must.[73] To Hegel this procedure seemed less a recognition of the limits of reason than irrationality.

Hegel had already expressed his preference for the Aristotelian view of life as entelechy, and it comes as no surprise that he returns to it here. Organic nature, life, is a self-moving and self-developing, end-directed, purposive process. Instead of isolating each organism and then dividing it up into an 'inner' and 'outer,' each one should be looked at as part of a species and then genus. By reproducing itself each organism contributes to the greater unity of which it is a member. For each is a manifestation of a species, of a genus and of life as such. As life is purposive so the self-preserving function of each part of each member is purposive ultimately. One must expand rather than contract one's conception of organic life to cover the entire earth horizontally and vertically until the place of each organism within the whole of living nature has been established. No one ever believed more firmly than did Hegel that the whole is prior to its parts. Life must be understood as an ensemble of species each of which contributes to the process as a whole by preserving itself in its integrity. Purpose not causality must therefore be the primary conception in approaching organic nature.[74] We have every reason to go beyond the bafflement of Kant. And indeed Kant did so, even if only very tentatively, by suggesting that we could hypothetically impute purposes to nature when he came to consider human history. To account for the

73. B294–321; H193–216.
74. It was a conviction in which Hegel never wavered. See *Lectures on the History of Philosophy*, II, 157–63. B321–5; H216–19.

possibility of human progress he ventured to guess that nature, though hardly generous to mankind, did indirectly support human perfectibility.[75] That was also Hegel's preoccupation. He made it quite clear that the life of mankind is purposive beyond mere survival. A man is a man as a member of a species, of mankind, in just the same way as a rose can be truly known only as a flower. There is, however, he hastened to remind us, a vast difference. The purposes of nature determine the being of every species except mankind which creates itself. That is why history is not like nature. It is made by self-determining free individual agents. The purposes of organic life stop at the level of the human species. There nature ends and history begins, an altogether different and unique form of life, the free life of the human spirit.[76] Both individually as free agents and collectively as an historical species, men stand outside the order of organic nature.

While Hegel had a point in noting the conflict between teleology and causality in biological thought, it cannot be said that he contributed much to the philosophy of organic forms here. That may well not have been his primary purpose in any case. He may well have been more interested in establishing the structure of ideas that reason brings to the observation of human nature. It is the study of man, psychology and above all those earliest forms of behaviorism, physiognomy and phrenology, that were the real objects of his concern. The contradictions of the categories of biology are a step toward the exposure of more glaring intellectual defects. Hegel had only contempt for Schlegel's rhapsodic philosophy of nature and his own ideas if not very profound were at least sober. Their main aim was in any case to establish the enormous difference between the processes of nature and those of history.

The next step taken by observing reason, Hegel argued, is again a sort of escape. In its puzzlement over the dual character of organisms and in its inability to turn from mechanical to purposive thinking, the instinct of reason turns inward. It feels forced to consider the human mind, since organic

---

75. *Idea for a Universal History from a Cosmopolitan Point of View*, trans. by L. W. Beck in his *Kant On History* (New York, 1963), 11–17.
76. B326; H219–20.

nature is so baffling. This again is not the history of science, but Hegel forcing his model of the movement of consciousness upon it. The first effort of reason now is to establish 'laws of thought.' That can be a purely formal epistemology. If a content were to be supplied to such a methodology it would have to be a history of knowledge.[77] We know from Descartes that history is just what this method of thought intends to avoid as insufficiently objective. The 'laws of thought' are therefore to be determined by an observational psychology. As usual description is the first step. The faculties of the mind are enumerated and classified. Then these 'bags of faculties,' which is what men now are, are compared to each other in terms of the strength and intensity of their faculties. These differences must now be explained. Their causes are sought in the environment. The climate, culture, religion, in short, the whole state of the world, is seen impinging upon each human organism to make it whatever it is. The 'inner' structure is here treated as the effect of external pressures. The great difficulty is that this does not explain the differences between people, each one of whom seems to react in his own way to a common environment. Each one seems to be in a different situation, or perceives his situation in an individual way, and internalizes it in a fashion peculiar to himself. 'Inner' and 'outer' man seem to remain apart. One would apparently have to consider not only what the general environment does to the individual, but also what the individual experiences and makes of it. That would mean two portraits of each man, one a picture of specific small world constructed by and for the self and another of the all-encompassing world that is said to affect him. The persistence of individuality appears to defy the psychological necessities postulated by the laws of an environmentalist psychology. The 'inner' and 'outer' man refuse to coincide in the picture of 'man the machine.' What has been left out is the universal element of mind, that which makes the individual a human being who works and speaks and has a purposive life in relation to others of his kind. That is however a part of the ego closed to observing reason which knows only 'things.' [78] As

77. B329–31; H221–3.   78. B332–6; H224–7.

in the inverted world of the understanding, reason shows its worst failures when it concerns itself with human conduct.

Unable to settle the universal laws of environmental psychology, the instinct of reason gives up its effort to explain external man. It turns to the 'inner' sphere, or to be exact, to its external manifestations which are all that can be observed directly. These, according to the 'science' of physiognomy, which was very popular in Hegel's day, are found in facial expressions. It is slightly more sensible than palmistry, Hegel observed, since we can register our feelings on our face, while the lines on our hands have no discernible relation to our mind. Beyond that there is little to choose between the two. Unhappily for the discerning physiognomist we can express, conceal or fabricate emotional expressions with our faces. These are means of communication, a language which we share and control, not the automatic manifestation of some mysterious inner force. Like the palmist the physiognomist is only looking for a short cut to Solonic wisdom. That sage had taught that it is only after death that a completed life can be known in all its dimensions. The physiognomist forgets that work and speech know nothing of an 'inner' or 'outer' man. Communication involves a whole person. It is interaction. A man is known to be a scoundrel or a decent fellow not by his facial expressions or 'inner being,' but by what he does and says to those with whom he shares a system of communications and shared meanings. We may not always be able to say or do exactly what we intend to, but these failures do not imply some mysterious inner being crying to be let out. Although the founders of physiognomy tried to get away from the materialistic environmentalism of Helvetius and La Mettrie with its 'man the machine,' they also failed to establish the identity of the individual. For they also looked at man as an isolated and static being – a 'thing' that does not grow, alter or interact with others.[79]

The low point of observing reason's view of man comes when it accepts the unreliability of facial expressions and turns to phrenology. This 'science' was generally accepted by the most advanced opinion for decades after Hegel wrote.

79. B338–50; H227–38.

This was no straw man. One need only recall the influence of Cesare Lombroso on criminology to recognize how important a part measuring skulls played in the development of the social sciences. It was Lombroso's belief that by measuring the skulls of prisoners one would determine who was, and by implication who was not, a criminal type. Traces of this sort of reasoning are, in fact, by no means extinct now. In any event phrenology, the science that measured skulls to know the character of man, was very much alive in Hegel's day and his rage is not incomprehensible.

The argument of phrenology is simple. The brain is the mind. Its shape and size, pressing upon the cranium, gives the latter its characteristic bumps. By measuring these one can, therefore, know the shape of the brain which determines the character of a man. Since the brain cannot be observed, one discovers the 'inner' being of a man by observing its external expression, in this case, the bumps on the skull. These are known, and define a man. In short, to all intents and purposes a man is his skull-bone. Since not all men with criminal bumps actually commit punishable acts, phrenology does not claim that the bumps cause behavior. They only demonstrate a general disposition. The trouble is that not only is this theory of brain activity a mere guess, there is also no causal link between bumps and behavior. It is not the bone that actually writes poems or robs the poor. Like 'the state of the world,' skull bones do not explain the behavior of men throughout their life histories. 'The individual can be something else than he is in his original internal nature and still more than what he is as a skull bone.' [80] Men change, but their bumps do not. That would be true even if phrenology were more than a bad guess. For not only do men learn, the character of their acts is not defined by their shape and physical motions. A man is not a thief or a poet because he makes certain motions or has a particular shape, but because he performs specific socially recognized acts and speaks in a mutually recognized manner.[81]

The instinct of reason has now reached its nadir. It has come to the ultimate implication of the view of man as a 'thing.' It began with observing the self as a datum that

80. B364; H248.   81. B351–67; H239–50.

thinks and ended with defining it as a bone. Is observation itself not also the work of a bone? Is the instinct of reason itself not a bone? Do bones communicate? Are we really bags of bumps? Such a level of silliness Hegel thought could not be endured. Reason must surely reverse itself now. There is nothing to be done now, but to repent. He may have been overly sanguine, for once. The assumption that the coincidence of two constant factors must imply a causal relationship had quite a future still. For Hegel, however, the story ended with the skull bone. He was also sure that he knew how we had come to this. It was the doing of the 'unhappy consciousness.' It had renounced the independence of man and so had induced men to think of themselves as 'things' to be looked at. The life of the ego ceases to be creative, and reason and knowledge are taken to be possessions. In fact, men are implicitly rational and knowing. Self-knowledge is its own purpose and the end of its own activity. To recognize that fully was not within the capacity of observing reason, which is now stuck in the consciousness of being both a thing and something other than that. Such is the psychic disintegration which the 'unhappy consciousness' has bequeathed even to modern rationalism.[82]

Rationalism is not the only remnant of the 'unhappy consciousness.' It has left an even deeper mark on practical reasoning, and this can be seen even in moral attitudes wholly at odds with any possible Christian teachings. The erotic half of reason that asks 'What shall I do?' is aware of itself as just as dissociated and just as passive as the theoretical self that asks 'What do I know?' This practical self is no longer a thing, but it is not social or active either. It does not actualize its own norms, because it fails to generalize itself; its aims are drawn from introspection. Modern practical reason is the product of private self-examination and private cogitation.[83] For we are not free members of a free people. That is a situation which we have not yet attained and may never reach. Ancient Athens is our only image of what such a life might have been. It is an intimation powerful enough to give us a

---

82. B368–72; H251–4.
83. B374–453; H255–312. As this section is to be treated at length in a subsequent chapter, I shall pass over it very lightly here.

ʰdeep sense of what is missing in a world of dissociated individuals, but it can give us no grounds for believing that we shall eventually recreate this 'happy state.' An isolated ego cannot perform the work of a social self. It is only the latter that recognizes itself in others and is recognized by them within a free community. Because the Athenians arrived at it spontaneously, their achievement proved fragile. An enduring free community would now have to be the explicit creation of knowledge. The independent ego is not able to develop such a consciousness. Just as the theoretical reason of the present world cannot attain full knowledge of its world, so practical reason is blocked from reaching social truth. Neither side of this cycle of rational consciousness can transcend its own limitation. The present is an incomplete age in ethics as in science.

To illustrate the misadventures of isolated moral men Hegel put before us a succession of morally unsuccessful types. It is a parade of human deformities. Although he claimed that they fell into the 'basic' pattern of consciousness from sense certainty to the limits of understanding, the traces of that pattern are feeble. The progress from hedonism to Kantian self-legislation is only occasionally related to that earlier model. Moreover, though Hegel keeps telling us that there is a connected development here, the successive states of mind are quite disconnected. Each mentality disintegrates and is followed by an alternative, but the latter does not emerge as a necessity from the experience of its predecessor. Each one is vividly painted and each is known all too well to all of us. Hegel presents us with a splendid survey of every kind of moral self-deception in which isolated, self-observing, and self-centered people indulge. Without the possibility of being part of a free people, the individual will only project his moral preferences or imagination, without seeking or finding a community. To try to know what is right and wrong is intellectually superior to an unthinking harmony, but it is an obvious social and emotional loss, which may never be repaired. We lack both the spontaneous integrity of the polis and the self-conscious ethical order which we would now have to create for ourselves. Whether we follow our pleasure, the law of our hearts, private virtue, intuitions, or the rules of reason we remain inactive, uncommunal and ethically stunted. All our moral striving is an assertion of the self against the laws and customs of society, which indeed mirrors this very state of mutual indifference. What we lack finally is character.

If we were to live in a free society the rules of society would not only be 'things' out there for us because we would also identify ourselves with them. We would see ourselves in the law and the law in ourselves. That is what Hegel meant by being free and there is not a single suggestion in the *Phenomenology* that this was a possibility open to us, his readers. Since it is impossible, the very suggestion that harmony might be achieved by political coercion would be absurd and no hint of such a thought is to be found here. Independence is our fate.

Theoretical and practical reason do not overcome the original cycle of consciousness to come to some resolution. They only reach an impasse. Hegel meant to show how pervasive the independent spirit of 'reason' was and how deep the inherited inner division of the psyche ran. He was, however, doing more than just lamenting and cursing the age. He was also introducing an alternative theory of knowledge. As a critique of modern science the discussion of observing reason is not very subtle. The distinctions between discovery and justification, hypotheses and proof, induction and deduction are not fully drawn, though they would have been relevant. However, it was not Hegel's purpose to find a new philosophy of natural science. He wanted to suggest a different way of thinking about knowledge. Knowledge need not be treated as accumulation and acquisition, rather it should be recognized as the transformation of the knower. That of course identifies learning and knowing. But since perfect truth has not been reached that makes sense. The experience of knowing becomes, as it was for Plato, an aspiration and a self-transforming ascent. That is really the alternative to observing reason which remains static as it piles up knowledge. It does not seem really to matter whether one thinks that truth is a final reachable end. The process of pursuing it could still be seen as either a quantitative or a qualitative change. Hegel made a case against the former. While introspective morality is not an accumulation of knowledge about right or wrong, it is the imposition of one's own self-devised conceptions on others. As proselytization and self-aggrandizement it also is without communion, or even concern, for the views of others. The path to learning is thus blocked. For in theory as in practice, observing reason is wholly unaware of any cultural setting. Yet culture is for man what nature is for all other living beings, the whole of which he is an active part. To ignore that is to lack the most elementary self-knowledge. It is also to renounce freedom which is to be found in the knowledge of that necessity. For the choice for consciousness is not to act or not to act, but to know or not to know. Hegel knew that his debt to Spinoza was great, but he could never fully admit it.

Politics in exile (spirit)

Hegel had now traversed three cycles of the human spirit. The first and ever-recurrent cycle of consciousness took natural mind to self-consciousness. The second led self-consciousness from the heroic duel to the disintegration of the 'unhappy consciousness.' The third followed the static, objectifying ego as it observed nature and man and as it looked into itself for morality until it reached its present dead-end. This last cycle had followed the intellectual fortunes of reason, the ungrateful offspring of the 'unhappy consciousness.' It is to the latter that Hegel now returns to describe the experiences of the ego enthralled by the 'beyond.' The misery of the erotic ego is inherent in its self division. While it vainly yearns for fulfillment in the beyond, it must remain here below in a world it despises. It is doomed to be a member of society and to work and speak within its burdensome confines. It is thus doubly estranged. In spite of all his longing to escape from it, the Christian remains a part of a culture, and the very negativity of his attitude to it gives that culture its 'spirit.' Hegel gave his fourth cycle the title 'spirit' which means the totality of attitudes, rules, institutions, habits and beliefs that make up a political culture.[84] 'Spirit' is polit-

---

84. Again, since I deal with this, the longest single section, in detail in two subsequent sections, I pass over it relatively quickly here.

ical culture or the dominant political values of a society revealed in specific deeds and words. The record of these gestures and speeches Hegel found in the most perfect works of literature of an age.

Throughout the earlier cycles Hegel had occasionally mentioned that the experiences of consciousness were expressions of an age and place. He now turns to that wider cycle directly. It is the travail of the erotic ego in its unhappiness. For although men do continue to communicate and to form political associations, they do so in ways that can only be called grotesque. To see fully just how horrible the public life of Europe from the rise of Rome to the French Revolution was, Hegel began by drawing a picture of the exemplary polis. We are confronted with our lost paradise, the ethical community of Athens as it is revealed to us in its dramas and in the pages of Aristotle. The second phase is that of *'Bildung'* or the secular culture of Europe from the rise of Christianity to the fall of the *ancien régime*. It is a radically despiritualized culture, sunken in 'crass, solid actuality.' [85] Its public values are a mere scramble for power and wealth. The real character of its nihilistic spirit becomes evident at the moment of its death in the French Revolution. The last phase of the spirit is that of the present: the age of private morality and the triumph of conscience. It is the age of Kant. We have come far, for we now do know what duty really is, but the will to act ethically and to assume the responsibilities of political action are still lacking. The erotic ego has not yet become a 'we.' It strives to find community but to no avail, for moral autonomy remains severed from society.

The cycle of culture is much the most original and vivid section of the *Phenomenology*. One cannot but feel the excitement of so novel an effort. Hegel was inventing nothing less than an historical psychology. He used the language of the various social groups and our incomparable literature to reveal the typical psychic states prevalent in our culture. It is particularly in conflict that these emerge with utmost clarity. For this is a world riven by social hostilities of all kinds. The paradigmatic struggle between master and servant is reenacted over and over again in different forms and circum-

85. B460; H315.

stances and by diverse individual actors. This was how the divided self came into being and this is the battle it must re-fight. The Revolution comes as no surprise. It is only the final illumination of the spirit that has prevailed through the ages.

At the beginning there was Athenian culture. It was the world of the free master.[86] For the master is more than just a slave-owner; he is also a member of a clan and a citizen. Only when he is no longer a free citizen does his slave get the better of him.[87] The victory of the slave is part of the Stoic consciousness which emerges in the course of the general decline of political freedom in the Roman Empire. Neither slavery nor slave revolts destroy the polis. The happy harmony of the master's city disintegrates when the family and the polity come into conflict. The former is the realm of women and piety, the latter of men and government. The equipose between these orders was a spontaneous one and when it collapses it cannot be restored. The individual liberated from ancestral religion asserts his own opinions. Social ties and customary values lose their binding power. Finally with Socrates we see the first man fully aware of himself as a free moral and intellectual agent. His is the voice of the future. The beautiful harmony of the polis is gone, to be followed by the cold, impersonal legal order of Rome. The slave asserts himself now and the 'unhappy consciousness' is at hand. To have seen the germ of the disintegration of Athens in the conflict between the gods of the netherworld worshipped at the hearth, and the state may seem fanciful, both as an interpretation of *Antigone* and of Athenian history. Hegel was, of course determined to show the social dangers inherent in any otherworldly form of religion. The struggle between Antigone and Creon is meant to foreshadow and epitomize all the subsequent wars between religion and politics.

The culture of the 'unhappy consciousness' is called *'Bildung.'* This word means both education in the academic sense and character building. Perhaps the title is meant to be wryly funny, for it is a task at which this culture fails utterly. It does not help its members to fulfill their potentialities. Its

---

86. For a development of this point, see Alexandre Kojève, *Introduction à la lecture de Hegel* (Paris, 1947), 98–9, 184–95.   87. B502; H343–4.

principle is to leave its various 'spiritual masses,' or groups, to set their own standards, since nothing in this vale of tears really matters. *Bildung* is what this culture needs, not what it achieves. Any culture shapes its members, that is merely a definition of culture. What Hegel meant was that Europe did it badly. It failed to educate its members to become perfected individualities such as the Athenians had been. A full education enables each person to rise above his purely personal, incomplete mind. A truly complete education is a liberation from our natural peculiarities and limitations.[88] Without it one is a mere specimen of humanity, not a many-sided personality with a sharply defined character. Education so conceived is not something one receives. It is a striving for the best, for the 'high culture' of one's civilization.[89] Athenians could reach it without much effort, because they were born into a harmonious society. In absorbing its values they were freed to sculpture their own characters in association with their fellow citizens.[90] They created themselves and each other in an unbroken interchange between each and all. But spontaneous culture is gone forever. *Bildung* would now have to be a self-conscious achievement and it appears to be unattainable.

Hegel was not alone in his obsession with the modern feebleness of *Bildung*. The passionate yearning for Greece that Winckelman's book on classical art had stimulated was shared by many German writers. However, even before their discontent took the direction of Hellenism, they had been acutely aware of the disjointed character of their society. The division of labor, the enormous distances between classes, geographic and political particularism, the isolation of the educated from the rest of the population and a privatizing piety, all seemed to contribute to a non-society held together only by mechanical coercion from the top. So it seemed to Herder, Schiller and many lesser writers. Hegel was far from being unique in noticing that modern *Bildung* produced neither self-development nor social cohesion.[91] The only spon-

---

88. B514–16; H351–2.   89. B89–90, 516–17; H26–7, 352–3.
90. B376–8; H256–8.
91. F. A. Barnard, ed., *Herder on Social and Political Culture* (Cambridge, 1969), 12–13, 319–23; Schiller, *On the Aesthetic Education of Mankind*, trans. and ed. by E. M. Wilkinson and A. Willoughby (Oxford, 1967),

taneously unifying bond in the secular culture of Europe
that he could discover was economic activity. Here each one
works to promote his own interests and yet necessarily suc-
ceeds in satisfying the needs of others. Man as a producer is
integrated into a system.[92] That, however, is as far as cohesion goes. The worst split is between faith and reason. That
is indeed inherent in the notion of culture that conceives itself as serving only man's immediate needs, or as we might
say 'secular.' It is a culture whose highest aspirations are concentrated on extra-human ends. That leaves a wholly despiritualized society.

The dominant values of this society are those of its military
aristocracy. These hold state service to be 'good' and economic activity to be 'base' and bad. They are not citizen-
masters who appreciate anything that contributes to the public good. They only value their own interests, their honor,
which becomes quite clear in their mutual battles. These end
in the victory of one of their kind, the new absolute monarch.
The nobility's merely rhetorical 'good' of the state becomes
actual as *his* self-interest. Deprived of their old pretensions
the noblemen now find themselves openly craving wealth,
just like their unequal, economic man. This 'base' type has
come into his own, and in the confrontation between aristocrat and bourgeois both lose. For the former has given up
his values and the latter is incapable of creating any, since his
whole life is confined to isolating activity and the satisfaction
of physical needs. That is not a situation that allows one to
visualize public purposes. The vacuum left by the mutual
paralyzing of aristocrat and bourgeois brings the third 'spiritual mass,' or group, into view, the intellectuals. These, the
bearers of 'pure culture,' are detached now from both power
and wealth. Their most perfect representative is Diderot,
who finally tells the truth about his culture, and reveals its
total futility and nihilism. Like all perfect nihilism it is self-
destructive. *Rameau's Nephew* is the liar who admits that he
is a liar. That is an insoluble paradox, which language cannot
endure. Language itself, the most essential kind of culture,

Letter VI and IX especially. Also, Roy Pascal, 'Bildung and the Division
of Labour' in *German Studies Presented to W. H. Bruford* (London,
1962), 14–28.   92. B520–1; H355.

has become meaningless. The moment of complete spiritual dissolution has arrived. The hour of philosophy may be at hand. The second confrontation is between faith and 'pure insight,' or the Enlightenment as it becomes popularly known. Pure insight is in the first instance a part of faith's own demand for spiritual purity, but it becomes hostile toward belief and turns to rationalism. Cartesian reason in its cultural dimension does serve a purpose: to destroy faith. It is 'pure' because it has no credal content. It exists only to eliminate faith. That is one of its strengths in its efforts to simply drive faith out of culture. When 'pure insight' reaches maturity in the age of Enlightenment, it does acquire a truth of its own. That is the idea of utility and it is nothing if not explosive. Like the understanding and observing reason, 'pure insight' reveals its worst features when it develops a social theory. For every man has his own notion of utility and the will to assert it. A war of all against all follows the collapse of the 'domestic arrangement' for which faith and reason had settled in lieu of a marriage of true minds. The Terror finally unveils the inherent drive of a society where each must assert himself directly or be crushed. But the truth of the Enlightenment does survive it all. We have returned to earth and will have to make our heaven right here as best we can. Above all, the shackles imposed by the 'unhappy consciousness' upon men's power to judge and decide have been shaken off. The liberty of the individual as an independent spiritual agent is now secure. It is, however, an aimless liberation, for the erotic ego, now back from the 'beyond,' is left to languish in yearning. It is not a part of a cultural 'we.' [93]

After the French Revolution the erotic ego retreats from the political arena and withdraws into personal spiritual life. It knows politics to be pure selfishness. This now is the 'moral view of the world,' or a moralism of Kantian provenance. It scorns action since it is the expression of physical need and occurs in the natural order. Duty is opposed to that and to the demands of law and convention as well. These are all experienced as sheer outer constraint, yet insuperable. Therefore no actual word or act can ever have pure duty as the sole

93. B590–8; H407–13.

motive. One has therefore only two choices: to be openly bad or to be hypocritical. The final confrontation is thus between the hero who recognizes the demands of politics, who acts and confesses his wickedness, and his hypocritical valet who condemns every action because he has found out the low motive behind it. Both these figures are essential, as are the necessity of action and the freedom of morality. Until these two are reconciled in some fraternal union there will be no spiritual harmony and the human ego will remain self-divided. We have reached self-knowledge. The hero and the valet, actor and judge, social and individual man are two sides of a single ego. However, until the 'world spirit' of history brings us to a new culture and ends the present stage of transition, there will be neither inner peace nor social freedom. That 'happy state' as Hegel had warned is long past, has been experienced and may never come again. The 'yes' that is demanded of the two halves of the present self is more a plea for tolerance than for a new society. It is a call to relax our private pretensions in favor of a greater expansiveness, and for a balance between our inherent need to maintain our individuality and our erotic drive toward culture and community. There is not a word here about the authority of an ethical state. The tensions of the spirit are not only cultural, but are also reflected within each individual. It is to the latter and to his self-knowledge that Hegel was here addressing himself. For men are finally not only parts of this or that culture but of mankind. As long as they cling to their independence, their old and insuperable illusion, however, they will not know it.

Religion and history

The final cycle of consciousness is that of religion. One might well suppose that Hegel had already said all that he could possibly say about Christianity. It might even seem that he had rendered it an irrelevant topic. The French Revolution had driven it out of politics and the Enlightenment had succeeded in bringing this culture back to earth even earlier. Nevertheless there was more to be said about religion. It is the most comprehensive and all-encompassing expression of human spirituality. In its scope it is a unique cycle of consciousness and the only one, so far, that attempts to encompass mankind in its entirety. As such it transcends the 'spirit of the laws,' of culture. This is the consciousness that knows itself to be a part of humanity and its destiny. All the previous cycles of consciousness were finite and could be tied up and knotted as discrete parts of our experience. Religion embraces them all. Religion must therefore be considered as a separate cycle of consciousness and as the all but final one. For there is something after religion: knowledge or Absolute Spirit. Philosophy has taken the place that religion once occupied. It is both the completion and the over-coming of religion. That makes this brief section on religion doubly necessary. It takes us beyond the spirit of culture and to the supra-religious consciousness of the present, to the point from which the *Phenomenology* set out and to which Hegel had promised us to return. The knowledge of all the cycles is the completion of self-knowledge.[94]

Even though necessary, the section devoted to religion is very brief and the *Phenomenology* ends abruptly. Hegel's manner in dealing with this last phase of consciousness is also rather different from his usual procedure, even though the primordial cycle of consciousness is retraced. Biblical religion especially is never allowed to speak in its own voice at all. Christianity is interpreted, given its 'real' meaning, explained and criticized without a moment's respite. As ever it is treated altogether differently from Greek piety. For after a few words about Oriental religion Hegel, as usual, does turn lovingly to the Greeks and to their 'religion of art.' Although Greek piety is inseparable from Greek culture and rooted in the myths of a people, it is ultimately expressed in works of art that have a universal meaning. Beauty in art, both plastic and poetic, transcends its origins. It speaks a universal language that rises above any one culture and the images and local beliefs of its creators. In art the Greeks were no longer conscious of their own peculiar character, but of 'the universality of human existence.' Beauty is a universal experience of the human spirit. The final form of Greek re-

94. B689–93; H476–80.

ligion is available to us, although we can never repeat or rival it. Without it we would not know what beauty is.

The Christian heritage is in this respect altogether inferior. Revealed religion is thinking in terms of pictorial images, but without beauty. It is, however, intellectually superior, at least potentially. It recognizes humanity as a single spiritual unity. That is implicit in the idea of God the creator, which must be translated as the presence of a universal spirit in the world. The Fall accounts for evil, or for man's self-centeredness which is a refusal to know himself as human. The divine wrath is, however, not endless. God becomes man and dies. The surviving holy spirit is to be understood as mankind's own redemptive power, the infinity of the self-creating mind. Christianity expresses this as the reunion of man and God through love. This love, however, is only a feeling and a groping. It is eros, the creative impulse alone that brings us to knowledge and community, not Christian love. The 'beyond' is not where we will find our ends. Erotic striving comes to the end of its search in the unity of mankind as the complete 'we,' and in perfected knowledge. The end of the 'unhappy consciousness' is in the unity of the self and others here and now. Religion has thus been intellectually transcended. For though it felt certain, its content was not true.[95]

Revealed religion did have a consciousness of the history of mankind. That was its great merit. However, it saw that history as a coming from and return to a 'beyond.' Now that we have done with that illusion we have come to the unity of thought and time. This puts an end to eternity. In the Christian view of history, time is always put in counterpoint to eternity. Now there is only time, defined by human development. Only memory contains and halts change. It has thus superseded eternity. This knowledge of our history, the total process of our coming to this present point, is the perfection of knowledge.[96] That is where Hegel has led us. It is not, however, an experience generally shared. Only when the world spirit, or to be more simple, history, will have actualized this speculative insight will it also be felt as true by all.[97] That only can mean some universal society commensurate with the universality of the human spirit. As we saw, Hegel

95. B798; H556.   96. B802–3; H560.   97. B800–1; H558–9.

had no expectations of any future 'happy state.' Knowledge defined now as retrospection is not prophetic. Hegel could claim to have come to the moment where knowledge would go beyond Athens and Jerusalem, but that was a purely speculative leap. Only when all will know that nothing human is foreign to them will the promise of humanism be fulfilled, but the philosopher can only show the intellectual necessity of this recognition, not its future probability.

The *Phenomenology* is then a justification of the history of philosophy, which now *is* philosophy, as the queen of sciences. The recollection of all those spiritual forms constitutes a journey to human self-knowledge, because it has taken one through all the transforming experiences that have brought the mind to the present. That is home, because the mind no longer strays away from its own world. History is a flux of past events but these are not external to us, they are our knowledge and when fully ordered and organized by the remembering consciousness they form science. It knows, as all rational knowledge does, its own limitations. And so its triumph is also its death. The end of the historical journey is a Golgotha, for it is only a completed past facing its end that can be so remembered.[98] The final transformation implicit in self-knowledge is at hand. In joining the heroes of the spirit, all dead and gone, the man who remembers makes their fate his own. That is the meaning of the promise Hegel had made at the outset, that the final act of the self-transformation of consciousness would at last make explicit *for* us all that had been implicit *in* our search for knowledge.[99]

Recollection is what really makes 'we,' as the end of knowledge, intelligible. The erotic quest reaches its end, self-knowledge, when it has expanded consciousness to absorb the whole of mankind's psychic development. The self knows itself by becoming one with this collective past. It can do this only when the end is known, and remembering is an ordering and illumination of the past. Then the individual mind can rise above its limitations and abandon the merely 'familiar' to know all that lies buried in its quasi-knowledge. The creative memory is a spiritual archeology and only at the end of its labors is it also a master dramatist. For the

---

98. B806–7; H563.   99. B142–4; H73–4.

mind that seeks knowledge is transformed in the process of uncovering these experiences. It produces its own maturity. That is its dramatic work. Like classical drama it does not discover new information, but retells a familiar myth in such a way that it becomes the vehicle of philosophy. That was one of the lessons, by no means the only one, that Hegel learned from the example of the Greeks.

Plato's erotic voyage took the lover upward in a hierarchy of stages toward knowledge. Hegel's erotic ego fulfills its destiny by an expansion in time. It becomes universal by moving through the human past to remember the history of the species. That is an enormous difference between them. However, both agreed that an awakened memory is the source of knowledge. For neither was this a spontaneous or intuitive mental activity. It must be learned. Although even Meno's slave can be shown that he can recall geometric relationships, the course of education that leads to philosophic knowledge is, as we know from the *Republic,* arduous in the extreme. It is a transforming process and ultimately leads to the 'beyond' of the myth of Er, which is the source of the knowledge to be recalled. Hegel's education is radically phenomenal and it is to master time but not to escape from it. In both cases, however, the individual finds truth in the most comprehensive vision open to the mind. For Plato that meant that the psyche must venture beyond history, while Hegel demanded that it encompass the totality of history. The first rejects the world of becoming, the second finds all knowledge there. The difference is very real and insuperable. Hegel claimed that he was not sure of Plato's meaning. If Plato thought that knowing is remembering something that has happened earlier in time or in another world, he was wrong. If he meant that knowing is a going inward to articulate and make conscious what is immanent in the mind then, Hegel thought, they were at one. Remembering is bringing the past into the present by recreating it. It is drawn out of a general, cultural, not a private consciousness, and made explicit.[100] Meno's slave, however, is not reconstructing history. He has a rational soul, even though he does not know it and Socrates makes him respond to it. What Plato and Hegel share is

100. *Lectures on the History of Philosophy,* II, 32–6.

mostly a manner of thinking of philosophy as an intense striving, as a force of eros.

Hegel, quite intentionally, moves his readers back to the Greeks, but we need not limit ourselves to that. The *Phenomenology* was also to be the herald of the future, though one much delayed. Its real second life is contemporary. That also is due to its mnemonic character. Perhaps because we are no longer enthralled by the future, Hegel has become more accessible to us. It may be not too much to say that biography and autobiography, whether as fiction or history, have taken the place of the social novel in our literature. We see ourselves so habitually in the past that we are no longer even aware of what we are doing. The *Phenomenology* is both a justification and an explanation of this sort of intellectual psyche. Because Hegel presents knowledge as bringing the half-conscious to full consciousness, an association with Freud has often been suggested.[101] However the relationship, if any exists, is remote. Hegel's picture of the semi-conscious mind is not that of a repressed sub-conscious. It is not a distortion of memory. It is potential knowledge that the individual can achieve by exercising his own intellectual powers. He needs *Bildung*, books and a critical cast of mind, not a psychoanalyst, to help him. It is not a past rejected and denied, but a past simply unknown. Education, not therapy, is the cure for ignorance of this kind. It is not a disturbing memory that has been covered and displaced, but incomplete thinking. Above all the unconscious that has to be recalled is not a personal, subjective past. Hegel's ego is the human self in general and the past is the history of mankind. He accepted the genetic uniqueness of the individual as a given, but it is not the subject of his inquiry. The knowledge of which we must become conscious is not private but public. Hegel was indeed more than occasionally aware of irrationality and madness, but he saw its roots in cultural disintegration, not in the personal history of a pathological 'case.' To escape from this sort of madness demands less not

101. E.g., J. N. Findlay, *The Philosophy of Hegel* (New York, 1966), 95, 117, 143, which also notes the resemblance to Proust. Others have written about this topic, but not very helpfully, while everyone interested in Hegel must be in debt to Professor Findlay's illuminating work. See also, Dieter Henrich, 'Vorwort,' *Materialien*, 32–3.

more introspection. Finally psychoanalysis is an explaining science of man. And as an exercise in observation it would not have met with Hegel's approval. However, to the extent that psychoanalysis is not passive, but an active endeavor involving a communicating patient and a therapist who together try to achieve a transforming self-knowledge in the former, it is not so unlike Hegel's own design. The archeology of the human psyche can take many paths. It may lead us to Hegel's natural mind which thanks to language is cultural in spite of itself. Freud's exploration led to layers of the mind untouched by logos. The difference here is as immense as that which separates Hegel from Plato. But again there is also a common mood. It expresses itself in a shared contempt for illusion and in fatalism. Both may be due to lessons learned from the Greek dramatists. Hegel would surely have been neither surprised nor shocked by Freud's discoveries.

Hegel's remembering is then neither that of Platonic idealism nor of Freudian psychoanalysis. It is not that of modern fiction either, although it is far closer to it in its style. When at the end of his masterpiece Proust declared that there is nothing in the work of art other than the personal experience of the artist, he was not necessarily proclaiming the primacy of a simply private memory. Such memories might not even be communicable. Proust is not talking about the ineffable, after all. The past recovered and transformed into art is social and shared. The greatest of the artist's own experiences is that of art itself. For Marcel, Balzac's *Lost Illusions* is a continuing creative principle in the mnemonic presence. It is as much a part of his recollections as any of the persons that weave their way through his memory. There was also a social world to be remembered. The past that has to be made into an ever-present consciousness is dominated by the Dreyfus Case. It is like a searchlight that seeks out implications and signs that it alone can reveal to the remembering mind. It is an altogether greater experience than the taste of a cake which stirs the memory so forcefully. That is only the trumpet that calls memory to its task and direction. It is not, however, the sensuous experience of remembering, but the creation of a world, here and now, made up of remembered bits and pieces. It is art and only art that can create this whole and give each of its moments an intense moral significance. Words and gestures are nothing in isolation. Nothing is just there. Memory creates a double reality, that of the fragments of experience and that of these episodes united into a single development. It is the record of events and their meaning within a single pattern. Proust's remembering was therefore very much like Hegel's in design, a going inward to create a new image out of the past. Proust's range was far greater. For though Hegel roamed over all ages and Proust over just his own time, Hegel described the adventures of the intellect, while Proust omitted nothing that men and women can experience. His was the more universal phenomenology of the soul.

There is perhaps little to be gained by comparing Hegel's *Phenomenology* to these more recent discoveries of the creative memory. Hegel's subject was history and the ways in which historical knowledge is both the creation of a coherent past and a transforming of its remembering creators. The present imposes itself on the past, but in doing so the living self is restructured from a self-ignoring to a self-knowing ego. It is not a 'useful' activity. It has no applicability to our future conduct. It is not an instrument of any sort whatever.[102] History has become an independent realm of experience. It may not be as Hegel claimed 'home.' Now there is no religion to return from. History is just there, a way of thinking and an independent self-sufficient manner of doing so. Hegel certainly did not invent history. There was much excellent history before he lived. The name of Gibbon need only be mentioned. Moreover, he has no techniques to offer the working historian. Historicism also owes him no debt, for Hegel did not conceive of history as an explaining science akin to the natural sciences. He was hardly interested in demonstrating the causes and effects of phenomena in an endless chain. He was in no danger of confusing history with nature or of inventing laws of history.[103] And while it is clear that Hegel's notion of 'spirit,' like that of Montesquieu, does subject

102. B131–3; H63–5.
103. Friedrich Meinecke, 'Historicism and Its Problems,' trans. by Julian Franklin in Fritz Stern, ed., *Varieties of History* (New York, 1956), 267–88, and Hans-Georg Gadamer, 'Hegel und der geschichtliche Geist,' *Kleine Shriften*, III (Tübingen, 1972), 118–28.

moral and political values to the logic of development, to becoming, there is for Hegel an ultimate aim: the knowledge that comes at the end of the ages. The teleological energy that Hegel discerned in the drive to history as historical knowledge is alien to historicism. As a traditional philosopher Hegel responded to the command, 'know thyself.' That had always meant, 'know your place in a universal order.' History was that order for Hegel, as well as the knowledge of that order, but it was not a fixed place. That is why the *Phenomenology* is not an invitation to passivity or to piety. It is a call to rethink ourselves now that we know that we ourselves, and not God, created mankind. That re-creation is the psychic activity left to humanists. Hegel's work is an incomplete map which we are free to fill out and redraw in our own time and place.

CHAPTER TWO

INDEPENDENCE AND DEPENDENCE

This history of the experiences of human self-consciousness is of necessity the history of ethics. Even the most defective views about mankind involve some thought about the relations obtaining among men in society. Hegel was intent upon showing that all the stages of self-consciousness so far were incomplete precisely because they were insufficiently aware of the cultural structure of the ego. The journey of the human spirit has been an errant search for social self-knowledge, for an expansive sense of the self as a member of a greater whole. Before the Greek philosophers wrote their supreme masterpieces, the citizens of the polis had been conscious of the political character of their lives. They lived in a condition of untroubled harmony with the rules accepted as simply given. Each citizen expressed the public ethos in his daily life, and each and all contributed to the creation of the laws by which they lived. When philosophy casts its disturbing shadow upon this world it is already disintegrating and the self-consciousness that philosophy creates is a part of that greater disorder. For philosophy is the unshakable knowledge that each individual is not just a social animal but also a discrete spiritual entity with his own life and purposes. From now on the thinker and society are no longer at one. As an external world the city is now subject to analysis and evaluation. The attitudes involved in these activities vary from age to age, as historical circumstances and the restless drive of the dissociated self demand, but they are not random. The chief pattern for men who have not learned to *know* what the ancient citizens simply believed as a certainty is to veer

from independence to dependence. That is so because they
are not free. The Greeks are our sole memory of what freedom might be. They are therefore a constantly felt presence,
a reminder that there is something other than various com-
binations of dominion and bondage.

Self-sufficient man: dominion and bondage

'Man is born free and everywhere he is in chains. The man
who believes that he is the master of others is nevertheless
more enslaved than they are.' Hegel's political philosophy begins with a restatement of Rousseau's immortal paradox. It
was for him the ultimate revolutionary challenge. Rousseau
had claimed that he simply did not know how mankind had
come to this monstrous state of collective bondage and self-
deception.[1] Hegel could not leave it at that. He had to account for the historical fate that the French Revolution had
revealed in the moment when freedom was both affirmed and
denied. To go beyond Rousseau was no simple task. It required a reconstruction of the entire experience of European
'self-consciousness.'

Self-consciousness is the second cycle of Hegel's model of
the mind in search of knowledge. It begins with the realization that the certainties of understanding are projections of
the categories inherent in man's intellect. When one reaches
the limits of natural reason one sees that the question, 'What
do I know?' can only be answered when one knows what one
is. In its first efforts toward that self-knowledge the now self-
aware ego divides itself so that one half is observed and desired by the other; for desire is awakened by objects that the
mind places before itself. And it is the desire to reappropriate
its other half, to know it by reintegration that moves the
ego. This procedure however can yield only tautological self-
certainty: the perfect assurance that ego = ego. This is subjectivism in its purity: an unending pursuit of the self by
itself. It does not lead on to knowledge. For that, as 'we'
know, a whole self must confront another entire self in a con-

---

1. Rousseau was being disingenuous here, since in the *Second Discourse* he
   had given an elaborate explanation of how this state of affairs had come
   about.

scious act of mutual re-cognition, that is, of knowing the self again in an other. This is the final, the erotic act, the equivalent of reproduction. It is the ego recreating itself fully in order truly to know itself. In this case that does not call for self-reincarnation, but for its intellectual equivalent. In mutual recognition men acknowledge their identity and overtly know each other as one 'we.'[2] This process is the perfection of communication and even its first steps require more than primitive utterances. It is possible only as part of an already highly articulate culture. The dawn of self-knowledge is Homer's poetry, itself an act of memory. His was the first 'universal song' that sets us off on our journey toward self-knowledge.[3]

The epic hero is certain of himself, aware only of his own self-sufficiency and autonomy. Achilles is beholden to nothing and to nobody. He is utterly alone in the knowledge of his own character and fate.[4] The existence of other equally independent beings is for him both a threat and a challenge. Since, as a hero, he must demonstrate his independence to reaffirm himself, he is determined to impose himself upon these others. Each one is driven to challenge the others to a duel to the death. Each one knowing only his own passive, consuming ego sees the other as a mirror of that half of his self-divided self. As such the other is a deadly threat that must be subdued to ensure the survival of the active, the self-conscious ego. He must therefore risk everything for the sake of ensuring this independence. The battle of heroic competition cannot be anything less than mortal combat. Hector and Achilles never consider anything else. They do go beyond self-certainty, however. A moment of genuine mutual recognition does occur. For it is peculiarly human to risk one's life for the sake of one's self-image.[5] It sets men radically apart from the beasts. The germ of the freedom of mankind is born in the battle between heroes. But it does not grow or endure. For no common bond is forged. Only a sense of a general fate, of inevitable death is shared by these warriors. One re-

2. B218–27; H133–40, and above, chap. 1.   3. B732–3; H507–8.
4. B229–34, 736; H141–6, 510. In the sections that follow I use the words autonomy, independence and self-sufficiency interchangeably.
5. H. C. Baldry, *The Unity of Mankind in Greek Thought* (Cambridge, 1965), 8–15.

calls that Homer's phrase for men is 'mortal beings.' Nevertheless there is one fleeting moment of genuine recognition:
when Achilles and Priam stand over the dead body of Hector,
they suddenly know their common humanity. Here is knowledge, but it is only the act of a passing moment.

The real defects of the self-sufficient self emerge in the inevitable consequences of heroic battle. If one of the warriors
is not killed, he is enslaved and reduced to passivity. The new
situation is now one that involves no heroes, only the slave
and his owner. The latter, considered only as a master, is
neither a hero, nor a citizen engaged in the affairs of the city.
The Aristotelian master knows that happiness is to be found
only in perfect contemplative self-sufficiency. To achieve this
he must have a slave to provide him with the necessities of
life. He also needs the slave to define himself.[6] Self-sufficiency
is the very opposite of slavery not only because the slave is
obviously constrained by his owner, but because he toils and
produces. He performs wholly degrading tasks which im-
merse him in the material world of which he is almost a
part. At most he is the supreme tool. For to the extent that he
is a part of the master, he cannot be called an instrument
of production, but one of action. As a true slave, however, he
lacks the capacity for deliberation and merely produces, he
functions as a 'thing.' He exists to supply the master with all
the objects that the latter desires. The master is a pure consumer. His desires are gratified effortlessly. He need not concern himself in any way with work or creation. Indeed that
would only impinge upon his independence. All he must
know is to command the services of a slave. What the slave
does is of no interest to the master as long as this instrument
acts in accordance with his wishes. If the slave were to be
considered a human being that would, of course, render this
arrangement impossible. Greeks, Aristotle remembered, cannot be natural slaves.[7] That does not render slavery any less
necessary. It is not only required for the self-sufficiency of
the master. Master and slave are, above all, paradigmatic, a
manifestation of a universal principle of order. It would be
difficult to exaggerate the importance of the image of master

6. *Nicomachean Ethics*, X, 1177a–1178a.
7. *Politics*, I, 1252a–1255b, 1259a–1260b; III, 1277a.

and slave in Aristotle's thought. It expresses the essential character not only of all relationships of superiority and inferiority, but of a pervasive dualism. Mind and body, spirit and matter, theory and practice, contemplation and action, all exhibit the necessity of ruling and subordination which originates in the very constitution of the universe.[8]

These considerations give Hegel's celebrated set-piece 'Lord and Bondsman' its central place in the rise and fall of the independent self-consciousness.[9] As a hero, self-sufficient man had a very clear, and within its limits, a true sense of himself. The lord who sees himself solely a master of others, is quite mistaken about himself and his situation. He thinks that he is perfectly autonomous, but in fact he relies utterly upon his slave, not only to satisfy all his desires, but for his identity. Without slaves he is no master. That is the implication of reducing the 'other' to a mere part of himself. He has defined himself in terms of the 'thing' he owns. The master is also deluded in thinking this toiling part of himself inferior because it works. The belief that producing is a less than human activity is wholly erroneous. It condemns the master to arrested development. Contemplation without creation, thought without learning, is pure passivity. As a pure consumer it is the master who becomes an idle 'thing.'

The active erotic consciousness is that of the slave. By working upon material objects not only does he learn skills, but he also develops an awareness that he dominates the matter that he moulds with his hands. He knows the difference between himself and the products of his labor. In his mortal fear of the master he also comes to know what it is to be human. Total fear teaches him self-discipline and self-mastery. Only this mixture of such fear and unremitting productive toil can give the slave his consciousness of autonomy. Work without fear is just vexing, while pure fear merely paralyzes. Together these two experiences make the slave the self-sufficient man that the master so falsely imagines himself to be. The slave now has a mind of his own that goes far beyond stubbornness. He is conscious of himself as a human being and demands that his master recognize him as such.

8. *Nicomachean Ethics*, V, 1138b; VIII, 1161a–b. Baldry, 88–101.
9. B234–40; H146–50.

When master and slave know each other as alike in their autonomy, neither one is liberated. The slave merely adopts the stance of the master as both flee inward. The master gives up his dependence on the slave, and indeed on all external things, while the slave comes to share the master's contempt for productive work. Both are now alike in their independence from the shackles of the entire physical order. This is the Stoic consciousness, a state of indifference to the external world that was implicit all along in the master's highest aspirations. The ultimate aim of his mastership was to give him the leisure to devote himself entirely to contemplation. He is the hero-as-philosopher. Had not Socrates already compared himself favorably to mighty Achilles? [10] Aristotle's master, the hero-as-philosopher, looks upon contemplation as the perfection of the self-sufficient life. It is the worst of his illusions, for the man who just waits for knowledge to come to him waits in vain. There is nothing out there to contemplate. The contemplative man is doomed to a condition of spiritual emptiness and immobility. This is the Stoic. He thinks himself unfettered in thinking and does not realize that his is the freedom of the void.[11] Ratiocination divorced from experience yields only formal platitudes: it repeats intuitions without advancing toward new knowledge.

With Stoicism Hegel, for the first time in the *Phenomenology*, chose to refer to specific political events directly. The inner emigration of the Stoic reflects the spiritless, atomizing, horrible despotism of the Roman Empire.[12] It is a world that repels everyone, from the supreme lord down to the lowest slave. Thought alone, the mind in isolation, seems the only impregnable spiritual fortress. Marcus Aurelius on his throne and Epictetus in his chains share the same philosophy. Both are 'wise men' in flight from a crushing external world. That is why Marcus Aurelius quotes Epictetus' remark that man is 'a poor soul burdened with a corpse' and pitied the great warrior heroes of the past for suffering from 'an infinity of enslavements.' [13] Epictetus' own view of slavery is an inversion of actuality, not a liberation. Slavery is not

10. *Apology*, 28–9.   11. B245, 752–4; H153, 523–4.
12. B242–6, 502–3; H152–4, 343–4.
13. *Meditations*, trans. by Maxwell Staniforth (London, 1964), Bk IV, s. 41, Bk VIII, s. 3.

really being owned by another man, but being subjugated to one's own ambitions and avarice.[14] The perfect independence that both these 'wise men' seek is really a rejection of otherness. To be sure, both emperor and slave acknowledge their common manhood, but they achieve this sense of universality only by turning their backs upon nature and history, labor and action. Theirs is a rationality abstracted from all possible sources of human experience. Their standards of judgment, drawn from this internal reason, is a dogmatism that issues commands directed at all men at all times and in all circumstances. Conduct prescribed for everyone in this way fits no one at all. All this talk about goodness, virtue and wisdom is very elevating, but it has no specific context or intent. In fact, the Stoic always does his painful duty, but for him that is only evidence of his irremediable bondage to the world. In acting he is not independent, for his withdrawal from the world is incomplete.

The Stoic uttering his various prescriptions from within does not actively justify the voice he calls reason. Such dogmatism exists, as it were, to be challenged and defied. Where there is intuitive rationalism there scepticism is bound to appear.[15] This is the spirit that denies, that doubts everything, the outer no less than the inner order. The scepticism of Sextus Empiricus is no mere Humean empiricism.[16] It is total uncertainty. It sees that all the objects of knowledge are fleeting. This scepticism knows all the exceptions to the rules, all the contradictions raised by every generality. This is free thought in action.

The Stoic's independence was entirely passive. To really assert the autonomy of thought one must deny the certainty of all sense experience. One must doubt everything in fact. That is why the merely complacent dogmatism of Stoic indifference to the world calls forth Scepticism. The Sceptic really means to put the autonomy of thought into action. Everything gives way to its doubts, its whys and wherefores. Facts, moral rules, data, all the certainties are swept aside.

14. 'Of Freedom,' *Moral Discourses,* ed. and trans. by H. D. Rouse (London, 1910), 200–16.
15. B246–51, 503; H153–8, 343–4.
16. *Lectures on the History of Philosophy,* II, 328–73; *The Logic of Hegel,* ss. 24, 32, 81.

The slave is cast out entirely. He is all that toil and desire that a liberated mind denies. For the Sceptic has completed the dialectical run from sense-certainty to the limits of understanding and knows all about the flux of appearance on which slaves work so painfully. He is, finally, not taken in by the Sophist's faith in man as the measure of all things. Those standards are just as open to doubt as the will of the sovereign or anything else that may present itself as a rule. The world, after all, is full of contradictory regulations. This, in short, is doubt for the sake of doubting. It is not the acquiescence of the baffled understanding confronted by infinity, but a deliberate doubting as an assertion of spiritual self-will.

The Sceptic doubts even his own doubts, his own ever-challenging ego, but he cannot altogether annihilate it. He needs it to doubt. That is one difficulty. The other paradox is inherent in the activity of doubting. The mind must always absorb and identify with the objects that it must deny. It must see to deny the certainty of sight, recognize rules to challenge their validity and hear in order to doubt sound. Such a mind is shackled to the world, because it needs chains to break, since its freedom is just the act of liberation.

In his awareness of the contradictions inherent in consciousness, the Sceptic stands at the gates of wisdom. Precisely because of his despair regarding common sense and 'the whole compass of the phenomenal world' he is qualified to approach truth.[17] However, over and over again, he turns away from this possibility. He does not move on to self-knowledge. This refusal of the Sceptic to forge ahead is a recurrent experience of consciousness. The radical scepticism of the Enlightenment, for instance, had been dissipated in the French Revolution, while the even more profound scepticism of antiquity had been succeeded by Gnosticism, Neoplatonism, and Christianity, all expressions of the unhappy consciousness.[18] This is not a logical necessity, but an emotional one. The psychic tension of scepticism is overwhelming and the distracted ego chooses some avenue of escape. It yearns for some point of spiritual peace far from

17. B136–7; H68. *Logic of Hegel*, s. 78. That master and slave taken together add up to nihilism is very ancient wisdom, as the Babylonian 'Dialogue between Master and Slave' show clearly enough.
18. B608, 754–6; H421, 524–6.

the world of doubt. It flees to some 'beyond' where it hopes to be free or goes inward to cultivate a 'beautiful soul.' In either case the ex-Sceptic now accepts self-division, ceases to be defiant and becomes a permanently unhappy conscious-ness shifting miserably between the bonds of this world and the ever-receding freedom above, out there, or within.

With this account of Scepticism Hegel had not only elaborated Rousseau's resounding sentences, he had gone well beyond them. For Rousseau had identified freedom with self-sufficiency. That is why he was not able to rise above the eternal see-saw between dependence and independence. Not only did he admire the inner autonomy of Stoic wise men, but he was also obsessed with securing the external, personal and social self-sufficiency of ordinary people. *Emile*'s model is Robinson Crusoe. He is dependent only on natural neces-sity, never on other people. The *Social Contract* is a scheme for combining that sort of liberty with the advantages of political society.[19] To Hegel, who identified Rousseau with the most anarchic tendencies of the French Revolution, that arrangement was merely the democratization of the autono-mous consciousness.[20] Rousseau's failure, and above all that of the Revolution, arose from an inability to grasp that inde-pendence and dependence are indissolubly linked parts of a single, self-divided consciousness, a continuation of the see-saw of dominion and bondage. These are not really alter-natives. The one cannot and does not overcome the other. Freedom must be found in a far more radical change of human self-consciousness, in a genuine 'recognition' among egos.

Hegel surely was mistaken about Rousseau's social ideas. They may have been closer to his own than he could bear to admit. One subject about which the two surely agreed was scepticism and its psychological burdens. Indeed to illustrate the self-estrangement of the unhappy consciousness, Hegel could have done worse than to quote 'The Creed of the Savoyard Vicar.'[21] The Vicar begins by confessing that in his youth he had been a complete Sceptic and a soul in despair.

19. *Emile*, trans. by Barbara Foxley (London, n. d.), 147–8, 436–7. *Social Contract*, I, 6.
20. B602–10; H416–22; *Philosophy of Right*, trans. by T. M. Knox (Oxford, 1942), 33, 156–7 (ss. 29, 258); *Logic of Hegel*, s. 163; *Lectures on the History of Philosophy*, III, 400–2.   21. *Emile*, 228–78.

Unable to bear this state of mind, he turned to God, for whose existence he found sufficient proof in the needs of his own heart and in the visible order of nature. The manner of his discovery of God is interesting, but the character of this deity is even more important. For the Vicar's God is pure will, omniscient and omnipotent. He is loved not as a benefactor but as a master who must be obeyed unconditionally. Unless the Vicar can feel His presence immediately he feels lost. Only when he is certain of his obedience to God is he at rest, and that is rare. Mostly he is totally self-divided, at war with himself. His life is therefore a constant yearning for the peace that only God's felt presence can give him. The belief that sustains him is that in an after-life he will be eternally reunited with God and so at peace. Until then he feels enslaved by his lower self, free only when he obeys the voice of God within himself. When he errs, he is a mere thing; when he is good, he knows that he owes all to God's will. At all times he desperately needs God for both moral and intellectual reassurance. For 'if there is no God, then the wicked is right and the good man is nothing but a fool.'

This is a perfect picture of what Hegel called the unhappy consciousness.[22] It is miserable and self-divided not because it is sinful, but because of the kind of God it has created for itself. All creativity has been vested in an unreachable master. Mind has left nothing but thinghood for itself here and now. This God who is master clearly is the God of the Old Testament. The basic situation is not altered when God is incarnated in an historical person, in Christ, nor when He is universal spirit, as the third person of the Trinity. There is still only *one* source of life and *one* 'beyond' toward which the believer aspires. The Vicar is a Christian, but he trembles before a God, even though he longs to be reconciled to him forever. As long as this God remains in charge, the relationship of master and bondsman prevails. What this unhappy consciousness cannot grasp, according to Hegel, is the meaning of God becoming man and dying. God is really dead, and the holy spirit is mankind's own spirit. The limits of a still primitive 'pictorial' imagination, no less than self-division, keep the Christian far removed from self-knowledge. By

22. B251–6; H158–62.

directing all its erotic energies toward a beyond, the ego is deprived of the possibility of integration.[23] The self-hatred of the Sceptic is simply frozen in this consciousness, but he has been relieved of the anxieties of total doubt. Instead of accepting assertion and negation as part of a universal process he gives up questioning and finds stability in a beyond that guarantees the structure of reality. He also condemns himself to a life of yearning. Half of him is always 'beyond' seeking God, the other must live below in the shadow. Although this ensures its misery, the unhappy consciousness needs this beyond and the master too much to return to the wholeness of here and now.

The 'figurative' or 'pictorial' awareness of God forbids any effort to make Him an object of thought. The believer cannot reach Him and attempts to do so, in any case, appear too self-assertive. Only the humble exercising of pious longing will do. To achieve the desperately desired unity with the divine object of devotion the unhappy consciousness tries at least four different ways of reaching God. All fail, but each one is a step toward ever deeper self-enslavement.[24] That, for Hegel, was the sum of the spiritual history of medieval Europe. First the unhappy consciousness tries to join God by possessing symbolic objects recalling Christ, relics especially. It seeks the tomb of Christ, for example. The Crusades, although they are acts of devotion, are also the occasion of the grossest brutishness. The quest for the Holy Land does not lead to God, but makes the crusader aware of himself and that in the most earth-bound form. The second effort is to toil and labor in the service of God in the hope of self-forgetfulness. However, just like the slave of a human master, this worker discovers that far from reducing the self, work gives him a strong sense of his own powers. Horrified by its pride, the worst of all sins, the unhappy consciousness practices humility and self-abnegation. God is credited with all the good work it has achieved. Whatever is well done is the work of Providence, not of man. The human consciousness eliminates itself from its work and thanks God. Even in these thanks there is pride and a sense of achievement. The

23. B778–85; H544–8.
24. B256–67; H162–71. E.g., *Lectures on the History of Philosophy*, III, 45–60.

unhappy consciousness is now so overwhelmed by the sense of
its own sinfulness that it gives up toil on God's behalf. Its
third effort to be at one with God is through self-mortifica-
tion and asceticism. The devil is within himself and uncon-
querably so. For the very suspicion that the devil has been
subdued is a sign of pride and proof of failure. This battle
cannot be won. Having failed in all its attempts to destroy its
own ego, the unhappy consciousness now comes to the most
desperate measure of all. It gives up its power of judging,
willing and knowing to another human spirit, the priest of
the Church. Now the believer is really a 'thing'; he has inflicted upon himself what the Greek master could never do
to his slave. It is not quite the end, however. The priest after
all knows that he is not God, that the Church is so only
implicitly. That is a crack in this destructive arrangement. It
is enough to permit reason to enter and eventually to undermine this order.

The drama of the self-sufficient consciousness is now complete. It is not ended, since it repeats itself though in
different ways and under other circumstances. In the age of
the French Revolution the cycle of Stoicism, Scepticism and
unhappy consciousness is repeated. From rebellious self-
assertion to the flight to a beyond by all sorts of yearning
'beautiful souls,' the pattern is displayed again. For Hegel
these last, the romantics quivering with longing as they turn
away from actuality, seemed particularly revolting.[25] In spite
of his scorn and contempt he knew these to be the necessary
final moments of the consciousness that begins by confusing
the autonomy of passive masters with real freedom. The self
that depends on its 'thing,' whether that be another human
being or its own body so conceived, is conscious not of freedom, but only of bondage. It must swing back and forth
between independence and dependence. The Sceptic under-
stands that perfectly well. He does not suffer from the
delusion of those who think that self-isolation is really autonomy. The psychological cost of his realism is, however, too
heavy and far from escaping both mastery and slavery he
sinks eventually into extreme dependence. Hegel clearly
thought that he was the first philosopher to have succeeded

25. B663–7, 675–6; H460–3, 470.

in going beyond this cycle, and in the works he wrote after the *Phenomenology* he set himself the task of explicitly overcoming it. Here he merely points to that possibility. For this is mostly an account of the experiences of incomplete forms of consciousness.

Free people

One of the reasons why Hegel was able to entertain the intellectual possibility of overcoming the recurring cycle of independence and dependence is that he knew that it had not always prevailed. Neither the epic hero nor the citizen of a free polity were in its grip, and these figures from the past allow one to consider the character of free men. The pre-civic consciousness, though incomplete, did have its moments of undiluted grandeur. The epic heroes, founders of states and creators of a vision of unbounded personal dominion, were undeniably glorious. Their fate was always lamentable, but they were neither self-divided nor self-deluded. To be sure the age of heroes can never return. They have no place in the civic order.[26] However, as men of action they remain exemplary, a reminder of what men can be. The hero is the very opposite of that consciousness which signs away its own will-power to others.

Hegel had already in an earlier essay compared the freedom of the heroes of Greek tragedy to the self-enslaved consciousness of both the Old Testament and of Kant. The latter are always subject to an external master, responsible to some power outside them. Even moral law within acts like an external master who lords it over the rest of the ego.[27] He re-thought and re-wrote those passages in his last years especially in his lectures on art and religion. In the *Phenomenology* the heroic consciousness is singled out, even if only briefly, for its stance in the face of fate, for its ability to act freely even under that shadow. When the hero acts – and it is always on a grand scale, for these are great noblemen – he

26. *Philosophy of Right*, 245 (addition to s. 93); *The Philosophy of Fine Art*, trans. by F. P. B. Osmaston (London, 1920), IV, 120–68.
27. 'The Spirit of Christianity and its Fate,' trans. by T. M. Knox, *Early Theological Writings*, ed. by T. M. Knox and Richard Kroner (Chicago, 1948), 224–38.

knows that he is challenging fate. He is the man who risks everything. He knows that he is asserting himself against a power that is superior even to the gods in the epic poems of Homer, and against the established religious and social order in the tragedies of Aeschylus and Sophocles. When he seeks glory, dominion, or revenge, he is defying powers he cannot control. To act boldly is in any case to incur the danger of error and evil. Innocence is not for man, not even for children. Only stones are innocent.[28] The Greek tragic hero knows that he can know only a part of all that is involved in his action. That does not deter him for one instant. For him the real tension is not between guilt and innocence in any case, but between guilt and destiny.[29] The Greek hero knows that he must suffer unspeakably as a result of his self-assertion. Achilles knows that he must die soon, but he does not shrink from action.[30] Neither do Oedipus, Orestes and Antigone, who expect to suffer as they do thanks to their inner destiny. The heroes of tragedy, moreover, accept responsibility for the 'entire compass' of their deed. They do not limit their responsibility to what they intended and could foresee. Their crime includes all the consequences and unknown aspects of their deeds. It would be beneath them to assume the lesser burden. They are not responsible *to* anyone, but *for* everything, even those circumstances that were beyond their knowledge and control. The acts of tragedy, unlike those of the earlier epics, are not controlled by an outer fate; their actions are compelled by their character, but necessity surrounds them and enhances their guilt. Indeed culpability is part of that necessity which is now called fate.

When Orestes and Oedipus commit their various crimes they are rebelling against fate. They arouse an enemy against themeslves. By destroying life they bring the furies down upon themselves. The fury of remorse and grief rage within the tragic hero. He knows that he is faced with necessity and accepts it. He does not deny his responsibility for his acts or the inevitability of what follows. It is so. The sorrow

28. B488; H334; *Lectures on the Philosophy of Religion*, ed. and trans. by E. B. Speirs and J. B. Sanderson (New York, 1962), I, 272–85; *Hegel's Philosophy of Mind*, trans. by William Wallace (Oxford, 1894), s. 472.
29. B489–92; H334–6.   30. B736; H510.

and regret that torment him, moreover, can be shaken off. They can be washed away. There are several things a tragic hero could do. He might commit suicide to find forgetfulness in Lethe. No judging god awaits him and the blot is wiped out. He might expiate his crime and put the furies to rest as Orestes does with Athena's help, or heal himself as Oedipus does in a mystical rite at Colonus.[31] At no time does he receive grace or forgiveness as a Christian might. He heals himself and frees himself from culpability. The age of heroes is gone, but the possibility of thinking of error and evil as fate remains. Not a punitive God, but the inherent structure of reality and of our individual natures make it inevitable. No one need fear action.

The Greek who knew necessity and said 'It is so,' 'It cannot be helped,' did not need consolation. For necessity is not coercion and it is not a tyrant or something imposed at all. It is simply inescapable reality. It cannot oppress once it is truly accepted. That is why the Greeks were never vexed as we always are. The reverent sense of necessity led the Greeks to create themselves into noble and beautiful characters. They internalized necessity, they made no effort to escape it. We, in glaring contrast, never say 'it is so,' but always 'It ought to be so' and are always petulant and dissatisfied with ourselves, thanks to bad conscience, to the fear of God and of law – all seen as willful masters over our selves. Finally, the necessity of Greek fate had nothing to do with the chain of cause and effect. The latter is also experienced as a loss of freedom and thus a source of frustration for which we require continual consolation. Real necessity is not an explanation. It is the sheer 'is-ness' of reality as given.[32] Heroic man, in short, is free.

This realism and untroubled acceptance of necessity, which is the heart of freedom, is not limited to heroic figures. It is shared by the far less ambitious and far more law-abiding chorus of citizens. The capacity to act without inner division, the undivided ego, is common to the united citizens of a free

31. B489–92; 739–43; H334–6, 513–16. In the *Philosophy of Fine Art*, IV, 312–26, Hegel made clear that he did *not* think of Oedipus' release as a Christian act of salvation, but as an ethical reconciliation.

32. *Philosophy of Religion*, II, 239–43, 256–67, 286–8; *Philosophy of Fine Art*, I, 214–15.

polity. The law is their fate. The master is neither an epic
nor a tragic hero, but he is more than a mere owner of slaves.
He is also a citizen. He shares in the spontaneous inner integrity of a whole people. Collectively these citizens are an
individual people, a whole which acts freely. It is a situation
that cannot endure. The inner harmony of such a people is
unreflective and that is its great defect.[33] When individual
rationality asserts itself against the common order the free
society crumbles. The Sophists shake it and Socrates is both
the product and voice of its dissolution. He already speaks
for the future ages of personal morality and public disintegration. Not even Plato could restore a civic order once it had
been destroyed.[34] Nevertheless, Athens remains our one and
only intimation of what a free people might be. As such, the
people, far more than the totally defunct hero, is a more relevant example of genuine freedom. As citizens they stand
outside the cycle of independence and dependence. They
are the only example of a happy consciousness. Their happiness is one that mankind has lost or *maybe* has 'not yet attained.'[35] In either case it is the 'utopia,' the nowhere, now
which alone illuminates what freedom, in contrast to lordship and bondage, would be. As the only picture of 'recognition,' it shows the self at home and the erotic ego satisfied.
It is not a state of self-knowledge, but it is its emotional
equivalent.

The master is *merely* a slave owner when he has ceased
to be the citizen of a free polity. Only then is he isloated.
He thinks he is independent because he is not owned by
another man and has achieved an aloof spiritual condition. Once, however, he had been an integral part of an
ethical culture and a free, rather than a merely independent,
man. Without being aware of it, he was an active citizen,
integrated into the political life of an autonomous city of
people who mutually recognized each other. The relationship among masters was freedom and reason realized. This
autonomy of the polis and the freedom of its people had
never been regained. The French Revolution had not been a

33. B462-3, 498-9; H317-18, 342.
34. B747; H519; *Lectures on the History of Philosophy*, I, 384-448.
35. B378-80; H258-60.

new beginning, but only the prelude to a new cycle leading inward and to the unhappy unconsciousness of romanticism, endemic in modern culture.[36] The culture of an ethical people is nowhere in sight. Yet Hegel thought that it might be in the future. However, prediction was never his business. The *Phenomenology* is devoted to remembrances.

Each one of the cycles of self-consciousness, that is, every section concerned with moral and political phenomena, begins with a lovingly drawn picture of ancient Athens and its free, ethical people. Hegel clearly places these passages strategically to remind us in each case of what had been lost and not yet regained.[37] He uses the Homeric hero, the single free man, to introduce the cycle of autonomy that ends with the unhappy consciousness. The story of the efforts of modern practical reason to develop a viable ethic is preceded by a long account of the happy people of the polis. The tale of the course of the European public spirit up to the age of the French Revolution opens with a discussion of Sophoclean tragedy. And finally, the pages devoted to religion, after a brief review of natural religion, go on to Hellas' religion of art in all its perfection. All these recurrent reminders of the Greek achievement are not just meant to give us an intelligible notion of what a free people would be. They are extreme contrasts which act as illuminations, like search-lights. The Greeks are called on to show us what has not been achieved, the distance between then and now. In each case one is forced to see that every cycle of self-consciousness is remote from self-knowledge. If one puts all these passages about Athens together, one sees that they are not presented as a goal to strive for, but as a judgment. Indeed, even as a young man Hegel had already known that Achaea could never be the Teutons' home, even if they were to forget Judea.[38] They belong neither to Athens, nor to Jerusalem. There can, however, be no mistaking the difference in Hegel's attitude to these two eternal cities. The first was regretted, loved and recalled as an enduring inspiration, the second was an experience to be overcome.

36. See below, ch. 4.
37. B230–4, 375–9, 462–99, 709–49; H142–5, 256–9, 317–42, 490–520.
38. 'The Positivity of the Christian Religion,' *Early Theological Writings*, 149.

That so much of the *Phenomenology* should be a lament
for Hellas is not surprising. Hegel was hardly alone in the
elegiac mood. It was shared by many German writers, but his
memories were far more political than theirs. This use of
antiquity as an instrument of political criticism to shame the
present was of course not new. Much of the radical utopian
literature since the Renaissance had relied on this contrast.
One need only remember Rousseau's use of Sparta as an
anti-Paris to see that Hegel's method was far from novel.
Indeed, much of what drew Rousseau to Sparta moved Hegel
toward Athens. Even though these two cities stood for quite
different ideals, neither resembled any modern place. The
happiness of the Athenians was due entirely to their being a
free people. No tension between the private and the public
self, the inner and the external world, or the here and the
beyond interrupted the undivided consciousness of free citizens in a free polity. They alone had laws and customs that
were the creation of each and all of them. And all and every
one of them expressed in his person the collective consciousness of the whole polity. The freedom of these citizens is not
the pursuit of personal self-sufficiency, but the preservation
of their collective autonomy and individuality against other
peoples. To that end war is not only an aspect of political
life, it is the supreme expression of citizenship and public
freedom. Freedom is affirmed in the Persian Wars. Indeed,
war has an educative function also. It tears the citizens away
away from the many private associations and groups to which
they belong.[39] The free people was for Hegel, as for Aristotle,
not a pile of bricks, but a single whole composed of a plural-
ity of types and groups.[40] The government, however, has the
highest and prior claim upon them. For its power is 'the will,
the self' of the people.[41] The laws express the active character
of each individual citizen. They are not impersonal rules
'out there' that impose roles on legal persons, as in Rome and
in the modern state. The law is such that each citizen can see
himself as a particularization of its general aims. For he has
willed them. That is why a free people is 'reason realized.'[42]

The Greek citizen does not enjoy the freedoms which the

39. B473–4, 497–8; H324, 341.   40. B709–10; H490–1.
41. B511; H348.   42. B378, 731; H258, 506–7.

subjects of modern states quite rightly expect as their due. They are not members of civil society with its multiplicity of legally recognized rights. In a later discussion of Aristotle's *Politics*, Hegel was to note that the Greeks had no notion of such a society. They 'were still unacquainted with the abstract right of our modern states, that isolates the individual, allows of his acting as such, and yet as an invisible spirit, holds all its parts together.' In the fully-developed modern state no individual can ever be fully conscious of the whole to which he contributes, quite in spite of himself, by projecting his individuality. The market economy is the perfect example of this unity of the disunited. It is exactly like a factory, Hegel added. The freedom of such men is that of the 'bourgeois,' not that of the 'citoyen.' [43] The modern state is so much less fragile than the ancient city just because it does not depend on anything so difficult to achieve as full citizenship. It can thrive with its stunted bourgeois. And stunted they are. Hegel was very much aware of that. Man for man they were simply inferior to the free citizens who knew their entire city and their place in it. That is why citizens had to possess character and not mere moral knowledge, as Aristotle had pointed out to Plato.[44] Personal morality as the individual consciousness of right and wrong is, to be sure, an advance toward human freedom, but it is learned at a great cost – the loss of spontaneous and complete citizenship. Civil society and the modern administrative state are to be cherished, but as political necessities, not as ultimate perfections. As Hegel had noted when he first began to consider Germany's political condition: there was now only the choice between the modern state and the helplessness of the Jews of the diaspora.[45] It is the best we can do without Athens.

In the *Phenomenology* Hegel did not mention civil society or the modern state directly. Indeed, there is no explicit consideration of law and politics in his own age. Even the basis for a modern legal and poltical philosophy, a discussion of the will, is notably lacking. All that was to come in the *Philosophy of Right*. This earlier review, a review of the

43. *Lectures on the History of Philosophy*, II, 209–10.   44. *Ibid.*, I, 414.
45. 'The German Constitution,' trans. by T. M. Knox, in A. A. Pelczynski, ed., *Hegel's Political Writings* (Oxford, 1964), 242.

'experiences of consciousness,' is, however, not indifferent to political phenomena. It shows with utmost clarity what the modern state is *not* like and what degree of civic integrity had once been possible. The free people does not owe its condition to invention, but to a unique social balance. The equipoise between kin and city is really what maintains it. The ethical spirit which sustains freedom has its roots in a precarious arrangement by which the polity preserves the kin and the kin raises citizens fit for freedom.[46] Hegel went well beyond Aristotle here, who had seen the family only as the economic base of the polis. Hegel also consigned it to an entirely separate sphere, but one far greater and very much less material. The family (or kin) group fulfills an ethical function in the life of a free people. While the polity remains prior to the family as the only realm in which men can reach their highest ends, it could not without the ethical family create the spirit of citizenship on which its survival depended. The ethical family ties the living to the dead. Its religion is ancestor worship. As such it is less than rational, with its deep belief in the nether-world. However, it serves a truly human and social function. It protects the individual against his most awful fear, the horror of extinction. Here the dead endure among the living, who continue to fulfill their obligations to their departed kinsmen. Hence the absolute duty to bury and avenge the slain kinsman. For women this family, with its rites and duties, is the whole of the social world. The men, however, must ascend to the realm of light, the upper world of the polity, as young citizens and warriors. The women in their educative and supporting task, as the guardians of the family ethos, also make their contribution to the civic order. Indirectly, but indispensably, they give men the strength to become citizens.[47]

The criminal law of the city has its roots in the family. That is also the source of its strength and its social immediacy. When the civic ethos at last claims the furies, the prosecution of murderers is left to the kin of the slain citizen. The community as such does not participate on behalf of either party in cases that call for vengeance. It only sets limits

46. B467-8, 481-2; H319-20, 330.
47. B468-74, 478-9, 739; H320-4, 327-8, 512-13.

to the process of retaliatory justice, but it does not deprive the kinsmen of their duties to their dead.[48] That is why they can devote themselves so wholeheartedly to the upper-realm, to the rational, distributive, man-created law of the city. It supports their familial existence, which in turn prepares them for the civic life. Again war, the necessary discipline and highest function of citizens, would be an intolerable slaughter if the warrior did not know that he would be buried and worshipped by the surviving kin, among whom he would thus remain alive. By insisting on the religious functions of the family in a free city, Hegel separated the household and the polity as completely as did those modern critics of the patriarchal monarchy, Locke and Rousseau. Their purposes were not, explicitly at least, his. He was far more concerned to show the necessity of separating the divine and human law, the realm of darkness and that of light, church and state, faith and reason.

The ethical family is the citizen's initiation into social life. Here he takes his first steps from 'I' to 'we.' The mission of such a family is not merely economic or biological. Its members are aware of themselves as belonging to a whole that unites past and present, and the family's 'Penates,' the gods of the hearth, symbolize that continuity. The ethical family has its own laws and spiritual ends. It also provides its offspring with the one and only perfect experience of recognition. Brother and sister are simultaneously opposites and yet as one. They belong to different sexes, but their tie is not a physical one. Their duties lead them in different directions. The sister is the guardian of the domestic gods and the rites devoted to the dead. The brother ascends, as a citizen and warrior, to the world of light and life. She sends him forth to that other world just by offering him the secure knowledge of her piety, while he is her protector. He brings her to his world, as she holds him to hers. This recognition, this untroubled 'we,' so intimate in content, nevertheless, does not depend on the individuality of the persons involved. Each one is sisterhood and brotherhood personified. It is in this relationship therefore that the mere 'this' of the self becomes general and finds its most personal, as well as its most

48. B480–1; H329–30.

public, occasion for discovering the humanity that embraces both sexes.[49] A common memory and an undisturbed love are thus a bridge between the individual and humanity, between two laws, two obligations, and two sexes.

Hegel, of course, did not deny that the family served sexual and progenitive purposes, nor that it was necessary for rearing the young. But as children grow up they leave the family, which thus dies when its purely natural and educative functions have been fulfilled. Its ethical character and the experience of recognition, especially between sister and brother, however, endure beyond life. The burial of the dead brother is the sister's highest duty. That is how Antigone's whole tragedy begins. In her perfect ethical consistency, she was Hegel's answer to the unethical family of his own age. He was quite familiar with the naturalism of the more radical libertinism of the Enlightenment and its sexual amoralism in which, if nature and not convention was to be the sole norm, then the traditional family was a questionable institution. Hegel was not the first philosopher to consider sisters and brothers. Montesquieu, whom he admired, had suggested in the *Persian Letters* that there was nothing in nature to prevent the perfectly happy marriage of such a pair. From there it was not far to the complete sexual anarchy of Diderot's imaginary Tahitians.[50] Marriage as a pure contract was also unacceptable. What, after all, is the substance of such a civil contract?[51] It ignores the entire emo-

49. B475–7; H325–7.
50. *Persian Letters,* XLVII; Diderot's *'Supplement' to Bougainville's Voyage* had already been published when Hegel wrote the *Phenomenology,* but he could not have known of the even more radical *D'Alembert's Dream.* Hegel was, moreover, familiar with the writing of La Mettrie and the libertinage of Schlegel's early novels. He was properly shocked by the whole lot. See e.g., *Lectures on the History of Philosophy,* III, 399, and *Philosophy of Right,* 263 (addition to s. 164).
51. Kant had, with his usual intellectual radicalism, faced up to the question of the content of the marriage contract. It was for the exclusive use of the partners' genitals. This suggestion, though not illogical, certainly gets the church out of the picture, as well as reducing the role of the state to a legal minimum. It secures the privacy of the relationship, but it cannot be said to be an adequate view of marriage. Hegel found it repulsive and so have others. *Philosophy of Right,* 58–9, 262 (s. 75, addition to s. 161). This part of Kant's *Philosophy of Right* (s. 24–7) has been omitted from the most easily available version of that work, *The Metaphysical Elements of Justice,* ed. and trans. by John Ladd (Indianapolis, 1965).

tional and social content and purpose of marriage and the family. Again Hegel was not the first philosopher to be alarmed by sexual radicalism. Rousseau had already been upset by it. He had hoped that a family, highly patriarchal in structure and living apart, might prove a quasi-natural refuge from the modern world. But he knew that the arrangement could not work, and was no substitute for the Spartan order, in which the family played a very subordinate part. In short, he could see no bridge between an impossibly moral and isolated family and one that served genuine civic purposes. It was thus left to Hegel to show that the family could serve not only civic ends but also natural and emotional ones. He saw such a family in Sophocles' tragedy. It was not only an example for him. The 're-cognition' between sister and brother, that is a premonition of ethical life, could, he seemed to say, survive even without an ethical polity. In later years he was to show that even in modern states the family provides a genuine proto-ethical experience. Even then, however, he quoted an old Pythagorean saying that the best education was to be a citizen of a state with good laws.[52] Clearly civil society is not the equivalent of an ethical city. The latter, however, was brittle. It would not survive the conflict between family and polity, and between the divine and human law. That conflict is, moreover, an inevitable step in the relentless drive of reason.

Sooner or later, then, the harmonious balance between the realm of family piety and that of civic law must give way. *Antigone* was the dramatic recollection of the final collapse, Hegel thought. But he saw tremendous tensions all along.[53] The heroes of other tragedies already show that to act politically demands a violation of the tranquil law of the hearth. Oedipus the Tyrant must, in order to rule, transgress the law against incest and patricide. He, who knows everything, must forget, or push into unconsciousness what the oracle foretold. In the end he expiates his crime against the divine law, but only at the door of death and after he has long ceased to rule. Here the old order is restored. Orestes kills his mother to avenge the death of his father the king. He is saved from the agents of the divine law, the furies, by Athena, in a triumph of the civic law; but again the two

52. *Philosophy of Right*, 109, s. 153.   53. B484–90, 737–8; H330–6, 511–12.

realms are reconciled. When Antigone defies Creon, no resolution of the conflict is possible. Antigone stands unwavering for the ethos of the kin. The brother must be buried, and to do this is her unquestionable duty. To punish the usurper, the disturber of the public order, is just as surely the task of Creon. He must assert the rules of the realm of light, indeed of reason, the human law made by human beings for their own fulfillment. If public law runs counter to the demands of the nether-world, to the ethos of family life, that is a disaster, but not one that Creon can avoid by giving way. The upshot is that both the family and the polity are destroyed. Fate in the form of destruction overcomes both.[54]

Now the individual ceases to see himself as wholly a social being, and neither family nor city can absorb him entirely. The struggle between two social claims degenerates into a war between the sexes, a concomitant of democratic societies that Hegel was exceptionally sensitive to have recognized. In Aristophanes' comedies he found how war had ceased to be the occasion on which citizens proved their freedom and had become, in the eyes of the women, a silly escapade provoked by male incompetence and stubbornness. The actors no longer wear masks to hide their individuality and to emphasize their social, impersonal roles. Now the stage is full of specific people, each one speaking for himself or herself. The sister who preserves the ethos of the family is replaced by the wife and mother who only wants her sons and lovers to stay alive and at home. As Aristophanes' Praxagora explains carefully, women have no use for war. Now that they speak as individuals and no longer as the guardians of the familial ethos, their hostility to the male world of so-called law and order and war becomes open and their weapons, ridicule and laughter, prove irresistible. They mark the dissolution of a free people, but it is an outburst of such healthy individual self-assertion that even Hegel could not solemnly condemn it.[55] Comedy is indeed the perfectly 'happy consciousness.' It is both the opposite and counterpart of the unhappy consciousness. Though it is our only reminder of spiritual

54. B490–6; H336–40.
55. B496–8, 745–9; H340–2, 517–20. *Philosophy of Fine Art*, IV, 327–30.

health, it thrives at the expense of the ethical order. It can laugh mercilessly at customs that have now lost their value, and ridicule all of them as pretensions. What is gone might as well be laughed at. Aristophanes was quite right to make fun of those who like Plato thought that a dead local ethos could be revived by translating it into 'universal' ideas. Healthy though that laughter was, it marked the death of freedom.[56]

To most contemporary audiences it would seem evident that the ladies of *Lysistrata* and *The Ecclesiazusae* enjoy far more freedom than Antigone, burdened with endless ethical obligations even before her conflict with Creon. That was, however, not Hegel's view, and not because he felt sorry for Aristophanes' beleaguered males. He simply had a very different notion of freedom. What, in fact, did he mean when he spoke of a 'free people'? He certainly did not mean that its citizens had rights against the polity. Quite the contrary, their freedom was due wholly to their being unaware of themselves as individuals apart from their social being. The freedom of the people is a state of mind, both individual and collective, that is marked by an absence of tension between the demands of the polity and personal beliefs and aspirations. The very possibility of such a conflict is unknown to the free citizen, or at least obscured by the harmonious transition from family to public life. For as soon as the ethos of the family and the duties of citizenship collide, the individual is emancipated from both, and now sees himself as a discrete entity for whom society is 'out there.'

It seems that the 'free people' is more easily recognized for what it was *not* than for what it actually was. This is entirely consistent with Hegel's purpose, which was to contrast the happiness of the socially integrated citizen, for every one of whom this was a spontaneous rather than a consciously chosen role, with the unhappiness of the restless, searching individualism of the modern world. The impact of the reproachful image of antiquity was heavy indeed. For Hegel used Antigone's example to expose the vanity of every form of modern morality. He was very far from admiring Antigone simply as a prophetess of the higher law. Indeed, when

56. B752–3; H522–3.

he quotes her celebrated lines about its obscure origins he made it clear that she did not understand the law that bound her, that she simply believed in its divinity.[57] She did not see the limits of kinship obligations and religiosity. Hegel was impressed with her ethical certainty, even though he rejected her claim along with every other higher law doctrine. Justice and law can only be created by public authority.[58] Creon's law, made by a government for a polity, was the most rational and most universal law possible. All other rules were less general and less valid because they served lesser groups. Hegel did not think that all actual laws were perfect. Far from it. The effect of Roman law was profoundly destructive to those who had to abide by it. The *ancien régime* was worthless in every way.[59] That did not, however, render notions of an extra-political or supra-human legality or justice acceptable to him. Law and justice, like every other idea, were entirely the work of men acting together.

The way men judge the rules that they have created for themselves, however, differs. It was Antigone's great merit that, although she did not understand the origins of the law which she so heroically defended, she never thought of herself as an individual expressing a personal morality. She spoke solely as a sister within an ethical family, as a social being, alone, yet expressing a universal order. That was the real source of her perfect certainty. She did not look into her heart or conscience to discover righteousness. She knew what had to be done, and always had known, because she was not making a moral choice, but obeying an unquestionable law.[60] That she failed to understand that law, that her allegiance to the nether-world was less valid than the law of the polity that expressed the rationality of the world of light, was irrelevant here. What mattered, above all, was that she had no notion of conscience, or personal conviction, or of individuality as an inherent claim. She was right, within her limits, because she represented an ethical group and its binding values. The universal significance of Sophocles' play and its enduring power to educate and move us is due

57. B452–3; H311–12.   58. B467, 473–4, 493–5; H319, 323–4, 337–40.
59. B501–6; H342–6. See ch. 3 below.
60. B452, 458, 484–6, 613–14; H311, 314, 330–2, 423–4.

to its social character. The drama is true because it presents two inherently valid social moralities and two conflicting sets of social mores. To Hegel the tension between personal conscience and reason of state was trivial by comparison, a mere accident. The confrontation of two dependent yet irreconcilable social claims, which go beyond a mere judgment of individual rightness or error, is a philosophical tragedy. It is tragic not because the protagonists suffer, but because they are not mere private individuals: they are each a personification of a social necessity. Creon is not a tyrant, but the voice of the polity and its priority, its claim to general social rationality, the end of men's striving. Antigone is neither a criminal nor a martyr to conscience. She also asserts a social, ethical claim, the validity of which had not been challenged until it collided with the demands of the public order. That is why her certainty is rooted not in personal conviction but in historical reality. The law 'is,' just as fate 'is so.' It would be unfair to Hegel to say that he was defending the supremacy of the modern state in the person of Creon. He would not have admired Antigone's personality so profoundly if that had been his aim. He was, rather, insisting on the perfection of character among men and women who knew themselves to be wholly members of established social orders and who lived and died ethically, that is, in response to the customs and beliefs of their peers.

Law and government are not the only aspects of civic life that are rational, in the sense that the most general public activities are freely accepted by the citizens, who recognize them as their own creations. Religion is also free, because the polity is its substance. Religion, by which Hegel at this point meant the collective beliefs of a community, is social and this-worldly among a free people. Its supreme expression is art.[61] And it is an open public art that is not an outpouring of the artist's personal inspiration, but an expression of the spirit of a whole people.[62] The rites of such a people are a daily part of their common existence. Unlike the Olympian religion over which Zeus presides, it is truly popular and local. That official pantheon is too feeble and distant, and in its unstable division of labor between gods

61. B709–11; H490–92.   62. B716–17; H494–5.

and men it is even ridiculous.[63] The real religion of a free
people remains particular, a part of its active, shared life.
The people has a god to unite it, but he represents not a
remote hope or a deferred fulfillment, but present, common
work.[64] The drama, which is a spiritualized and universalized
rite, abandons all the crudities and improbabilities of local
and Olympian ritual, but it is still rooted in common experience and is shared by all.[65]

The only powers that are not encompassed by the polity
itself are those ascribed to fate. Heroes defy it, but the demos
does not. For them fate is the whole of that dire necessity to
which men must submit. They bow before all that defeats
and defies them. The common people is aware of its helplessness and finds its voice in the chorus which, as it warns
and laments, reminds men of their limits, of fate. However,
fate is not for the people either a deity or an object of reverence. Eventually they also understand it to be character, and
the circumstances created by men in their complexity.[66] What
mattered most to Hegel was the integrity and freedom of the
religion of a free people. It was uniting, not divisive; common, not private. It encouraged action, not passivity. In short,
it was everything the unhappy consciousness is not.

Ancients and moderns: a lament for Hellas

What is freedom, considered as public and not as personal
independence? The Athenians were a free people because
each citizen was perfectly integrated into *his* society. As long
as the family and the polity form a single continuum, the
citizens enjoyed an undivided consciousness. The erotic ego
found its strivings satisfied as it moved from membership in
an ethical family to participation in an ethical polity. From
birth to death the citizen knew himself to be part of a community of mutually recognizing people. His ascent from kin
to city was a process of public education. Nothing here was
done simply for the sake of the individual. His *Bildung* was
a preparation for the tasks of citizenship and warfare. The
particular was generalized, given a political self to replace

63. B733–5; H508–10.   64. B723–4; H501–12.   65. B736–45; H510–17.
66. B685–6, 735–45; H473–4, 510–20.

the merely natural. By emptying himself of his own self and internalizing the customs of his people, the citizen gained powers far greater than those given him by nature and mere talent.[67] It was the power of an implicit self-knowledge, of what is universal in the individual. It is the realization of one's highest purposes. In Athens that consciousness was gained effortlessly. Its citizens lived in the secure certainty that the spirit of the laws was also their very own spirit and consciousness. They were free because they were not under the dominion of a master, either external or internal, man or god. The happy people was free because it did not suffer from the yoke of either lordship or bondage. Those chains are imposed not only by men upon each other, but also by the divided ego that reduces one part of itself into a mere thing.[68] To Hegel the enslavement of the mind by illusion and superstition was the same kind of slavery as legal and economic subjugation. The freedom of an ethical people, correspondingly, is also just as psychological as it is political. It has nothing to do with modern individualism. Indeed, the urge toward personal autonomy which begins with the contemplative lord is both the harbinger and mark of the collapse of public freedom.

The account of ethical freedom in the *Phenomenology* is hardly elaborate or complete. That is not altogether surprising, since Hegel seemed more concerned with what the polis was *not,* than with what it was like. He was, after all, not even quite sure whether mankind had left it behind or might not yet attain it. Indeed, if his defense of Antigone and Creon had only thin ties to Athens' historical actualities and even to Sophocles' play, that was not fatal. The purpose was to show up the flaws of every aspect of the unhappy consciousness and its world. If much of the *Phenomenology* is a lament for Hellas, that is not due to pure nostalgia, but mainly to Hegel's polemic against the false consciousness of subjectivity and isolation. The differences, especially the political ones, are meant to disturb 'us.' For the greatest difference between a free people and all others is in the quality of justice that renders its ethical life so valid and certain.

67. B515–17; H351–3.
68. See especially *Philosophy of Right,* 52–3, 241 (s. 66 and addition).

Athenian distributive justice was not an alien imposition, like the law of Rome and of the modern world. It was not the haphazard outcome of the judicial resolution of individual conflicts. It had intelligible guiding principles which corresponded to the actual 'self-conscious will of all,' and thus integrated the various groups and citizens within the polity into a single whole.[69] There was no room for the rampant self-assertion of the modern world. People found their pleasure in the family, not in the defiance of social convention. When they rose above the pursuit of pleasure, they turned to active citizenship, not to introspection. The law of their hearts was not a self-centered tyranny, but a sense of the uniformity of all hearts in an ethical society. Virtue was a civic act, not personal edification pitted against the course of the world. The individuality of the members of an ethical family was not like that of self-expressing members of an intellectual zoo in which each 'genius' has no end in view except to nurture his 'original' nature. Individuality was not treasured for its own self. Each brother and sister was different, but all strove to achieve a general aim of fraternal recognition and to prepare themselves for their place in the domestic and civic order. Each one was realized by pursuing set and wider social purposes. In an ethical household 'a woman's relationships are not based on a reference to this particular husband, this particular child, but to a husband, to children *in general* – not to feeling, but to the universal.'[70] The family interrupts the work of nature, the city completes that act of denaturation. The object of this final ethical act is not designed to form an individual, but has the community and *its* law as its aim.[71] Nothing could be more remote from the Rousseauian and romantic 'natural' education of *Emile*. The ethical order pays no attention to the nature of the individual, and it does nothing to nurture it. That is why, by forcing men to measure themselves against the objective demands of their city, it in fact produces strong, highly developed individualities. The education that caters to the natural endowments of each child only produces mere 'specimens' of humanity. It is self-defeating. By

69. B479–80; H328–9.   70. B476; H326.   71. B469; H320–1.

concentrating solely on natural gifts, it develops people who differ only in the strength and energy of their common gifts, not genuine individuality. Clearly, Hegel had no use for Rousseau's educational theories, though he had the same end in view: psychic and social unity.[72]

The citizens who receive this ethical education, so remote from every form of modern *Bildung,* demonstrate their superiority in their every social act.

When they concerned themselves with a cause, it is a matter of concrete policy, not chimerical dreaming. They weighed actions within a stable context of law and justice, instead of forever questioning and testing the validity of the laws in terms of some purely personal or abstract rule. Instead of the ever-unsteady voice of conscience, they had objective ethical laws to guide them. Not for them the 'pompous' rhetoric about the good of all mankind and the oppression of humanity; they pursued the public good of their city, a task within their reach.[73] The great conflict that ethical people experience, like that between Antigone and Creon, is not the 'comical' conflict between two abstract duties. It is a collision between two laws and two social groups and their respective ethical orders.[74] Antigone's claim may be inferior to Creon's, but it is the expression of a complete 'character' and of an objective social situation. That is far superior to that modern (Kantian) morality, which is merely a matter of abstract knowledge. She may have been less self-aware, but she completely lived her law; she did not have to think.[75] Modern morality, with its empty and universal 'ought,' forces the individual to give his duty any aim his conscience may choose. As such it hovers between tautology and arbitrariness. Antigone knew right and wrong with perfect certainty – that is her greatness and that of her society. Modern morality knows nothing of such poise. It dooms the individual to testing every law, every choice, by matching it against formal maxims that lack all specific content. This syllogistic practice reduces duty to a self-evident generality and moral action to an exercise in formal logic. In practice it can yield no guidance. The individual is left to his own confusion, apart

72. B514–16; H350–3; *Philosophy of Right,* 124–6, 268 (s. 187 and addition).
73. B409–10; H280–1.   74. B446–53; H306–12.   75. B613–14; H423–4.

from, and indeed opposed to, the sole source of genuine morality: social rules.[76]

It is a devastating set of indictments, but not novel in form. Many a utopia drawing on classical republican visions had said as much and more about the state of modern Europe in just that style. Hegel's book was, however, in one way entirely new. He was caught, as it were, between two quite incompatible types of classicism. On one hand, there was the highly political republican tradition perfected by Rousseau, which the Jacobins had utterly discredited. On the other hand, there was the aesthetic Hellenism of Hegel's German contemporaries which was completely apolitical. Since Hegel knew as well as Rousseau had that everything depends on politics, he could not accept the latter. The Jacobin effort to return to Sparta he knew to be absurd.[77] The Jacobins were nevertheless the legitimate heirs of a long line of political radicals who had looked to the classical republics as models of civic virtue. Pagan patriotism in peace and war had been extravagantly admired for centuries in monarchical Europe. Machiavelli comes to mind at once, but one ought also to remember Harrington and other radical republicans who emerged in the course of the English Civil War. Mably was only one of Rousseau's disciples to supply Jacobin rhetoric with Spartan themes. All these neo-Spartans and neo-Romans were intent upon stressing the civil–military glories of classical antiquity, not its intellectual and artistic achievements. Machiavelli scorned those who treasured classical statues but ignored the political science of the ancients, while Rousseau preferred Cato the Elder to Socrates.[78] The Jacobins, by trying to put these lessons into practice, revealed their utter inappropriateness for the modern world. Subsequent generations of radicals discarded them altogether. Marx was willing to admit that at most Roman austerity had provided the Jacobins with the illusions they needed to do the heroic work of establishing the bourgeois order. No revolutionary would ever need that sort of self-deception again.[79]

76. B446–53; H306–12.
77. *Vernunft in der Geschichte,* ed. by Johannes Hoffmeister (Hamburg, 1955), 19. See below, ch. 4.
78. Machiavelli, *Discourses,* Bk I, 'Introduction'; Rousseau, *Discourse on the Arts and Sciences,* especially.
79. *The Eighteenth Brumaire of Louis Napoleon.*

To judicious admirers of the ancients it had long been clear that Plutarch was no guide to modern politics. In all fairness it ought to be said that Rousseau knew that as well. He followed Montesquieu, the master of political reality, who had already exposed the gulf between the ancients and the moderns. Much as Montesquieu had admired the ancients, he was not blind to their flaws. The one great lesson to be learned from them was moderation, the principle of aristocratic republics. But if modern commercial monarchies were to avoid despotism, England was the example to follow, not Rome. These lessons were not lost on Hegel's generation. Benjamin Constant, who was Hegel's almost exact contemporary, was to take up Montesquieu's themes. If he did not have to worry about the despotic tendencies of the *ancien régime* any longer, there were those phony Lycurgwses and Charlemagnes, Robespierre and Napoleon, to consider. Both had been raised on the *Social Contract*. Their efforts to foist ancient liberty upon modern men was the great ideological menace of the age. Constant accordingly set down carefully all the differences between ancient and modern liberty. He was far from denying that the ancients had been admirable, but he meant to show that any effort to imitate them was now self-defeating and likely to lead to terror and despotism. In their small polities these peoples had been able to find all their happiness in public activity. The subordination of the individual to the polity was no burden therefore, especially given the general simplicity and equality. In the large, diverse, commercial societies of the present none of these conditions obtain. Now people seek and find their happiness in their private lives, and they need governments that can secure them the freedom to prosper, to develop, and to achieve individual ends. They neither desire nor need much political activity. Participation was the freedom of the ancients, private liberty is that of the moderns. War no longer ennobles men, who now do not demonstrate patriotic valor but only a disruptive and demoralizing savagery. The impersonal state can be just, but it cannot edify or enhance the lives of citizens, as did the small, cohesive and pre-commercial states of antiquity.[80]

Hegel knew all this just as well as Constant did. In the

80. *Oeuvres* (Paris, 1957), 1010–24.

Phenomenology however, it is clear that he found far more
to lament in the modern situation. The fact that Germany
had no recent political history comparable to that of France
may well have sharpened his regret. In any case he could not
console himself, as some other Germans did, by imposing a
purely spiritual mission on Germany. For them Germany
was to be a republic of letters. *Bildung,* as the perfection of
individuals, was to be its task, not politics. With this essentially aesthetic ideal came a new Hellenism, and it influenced
Hegel deeply, though he never shared the apolitical mood
that inspired it. Indeed, he despised the latter as just another
manifestation of the unhappy consciousness.[81] The 'yearning' for ancient Greece as the home of beauty was not, however, foreign to him, even though he rejected the social
passivity that accompanied it. One need only look at some
of the best of the works written in the 1790s on these themes
to see that Hegel absorbed their spirit along with much else
from the Weimar circle of Goethe and Schiller of that time.

The Hellenism that longed for Greek beauty, cheerfulness
of spirit and energy was directly inspired by the sense that
modern Europeans generally, and Germans especially, were
unfit for politics. Constant had only argued for a limited
state, but one in which public opinion and parliamentary
institutions would provide modern men with suitable forms
of political activity. It was neither Rome nor Sparta, but it
was politics. When one looks at the liberalism of Wilhelm
von Humboldt the difference is striking.[82] Because modern
men lack the energy of the Greeks, any sort of public life is a
threat to their individuality. The state should therefore all
but disappear so that each one might devote himself to the
preservation and cultivation of his unique personality. It
was, in fact, from Humboldt that John Stuart Mill all but
copied the passages devoted to individuality in *On Liberty.*
Unlike Mill, Humboldt had some very immediate and just
cause for seeing the administrative state as a threat. The
mania of many a German prince for administering everything did little to encourage personal independence in his

81. For this phase in German's intellectual history, see Friedrich Meinecke,
    Cosmopolitanism and the National State, trans. by R. B. Kimber
    (Princeton, 1970), 34–48.
82. *The Limits of State Action,* trans. and ed. by J. W. Burrow (Cambridge,
    1969), passim.

subjects. It was therefore not the general character of commercial life, which had preoccupied Montesquieu and Constant, but the extreme division of labor in the interest of efficiency as it was defined by governments that terrified Humboldt and inspired his call for individuality. The Greeks were, however, not forgotten, even if in their energy they were too remote to serve as public examples. They remain for the present an object of longing 'outside the circle of history' as he put it.[83] That is, they were a pure myth and to be treasured as such. Their value was to be models of self-perfection, of heightened individuality.

Rousseau's immense concern with the psychological destruction produced by the division of labor clearly had a deep influence upon his German readers. Indeed, they saw not only emotional and moral, but also aesthetic damage. Many were far more extreme in these feelings than was Humboldt, who was after all an essentially practical man and political to a degree, compared to some of the other Hellenophiles of the 1790s.[84] Not only bureaucratic and economic division of labor and psychic stunting, but artistic decline and intellectual specialization also were sources of distress. These also were expressed in a longing for Greek vigor and wholeness of spirit. The greatest work expressing all these currents of thought was Schiller's *Letters on the Aesthetic Education of Mankind.* Intellectual atomization and moral chaos clearly made political reform an impossible goal, in Schiller's view. In a world composed of effete barbarians and crude savages politics was pointless. Only an aesthetic education reviving the 'play instinct' in man could restore men to any degree of fitness, even if the Greek youthfulness of imagination and maturity of reason were to escape them. At first it seemed that this new *Bildung,* joining the impulses of nature to the demands of reason, was to prepare men for some sort of public life, but eventually it became clear that *Bildung* for beauty is an end in itself, the highest and the best.[85]

83. Miriam Cowan, ed. and trans., *Humanist Without Portfolio: An Anthology of the Writings of Wilhelm von Humboldt* (Detroit, 1963), 78–98.
84. Both Schiller and Schlegel, when young, had undertaken detailed comparisons of the moderns and the ancients, much to the disadvantage of the former. See A. O. Lovejoy, 'Schiller and the Genesis of Romanticism,' *Essays in the History of Ideas* (New York, 1960), 215.
85. *On the Aesthetic Education of Mankind,* Letters II, IV, VI, VII, X, XXVII.

Hegel also knew that without Greek art we would not even know what beauty is. Greece *had* been the spiritual paradise of mankind.[86] Man for man the Athenian *was* a better man than the modern bourgeois. He quite agreed with all that. However, poetry must not be permitted to threaten philosophy. The demands of the intellect were not to be denied their primacy. That is why the unself-conscious, spontaneous harmony of Greece did have to go under.[87] Knowledge required it. And this had to be endured without tears. Beauty, he wrote bitterly, 'hates' the understanding, because it cannot face the death inherent in the growth of knowledge.[88] Moreover, much as he agreed with those who saw the modern division of labor as destructive of human character generally and of art especially, he never forgot that it was the cement that now held society together.[89] There was no point in longing for a piece of the past. Since the whole has been lost, none of its parts could now be revived. Greece's religion of art was indeed a supreme moment of human consciousness, but even that was inseparable from the totality of its cultural life. If Greek *Bildung* could not be imagined apart from its political and religious life, then it was impossible to imitate it by reducing it to a purely personal ideal. Hegel had never warmed to the Spartanism of Rousseau, nor to the radicalism of the old republicanism, but his Athens was that of Pericles' Funeral Oration and of Sophocles' drama, not that of apolitical sculpture and lyric poetry. He ultimately agreed with Rousseau that the integrity of the ancient psyche was inseparable from politics. The very idea of an apolitical *Bildung* was the expression and perpetuation of the unhappy consciousness in all its self-division. Europeans, Montesquieu had observed, received three different educations, from their fathers, their teachers, and the world. The last tends to undo everything the first two attempt to achieve. 'This is to some degree due to the contradiction among us between the obligations imposed by religion and the world – a thing unknown among the ancients.'[90] Hegel

86. 'On Classical Studies,' *Early Theological Writings*, 325.
87. B378–9, 498–9, 747; H258–9, 342, 519.   88. B93; H29.
89. See especially, *Philosophy of Fine Arts*, I, 241–63, and *Philosophy of Right*, 122–34, 266–71 (ss. 182–208 addition).
90. *The Spirit of the Laws*, Bk I, ch. IV, s. 2. My italics.

may not have put it so elegantly but he certainly meant to say the same thing. *Bildung* must be of this world and it could be effective only if pursued without illusion. The notion that one could form strong, integrated individuals in isolation from the political life of one's people was one of the endless self-deceptions of the unhappy consciousness. Indeed, in his contempt for the self-delusion of the unhappy consciousness Hegel revealed an affinity for the age of the French Enlightenment that was to separate him permanently from his German contemporaries.

Hegel was then at one with the old republican tradition in celebrating the active down-to-earth, social spirit of Greece, and pitted it against all forms of individuality. The spiritual health of the Greeks was in their ability to create collectively a religion, a polity and an art here and now. Nor was their happiness a matter of personal gratification. It also was a social state, as was their freedom. War was its highest manifestation, and not because it was enjoyable. It was the absence of romantic individuality among a people who knew collective self-mastery, limited only by necessity, that appealed most to Hegel. It was no doubt for the benefit of the romantic poets that he chose to stress the religious, public character of Greek art, so remote from the modern cult of genius. Yet Hegel was himself surely no example of Greek wholeness. The mood of the *Phenomenology* is not one of resignation, or moderation. Hegel had not really absorbed the lesson of Sophoclean drama as thoroughly as had Montesquieu. Hegel's nostalgia was altogether too obvious, his contempt for his own age too violent. He also was a fine example of the maladjustment of the age. There was nothing in the spirit of his own age that could possibly act as a self-conscious successor to the 'ethical substance' of Athens. That substance is only 'a floating selfless adjective' for us now.[91] In his rage at the work of the unhappy consciousness he never considered, as Montesquieu had, the psychic costs of ancient fraternity and the military costs of heroic patriotism. He also did not really face the fact of ancient slavery. He could not bring himself to accept Rousseau's paradox that slavery, al-

91. B380; H260.

though totally unjust, might be necessary for real liberty.[92] In later years Hegel was to say that slavery was, like all institutions, to be judged in terms of the prevailing stage of historical consciousness. Slavery became intolerable only when men were far removed from primitive nature. That, of course, does not say anything to the slavery of the Greek world, which was far from primitive.[93] A second explanation was to say that the wrongness of slavery could emerge only with Christianity, because only then were all human souls known to be equal in dignity. The Orient had believed that only One was free, the Greeks that only a few were free, but only Christianity knew that man as man was free.[94] That was not, however, what Hegel said in the *Phenomenology*. On the contrary, he clearly not only identified the self-imposed slavery of the early Christian believers with the economic and legal slavery of Rome, but seemed to find the former far more horrible than the latter.[95] Yet he also insisted that the unhappy consciousness arose out of the experience of lordship and bondage. The tension between the master's contemplative, self-sufficient consciousness and that of the laboring, fearful slave occurs only when philosophy has come to preside over the decline and death of the ethical people. The master as citizen did not suffer from the destructive impulses of the autonomous consciousness. He still stood outside the cycle of dependence and independence. For him there was only the immediate, confiding trust 'in spite of differences of class' that 'they' are a 'we.' [96] His wisdom was not that of the independent master, but that of 'living in accordance with the customs of one's own people.' [97] Nevertheless this happy master *was* a slave owner and did depend on his living tool. Hegel found no paradox in this. It is the distinctive necessity of the intellect that forces the happy master to yield to the unhappy lord, and to the endless cycle of the self-divided consciousness. There are no successive stages of the ancient

92. *Social Contract*, III, 15.
93. *Philosophy of Right*, 48, 239 (s. 57 addition).
94. *Vernunft in der Geschichte*, 62; *Hegel's Logic*, s. 163; *Philosophy of Mind*, s. 482.
95. Hegel's anti-Catholicism endured; e.g., *Philosophy of Right*, 53, 241 (s. 66 addition).   96. B731; H506–7.
97. B378; H258.

consciousness then: one Greek, the other more specifically Roman; one of free citizen-masters, the other of merely autonomous lords.[98]

There is something deeply troubling about Hegel's silence about pre-Roman slavery in the *Phenomenology* and his failure to make any effort to come to terms with Rousseau's paradox or to deal with the difference between slavery as physical and political coercion and as a psychic state. The reason for this equivocation, which Hegel never gave up, is easy to understand.[99] Greece had to serve him as a utopia if he was, so soon after the French Revolution, to believe that the cycle of the unhappy consciousness *could* be overcome, that it was not impossible. Greece, however, is also the real historical origin of European culture. It was there that most of it began, including slavery. To salvage the utopian function of antiquity Hegel chose, as did most of the classical republican utopists, to avert his eyes from that institution and to dwell upon civic freedom. Hegel needed that, if the 'has been' was not to become a simple 'never again.' The *Phenomenology* is not, however, given over to prophecy. It is a work of elegiac re-membering, a re-integrating of the past into the present and that in a mood of profound sadness.[100] But the 'perhaps not yet' had its function: it was the spiritual magnet that drew reason onward in its still very incomplete journey toward practical knowledge. To say that a free people could be thought of as 'perhaps not yet' made it possible to assign an aim to that voyage.

98. *Philosophy of Right*, 221 (s. 375).
99. In later years, he simply discussed the two slaveries apart from each other; e.g., *Philosophy of Mind*, s. 432–5, 482.
100. B753–4, 807–8; H524, 563–4.

CHAPTER THREE

THE MORAL FAILURES OF ASOCIAL MEN

The beautiful ethical polity is now only a memory. However intensely one may long for its resurrection, it is dead. Its art, 'beautiful fruit broken off the tree,' has been preserved for us by a kindly fate, but the culture that gave it life is gone forever. 'The spring and summer of that ethical life' are for us a 'veiled remembrance.' We can remember that past and internalize it to make it part of our spiritual world. That gives the dead polity a more general scope than it had when only its living members knew it. That is however a purely intellectual gain. It offers no hope of a social return.[1] We have no reason to believe that the 'happy people' has 'not yet' arrived and is visible on the horizon. We can only recall the polity that 'has been,' but there is no sign of movement toward that ethical end. In contemplation, the past has been regained, but in practice independence, not freedom prevails. We are not however to feel nostalgic. Mankind had to go beyond the naive and spontaneous condition of the classical polity in which each citizen saw himself in his fellows, and them within himself. The force of reason cannot endure this unreflective life. In the post-classical world freedom could only exist in a consciously established political order. The real difficulty is that no real polity is anywhere in sight. Only the market economy exhibits any degree of cohesion. The division of labor ensures that each one by working only for himself also works for all and that by satisfying his own needs he also supplies those of others. That is only the bond of natural necessity and conscious purpose plays no part in it. A

1. B753–4; H523–4.

society of course does exist, even if it be composed of independent persons. They have their rules, but as long as they think of themselves as dissociated beings their network of exchanges will not constitute an ethical or a free order.[2]

Hegel had no grounds for political hopes. Europe has been in a dissociated condition since the emergence of the independent consciousness. Christianity sanctified social estrangement and its successor, rationalism, is the very epitome of self-reliance. As such it is not capable of restoring the shattered social reason of an ethical polity. Cartesian reason does bring the human mind back from the 'beyond' to the here and now, but not to a social home. The rational ego that is intuitively certain that there is a perfect harmony between it and the world it surveys is an entirely isolated self. 'Reason is the conscious certainty of being all reality.'[3] But ethical life is not included in this reality. The ratiocinating ego has no awareness of the society of which it is a part. Its activity is limited to observing objects. In this the 'I' is sure of itself, knowing that 'my object and my essential reality is ego.'[4] 'I' contemplate 'myself' thinking and 'I know' myself as a reasoning being capable of analyzing and knowing the external world. However, such looking and explaining keeps each observer in isolation. It yields no self-knowledge for no 'we' can emerge from such preoccupations. The final débâcle of observing reason reveals that. The sciences that observe man along with everything else reduce him to his basic material element: the skeleton. Phrenology, pure positivism, puts reason itself in danger of being a mere bone.[5]

Observing reason cannot escape its self-imposed limitations but the erotic side of the rational ego rebels against the wooden deadness of such a state of mind. Analyzing things becomes wearisome, and erotic impulses finally assert themselves to dispel this dim and dull rationalism. It is discarded in the course of an emotional revulsion, but it is not dissolved from within. Hegel knew that romanticism with its cry for more feeling and vitality was a psychological reaction against a constricting rationalism. Men of feeling simply turned away from ratiocination without touching it. The two

2. B376–9; H256–9.   3. B273; H176.   4. B275; H177.
5. See above, ch. 1.

exist side by side. Faust's need for 'green' life instead of 'grey' theory was a reassertion of the long-suppressed erotic needs of the self.[6] The voyages of that newly activated side of the rational ego is, however, no Faustian quest.[7] To be sure, 'practical reason' which now steps forth is not satisfied with merely absorbing the world through observation. It means to impose itself upon that world, but its efforts are all unheroic failures. We are treated to an account of a series of misadventures. Hegel could see nothing in the moral attitudes of his contemporaries except self-oriented poses. Not one of them was capable of achieving its professed ends. All were doomed to failure, because they did not aim at recognition among men. Each one was an attempt to pit the self against the prevailing social world, the real character of which was wholly incomprehensible to these utterly self-absorbed, introspective people.[8]

One may well wonder why Hegel called these highly irrational expressions of subjectivity reason at all. He did so because they shared all the defects of rationalism. The practical ego turns to other people and to society with the same assumptions that observing reason brought to bear upon nature. Practical reason does not merely look, it acts, but with the same intuitive certainty as observing reason that there is a world out there that corresponds exactly to its idea of a rational order. There are only a few obstacles to be removed, and a 'rational' society will be achieved. The ego makes a model of social life which it expects to actualize. Since this hope of perfect accord between personal consciousness and the world promises happiness, 'the individual is thus sent forth into the world by his own spirit to seek happiness.' However, in the absence of any 'ethical substance,' that is, social bonds, these lone individuals will have to 'fill up their universality through themselves and to provide for their destiny out of the same source.'[9] They can only actualize their social urges as discrete solitary individuals, which is clearly unthinkable. They have only themselves to blame, for

6. B384–5; H262–3.
7. Goethe had published only a fragment of his great drama when Hegel wrote these lines.   8. B379; H259.
9. B380; H259–60.

it is they who have left custom and usage, even such as exist now, behind in order to replace them with values of their own devising. Each one, moreover, acts alone in the false expectation that the world is waiting for him to 'restore' it. In fact, there is only an isolated self confronting a world which it wants to refashion. This ego does not in fact know the object of its exertions. In this it is much like its observing partner. Both long to know and so to be at one with the world lying before them, but neither is willing to give up its independence in order to do so.

In a later work Hegel was to say that theoretical reason closes the gap between the self and the world by an act of appropriation. Like Adam speaking to Eve, the self says to the external world 'Thou art flesh of my flesh.' Theory dissolves the world into thoughts and is united with it. Thinking and organizing thoughts are transformations of what theory finds before it. Practical thought is more erotic. It sets itself objects of desire and pursues them. It is the will that propels thought. Theory and practice are both part of a single ego, but the latter is dominant. The will is the master of thought. It initiates the responses of the mind and induces it to move. All thinking is thus action. That also defines the will's freedom. It dominates the mind. An Indian mystic can empty his mind of all content. A fanatic can concentrate his entire mind upon a single fixed idea.[10] The failure of observing reason is due to its refusal to accept its own limitations. By forgetting the creativity of the ego, observation imagines itself to be complete knowledge. Active reason does not suffer from that defect, but by keeping itself isolated it dooms itself to failure. It does not know that the real end of its striving is communication. Each half of the rational ego is self-imprisoned by illusions generated by isolation. Such a view of the faults of subjectivity is, in its own way, extremely individualistic. Hegel often tended to reduce subjectivity to a personal mistake, something which an individual could readily avoid. In presenting the difficulties of uncommunicative people in that way he also was all but ignoring that anarchy and anomie are also cultural phenomena. He certainly knew better, but he was so contemptuous of his contemporaries that he could

10. *Philosophy of Right*, 225–8 (addition to s. 4 and 5).

not refrain from blaming and upbraiding them. In doing that he seemed to forget those actualities to which he was trying to recall them. Reproach is perhaps inherently individualizing, even when it is directed at collective states of mind. His very anger at his asocial contemporaries revealed Hegel's resemblance to them.

To demonstrate the deformities of practical reason Hegel chose to parade before the reader a series of socially incompetent individualities. Each one represents an aspect of the detached ego. At first that ego still thinks in terms of 'things.' This is the consciousness of the pleasure seeker intent upon appropriation of a world he desires. His efforts end in frustration and he is succeeded by a man of feeling who knows himself and others to be sentient, not mere 'things.' Sentiment, 'the law of the heart,' is now projected upon a cold world which is to be made more feeling and humane. That also ends badly and a third man, the stern prophet of virtue, tries his hand at bringing the world to order. He does not, however, mean business, especially when he discovers how misplaced he is in the actual world. With that practical reason gives up the battle against the world and turns inward to contemplate itself. The world is no longer treated as an opponent. It is simply ignored. The self, like any member of the animal world, treats society as if it were a natural environment to be used, but not to be altered or even investigated. There is no hindrance to a free indulgence in self-expression, which is the sole activity enjoyed by the self-absorbed ego. When this self discovers that even this self-display is productive, it must learn, painfully, to cope with the fact that its artifacts inevitably lead it into contact with other people. No man can avoid engaging in purposive conduct and others will respond to it. However, because it is unthinkable for this ego to limit its independence, it does not learn to communicate with others and to recognize and be recognized by them. It cannot go beyond autonomy and capricious assertions of its own will. No 'we' is ever conceived. Kantian moral self-legislation is the pinnacle of this development. With that Hegel's devastating review of subjective reason ends abruptly. The image of Antigone is suddenly invoked to illuminate by the force of contrast all modern faults. That confrontation is also a sign-post. It shows why Hegel and so many of his contemporaries turned their minds from Kant back to antiquity, to the only spiritual alternative they knew.

The course of practical reason is patterned somewhat loosely on the original cycle of consciousness. In striving to actualize itself practical reason seeks universality. That is inherent in speech and action, word and work. More specifically, hedonism is meant to correspond to sense-certainty, the law of the heart to perception and virtue to the understanding that does not know that explanation is really an act of self-projection. From there consciousness must move on to self-consciousness, and the isolated ego does seek self-realization in art, in politics and even in moral rule-making, but it really only plays a number of variations on a single theme: aloneness. It never makes a move toward recognition.[11] Purposeless self-display and self-rule are all that can be achieved by so dissociated a mind. Actuality remains foreign to it, since it creates a moral order for itself out of its own resources. Even Kantian autonomous law-makers project social rules as if they were categories of individual reason.[12] There is no way in which this kind of self-consciousness can escape from its own confines.

Since Hegel could see no avenue out of the dead-end to which reason, whether observing or practical, had come, he could not speak of the ethical world as a prospect. It could exist in consciousness only as the memory of something that had once been. That memory was not insignificant. It served as a standard which Hegel applied to judge and condemn modern morality. It also revealed what the errant moral ego was too blind to see as its real end. To think of freedom as 'not yet,' one would have to believe that the restless movement of the dissociated self was a ladder of ascent and that its aims were genuinely social values that could serve as real steps toward general happiness. The instinct of reason would then appear to have moved from brutish impulse to increasingly public and refined forms of social consciousness. Modern morality would then be a highly developed social state of mind, far removed from the crude hedonism it had overcome

11. B374–5; H255–6.　　12. B414; H283.

and rejected. In short, one would have to believe in ethical progress. Hegel saw not the slightest justification for any such belief. The 'happy people' has been, and our intense remembering of that past is not a social advance. Morality is indeed a step ahead of hedonism, since it is a more perfect awareness of what individual autonomy is, but it is no more social. That is why it forces one, in sheer despair, to remember that lost happiness. Such, at any rate, was Hegel's own experience and that of some of his contemporaries, notably Schiller, who also found Kant emotionally unbearable. Our enhanced consciousness of the past, our awareness of the superiority of ancient ethics has given 'us' a more universal sense of what 'we' are and might be. It does not allow us even to guess whether we will be able to rise above independence to a communal consciousness.[13]

A mirror for egoists

While it was Hegel's declared plan to show practical reason trapped in the treadmill of the primordial cycle of incomplete consciousness, he all but abandoned this scheme in developing his theme. The satirist in him simply got the better of the philosopher. We meet a succession of human types, a gallery of personified moral disasters. Hegel's inventory was comprehensive. Few, if any, forms of moral subjectivism escaped his scornful eye. His bitterness comes as no surprise, nor do his characters astonish one. The figures paraded before the reader are as familiar to us as they were to him. The links between them seem often a bit contrived. There is no pattern of development from one to the other. These are not really stages in the movement of the independent ego to generalize itself through action. Hegel is presenting a series of portraits. Each one reveals something about the impotence of subjectivity, for each one is a special manifestation of the same defect. That is why the story of their experiences has a real psychological and literary unity.

The first and most primitive figure of moral isolation is the hedonist who looks only for 'private and particular pleasure.'[14] He appears typically when social ties are at their

13. B379-82; H259-61.   14. B392; H267.

weakest. The Cyrenaics in ancient Greece and the Roman Epicureans were the earliest philosophical spokesmen for this attitude, while English philosophy since Bacon has taught the same doctrine. It is, in fact, the moral application of empiricism, the twin of observing reason. Goodness and evil are identified with the sensations of pleasure and pain, as all knowledge is a matter of sense experience.[15] It is not, however, these philosophers whom Hegel recalls initially. He begins with a far more striking personage, Goethe's Faust, who, repudiating science and reason, plunges directly into life to find his happiness there. As all pure sense knowing is a sort of 'grasping' of objects, so is Faust's greedy hedonism. He wants to take life as if it were an apple to be enjoyed, but Hegel's readers knew, and were meant to recall at once, that Faust's quest ends in crime and despair.[16]

To be sure, the pleasure seeker does not want to consume other people, even though he sees them solely as sources of pleasure to himself. He wants them to find their pleasure in him also. He does not, however, expect to lose any of his independence in this exchange of pleasures. Faust does not know that when he seduces an innocent girl he or she will experience anything but bliss. Instead circumstances lead her to kill first her mother and then her unwanted child. When she lands in prison, a convicted murderess, Faust discovers that he is not indifferent to her fate. He suffers with her without being able to save her, and he learns that the consequences of his conduct are not really his own deeds. He only looked for personal pleasure, but he found mutual dependence, a 'we,' not two 'ones' who owned and enjoyed each other. In finding his pleasure, he lost himself. The dissociated freedom of the pleasure seeker is destroyed by the experience of genuine human association. He is not alone: other people, however loving and ignorant, are not just objects. Even pleasurable relationships create a unit, a society, that is a new, trans-individual situation for each person involved.[17]

The very existence of other people thus brings the plea-

15. *Lectures on the History of Philosophy*, I, 469–75; II, 276–311; III, 170–88, 295–314.
16. B384–5; H262–3. The fragment of *Faust* that Hegel knew ends with Gretchen's imprisonment and Faust's desperate failure to save her.
17. B385–6; H263.

sure seeker up against necessity and a shared, general condition, though isolated freedom and individual self-enjoyment were his only aims. That is, however, only one way in which hedonism fails. By conceiving of himself as an object, as part of the natural order, he is subject to the necessities of natural life. At the end of the natural life of any organism that has no purpose beyond its part in the natural order, is death and extinction. That is why he who takes life, in fact takes *his* life, commits suicide. For a life of pure sensation is only a path to inevitable death. Mere life is dying.[18] In conceiving of himself as an atom, unrelated to other human beings, and as a part of nature only, rather than of mankind, with specific human, social and spiritual ends, the pleasure seeker lost all that might have separated him from the natural cycle of life as death. He misunderstands his individuality by thinking of himself as a purposeless, self-contained pleasure and pain feeler and giver, and as such a part of a natural world. That world becomes quite incomprehensible to him. It is now a dark realm of fate and brute necessity. His own life becomes a riddle to him. He had eagerly looked for life and he found death. He had pursued liberty alone and for himself and discovered that he was as much subject to necessity as a plant. Nature as pain and pleasure is a relentless sovereign, as Hegel's contemporary, Bentham, noted, even if he drew different conclusions from that insight.[19] To Hegel the central paradox of hedonism was right there. Hedonism claims that men are bound to seek pleasure and to avoid pain, and yet one finds everywhere that they pursue misery. That, as the pleasure seeker learns, is so, just because pain and pleasure are such harsh taskmasters.

The defeat of hedonism is analogous to that of the crude

18. B388; H265.
19. B387-8; H264-5. The degree to which hedonism is not conducive to freedom or to individuality can be readily recognized in the celebrated first two sentences of Jeremy Bentham's *Introduction to the Principles of Morals and Legislation:* 'Nature has placed mankind under the government of two sovereign masters, pain and pleasure. It is for them alone to point out what we ought to do as well as to determine what we shall do.' Hegel had more in common with Bentham than one might suppose. In spite of great philosophical differences, they shared a very considerable number of dislikes, among which anarchism of any kind was the most important.

empiricism of sense-certainty in the primary cycle of consciousness. The certainties of the latter are also derived from personal sense experience. The hedonist's activity removes him from the immediacy of 'life,' just as speech destroys the self-assurance of 'natural' consciousness. Both die in the arms of 'empty abstractions.' 'Lifeless actuality' overcomes both when they are forced to deliberate and communicate. The direct experience of the senses and of pleasure are lost.[20] At the root of their trouble is the false notion of the self as an isolated unthinking atom limited to its purely personal sensations. As soon as the limits of such activity reveal themselves perplexity and futility overcome the victims of these errors.

If Bacon and Locke were not philosophers whom Hegel could admire, he was perfectly ready to admit that they had their uses and that their popularity was, regrettably, immense. Like their Epicurean ancestors, English philosophers had done valuable work in dispelling religious superstition. Moreover, they had provided the basic conceptions of the natural sciences. That alone made them the masters of modern thought. Later Hegel was to add another, and an unflattering explanation, for their success. Theirs was an outlook fit for shopkeepers and laborers, men wholly immersed in materiality and actuality. That was the typical condition of most men and it amply accounted for the ready appeal of this poor substitute for philosophy.[21]

There are always men who will feel the shortcomings of the pleasure principle. According to Hegel's account they reject unthinking life and its constrictions in favor of 'the law of the heart,' or a morality of loving. There does not seem to be any logical or psychological necessity for this movement, and Hegel shows none in the *Phenomenology;* to find it one must look to some of his other works. The real connection between the flight from hedonism and the turn to the inner voice of feeling is historical. The paradigm for this recurrent pattern of spiritual change was the rise of Christianity in the Roman Empire. In a brilliant theological essay of his youth Hegel had already identified Christianity as the religion of

20. B387, 151–60; H264–5, 279–89. *Lectures on the History of Philosophy,* III, 176, 182, 304–6. See above, ch. 1.
21. *Lectures on the History of Philosophy,* III, 172–3, 186, 295–8, 312–13.

the law of the heart and as a retreat from an intolerably cold order. Originally that was the world of Jewish legalism.[22] When he returned to the subject in the *Phenomenology* the Jews were replaced by the Romans. Later on he explicitly noted the similarity between Rome and the modern world. Both were marked by 'unspiritual subjectivity and subjectivity without thought.'[23] Even Roman religion was a calculating egotism, a religion of utility. Personal advantage was its principal and only aim. The Roman's gods were private deities whom he tried to bribe. This procedure only yields a sense of dependence on fortune, a general frustration and a fearful resort to superstitious devices and beliefs. Power becomes the reigning obsession. The state inspires a cold patriotism. It stands for collective power and power is the great object of worship. That these victims and worshippers of power should succeed in conquering the entire world was altogether consistent, as was their deification of their monstrous emperors.

Like all hedonists the Romans discovered that the consequences of their acts escaped their control. Having destroyed all the polities and religions around them, these egotists were now surrounded by a cold indifference. They were heirs not to pleasure, but to all the sadness of an ancient world.[24] In this world Christianity is the great hope and spiritual awakening. As the Empire stood for necessity and power, the new faith of the heart promised liberation and truth. It was, however, also a total rejection not only of the immediate environment, but of the world and of all its cares in general. That was its fatal failing – and one that emerged again and again in European history, especially in Hegel's own world.

Christianity in its 'negative' aspect, as a rejection of the world, was to remain for Hegel the original source and model of ethical egomania. Its morality of 'the heart' had become an endemic phenomenon in Europe which had spread far beyond its religious roots. Hegel was, in fact, obsessively irritated by the flourishing sentimentality of his own age. In art, in

22. 'The Spirit of Christianity and its Fate,' *Early Theological Writings*, 182–224.
23. *Lectures on the Philosophy of Religion*, II, 331; III, 150. The translation is not really adequate.   24. 'The Spirit of Christianity', 298–323.

philosophy and in religion 'beautiful souls,' worshippers of sincerity, and other types of self-cultivating sensitive spirits abounded. Hegel's response to all this was a sustained defense of sanity against what he regarded as pure lunacy. Most of his major works after the *Phenomenology* contain at least one attack upon those who preferred their feelings to the disciplined activity of thought. The dissection of 'the law of the heart' in the *Phenomenology* is, however, his most sustained review of the failures of this manifestation of subjectivity. It more than amply explains Hegel's enduring contempt.

The flight from brute necessity to the heart and the abandonment of hedonism are, in one respect, moral advances. The man of feeling recognizes that one must follow rules in one's relations to other men, not mere impulse. The law he accepts is, however, of a very peculiar sort. It is the creation of his own feelings and it is defined by its utter hostility to all prevailing conventions and laws. In its overflowing concern for other men the heart calls out to all other people to follow their hearts also, and thus to free themselves from the social oppression which stifles individuality by imposing cruel and alien constraints upon it. These spontaneous expressions of the heart, naturally, give much pleasure. They 'pass for a display of excellence' and show a fine concern for bringing about 'the welfare of mankind.' [25] It would seem that the men of feeling must truly enjoy their own perfection.

Unhappily for those who profess it, the law of the heart contains a double contradiction which becomes clear as soon as it is made effective. Since it has no content other than the rejection of convention, it cannot endure its own success. As soon as other men agree to follow the law of the heart, this formula becomes a general convention in its own right – and so ceases to be the private, sacred, personal innermost possession of the individual. It is no longer *his* law, it is now also 'explicitly alien and external,' a new, independent common and shared reality. In this difficulty the man who insists on the primacy of *his* heart as the sole source of moral truth rejects his fellows, and simply denies that 'his excellent intentions' could possibly be those of these 'detested and detestable' people. It becomes clear that the very notion of a pri-

25. B391–2; H266.

vate law is self-contradictory and that the law of the heart is not really meant to be a rule at all. It is not a law to be generally accepted by all. Its concern for the liberation of others is a sham.[26] 'The heart-throb for the welfare of mankind passes therefore into the rage of frantic self-conceit, into the fury of consciousness to preserve itself from destruction.' The religion of the heart when it is institutionalized must appear to the archetypal Protestant as a sinister conspiracy of fanatical priests and of 'degraded and degrading despots.' Mankind remains deluded as long as there are conventions, even if these acknowledge the law of the heart.[27] For some Christians any social structure, even a church, a community of the faithful, is a betrayal of the pure faith.

The second crisis of the law of the heart arises from its inherent contradiction and it leads to a kind of madness and conflict. There is an insurmountable contradiction between the 'heart' and 'law' of any conceivable sort. The heart stands for the supremacy of uniquely personal feeling, while law expresses general rules. The first is justified by its peculiarity, the latter by its common applicability. The two simply cannot be reconciled. The 'law of the heart' must be valid, either because it is one's very own, or because it is everyone's, but it cannot be both. The lunacy that comes from an inability to choose between the two is not a case of delusion, but of inner distraction. It is also a megalomaniac self-infatuation.[28] That becomes clear as soon as several hearts stake out their claims for general validity. Each insists on *its* own validity, but because of their personal character each one of these laws of the heart is different. Since they are by definition intransigent, a war of each against all others must ensue.[29] Inner conflict between irreconcilable pretensions is thus matched by external conflict between the many laws of many hearts. Here, more poignantly than in the case of the pleasure seeker, is the failure of self-generated morality. The heart seeks a fellowship it cannot accept. It is not capable of the self-surrender that any law demands. Without that, a state of war, psychic and social, is inevitable.

The 'law of the heart' had for Hegel two histories: that of

26. B393–6; H269–71.   27. B397; H271–2.   28. B396–7; H270–1.
29. B399–400; H273–4.

the 'fate' of the Protestant impulse and that of post-Kantian religious irrationalism. In his earlier essay he had commented at length on the theme of 'He who shall save his life shall lose his life.'[30] In the quest for personal salvation the original Christians rejected all morals. Neither duties nor rights had any meaning for them. Only forgiveness of sins, both one's own and those of others, was to remain. The law of the heart, the call to universal love, here meant total dissociation. In trying to preserve only his own inner purity the Christian, however, lost the objects of his love: other people. His life, the saving spirit of love, was lost, because he looked only to his own inner state and to his own salvation. Less self-absorbed Christians interpreted love to mean a community of the faithful, a group of worshippers who shared a common body of beliefs and customs. They thus returned to the world and to the universal condition of humanity. Jesus himself rejected this compromise and his anger finally drove his original great love from his heart.[31] He also suffered the inner destruction that must afflict all who turn their back upon the world to follow the law of the heart. That was, in Hegel's view, the ineradicable weakness of Christianity. It emerges again and again, especially in the sectarian impulse of Protestantism. For all their superiority to Catholics, Protestants tended to the madness of self-infatuation. In North America, where religion was free from all traditional and political restrictions, this inherent proclivity had now displayed itself in the crazy multiplication of uninhibited sects.[32] The pure of heart cannot endure the social discipline of a congregation or of organized worship. To break off from fellowship is part of their inner light. It is simply anarchic.

When he came to contemplate the claims of the Anabaptists, Pietists and Quakers, Hegel suspected the worst. Theirs was merely a stubborn refusal to obey the law under the cloak of religious piety.[33] However, his opinion of these sects would not have been higher had he regarded them as sincere. Sincerity did not, in his eyes, excuse their contempt for civic

30. 'The Spirit of Christianity', 236–7.   31. *Ibid.*, 281–7.
32. *Vernunft in der Geschichte*, 206.
33. *Lectures on the History of Philosophy*, III, 439; *Lectures on the Philosophy of Religion*, III, 140–1.

duty and common social usage. For Hegel holy self-concern was just as selfish as less pretentious forms of egotism. The pious anxiety for the purity of one's own soul extinguishes love.[34] To attempt to rise above the common standard in these matters only puts one below it. That was Hegel's most constant theme.

This unremitting rancor would be aberrant if Hegel had been concerned only with the world-denying ways of primitive Christianity and inner-light Protestant sects. The main object of his scorn was, in fact, far more contemporary and widespread in its challenge. Jacobi and his disciple Schleiermacher were contemporary prophets of a religion of feeling that impinged not only upon conventional Christianity but upon philosophy.[35] It postured as a substitute for serious thought by offering a soul-satisfying and easily accessible road to truth. Intuition was to replace the work of the reflective intelligence, at least among those chosen few who could hear its ineffable message. It was of these notions that Hegel wrote bitterly that 'apocalyptic utterances' of enthusiasts inspired by some 'vague and indeterminate Divinity' were threatening philosophy. This god, who is known directly, without reflection, remains the 'esoteric possession' of a few 'beautiful souls.' And they misrepresent this closed incommunicable insight as philosophic truth. Philosophy, however, is not personal knowledge, but potentially open to all mankind. Thought is 'the activity of the self in general.'[36] The voice of feeling is private. Intelligibility is the whole aim of philosophy, while the flowery expression of personal insight merely hints at esoteric feelings. In fact it communicates nothing, because it is an arbitrary combination of imagination and ideas, 'neither fish nor flesh, neither poetry nor philosophy.'

34. 'The Spirit of Christianity', 289; *Lectures on the Proofs of the Existence of God* in *Lectures on the Philosophy of Religion*, III, 180–7; *Lectures on the Philosophy of Religion*, I, 68–70.

35. In the 'Introduction' to his *Lectures on the History of Philosophy*, Hegel mentions Jacobi several times, more frequently than some of the philosophers whom he esteemed far more, and made it clear that the pervasive cultural character mattered more to him than the intrinsic strength of these views; e.g., I, 13–14. In 1817 he had written a long review of Jacobi's newly published works, which was kinder than his usual remarks, because it dealt with his abstractness and one-sidedness rather than his sentimentality. Hegel's *Sämtliche Werke* (Stuttgart, 1927), IV, 313–47.

36. B72–8; H13–18.

Because it thinks itself too good for conceptual thought, this sentimentality is really 'anti-human.'[37] Here, Hegel was to say years later, 'the glory of philosophy is departed, for [philosophy] presupposes a common ground of thought and principles.'[38] What cannot be said rationally is not open to others, to men as men. The religiosity of feeling is thus asocial *because* it is irrational.

The betrayal of philosophy was perhaps Hegel's main objection to the highly popular style of Jacobi and Schleiermacher, but there was something even more worrisome. The great appeal of their excesses was itself significant. It expressed a recurrent and deeply felt spiritual mood among the cultivated classes of Europe. The longing for instant certainty, for immediate edification, was itself the product of European education, an offspring of that very culture that the law of the heart rejected. This 'law' was of course not a response to some eternal, inner human essence, as its prophets claimed, but, in fact, a reaction to sentiments nurtured entirely by an old culture. It was indeed one of the paradoxes of this culture that it should generate such hostility to itself.[39] Moreover, the causes of these feelings of dissatisfaction were real enough. As the Roman order *was* cold and destructive, so modern society *was* unspiritual and harsh. The social order from which 'unhappy' souls turned to attend to their self-beautification *was* constrictive and frigid. That is why Hegel presented the 'law of the heart' as an historical reaction to hedonism and to its pervasive sense of necessity. It was, after all, to escape from 'the slavery of Time and Necessity,' and from all the stimuli which drive the pleasure seeker, that Schleiermacher chose to 'fix [his] eyes upon [his] true self' and to practice 'endless introspection.' It was explicitly a flight from 'mere legality,' crudeness, and materialism. This clearly was an excessive reaction that looked even upon friendship as a threat to freedom because the fear of constraint had become so extreme that even rational discourse was an imposition on the self. Only imagination and intui-

37. B126–7; H55–6.
38. *Lectures on the History of Philosophy*, III, 508–10.
39. *Hegel's Philosophy of Mind*, s. 470; *Lectures on the History of Philosophy*, III, 421–2; *Lectures on the Proofs of the Existence of God, loc. cit.,* 179.

tion were really free.[40] In Hegel's opinion they were also
vain. For our thoughts are not self-generated. Even intuition
and imagination are the work of collective experiences. By
cutting himself off from the very sources of his experience,
because these are shared, the man of the heart destroys himself. He becomes the victim of his inability to recognize the
social character of his own attitudes. As such he is a witness
to and the culmination of the suicidal impulses of European
culture.

Finally, Hegel was deeply aware that modern philosophy
had itself been the cause of these anti-philosophic phenomena. Philosophy had set in motion psychological dispositions
that had flowered into a literature wholly antagonistic to
the philosophic spirit. Philosophy now denied men certain
knowledge. Locke had told them to settle for probability and
Kant had rendered certain knowledge of God inaccessible.[41]
However, people went right on yearning for certainty. They
found it in feeling. To be sure, the mere feeling of certainty
is no guarantee of truth, as Hegel had already shown.[42] We
are bound to have feelings, but that is a mere description of
our condition. Unhappily for philosophy we can have very
strong feelings about God, morality and law. These feelings
may be decent or wicked, but they are no substitutes for
thought.[43] Indeed, they must remain subject to the judgment of the intelligence. The truly simple heart is in no danger. It submits to authority and is safe.[44] The peculiarity of
the philosophically educated is that their hearts can turn
against both convention and reason when these appear too
exigent. It is a sophisticated reaction, possible only to people
who find that philosophy is a threat to their already drained
emotional life.

40. For samples of Schleiermacher's rhapsodies on these themes, see his
   Soliloquies, ed. and trans. by H. L. Fries (Chicago, 1926), 15–22, 29–30,
   36–7, 56–7, 60–2; and his *On Religion*, trans. by John Oman (New York,
   1958), 80–1, 90, 93, 98.
41. Locke was for Hegel solely the author of the *Essay on Human Understanding* while for the attack on Kant in the *Phenomenology* no work
   was more important than *Religion Within the Limits of Reason Alone*.
42. B665–6; H461–2. See above, chap. 1.
43. *Philosophy of Mind*, 471; *Lectures on the Philosophy of Religion*, I, 276,
   288; *Lectures on the Proofs of the Existence of God, loc. cit.*, 181.
44. *Ibid.*, 183–5.

The practical consequences are just as troubling as the speculative. Kant's moral philosophy made demands as extreme as his epistemology. Hegel had long recognized that it had a psychological impact quite like that of Jewish and Roman legalism.[45] Schiller had indeed complained that Kant was the Draco of his age, having found it not yet fit for a Solonic dispensation. That, Schiller went on, was to denigrate mankind and to force upon it a punitive and monkish burden. Kant had replied that this was not his intention and that a man who had performed his duty for its own sake would surely be happy in the knowledge of his own virtue.[46] Whatever one might think of this hope, it cannot be said that Kant had met the psychological issue. The feeling of being open and sincere in one's relations to others gives one an immediate and certain feeling of one's own purity and goodness. It offers a sense of one's liberty which no amount of rational obedience to duty can rival. However, the consequence of sincerity as the sovereign moral norm, as Hegel duly noted, is disastrous. Woldemar, the hero of Jacobi's novel, is so sincere, so sensitive, that he finds he simply cannot endure other people. He longs for their approval, but it is never enough.[47] Sincerity, the display of one's own beautiful feelings, is not a bridge to other people. It may even turn, in its disappointment, to crime and madness. For the great mistake of the sincere is to believe that spontaneity implies goodness. Ferdinand, the hero of Schiller's *Kabale und Liebe,* finding his sweetheart less wholly committed to a rebellious sincerity than himself, kills her in a rage of jealousy and suspicion. Sincerity and contempt for others are intimately related, Hegel felt. Egotism in its moral forms is still selfishness.[48] That was, in a word, the first and the last of Hegel's countless comments on the 'law of the heart.'

The egotism of the law of the heart must lead to mutual destruction and scorn. That is the point also at which its

45. 'The Spirit of Christianity', 244–5. Hegel spoke here of 'the self-coercion of Kantian virtue.'
46. See Schiller's *Anmut und Würde* and generally R. D. Miller, *Schiller and the Idea of Freedom* (Oxford, 1970), 52–3. Kant's reply is in *Religion Within the Limits of Reason Alone,* trans. and ed. by T. M. Greene and H. H. Hudson (New York, 1960), 18–19.
47. *Philosophy of Fine Art,* I, 322–3.   48. *Ibid.,* I, 261–3.

failure becomes manifest, even to its adherents. The man of republican virtue thus follows the sentimentalist in the *Phenomenology*. Hegel argued that if the man of feeling recognizes the full implications of the law of the heart he will decide to abandon individualism altogether. Seeing that the war of competing impulses is devoid of morality, he turns away from selfishness altogether. For him it is now merely 'the course of the world' in which egotism reigns uncontrolled and destructively.[49] In disgust the disabused heart throws itself into the opposite extreme. Self-edification is now rejected in favor of stern public virtue. Classical discipline, a Roman rigor in the interest of the public good, is to replace individuality and its claims. Nothing would seem more remote from subjectivity than this morality. However, to Hegel it appeared clear that this fantasy, in its indifference to history and its necessities, was a private utopia just as self-willed and self-centered as the more obviously subjective forms of morality that had preceded it. He may not have detested it as vehemently as the law of the heart, but the futility and vanity of republican virtue did annoy him intensely. It also disturbed him, because he identified it with the heroes of Schiller's later dramas, and he admired Schiller as much as he despised Jacobi. To be sure he could not agree with Schiller's moral philosophy, but his debt to the poet was in many ways profound. His philosophy of art shows Schiller's influence on every page. In any case, Hegel was perfectly capable of recognizing Schiller's genius as a poet and thinker. Schiller's dramas were obviously immensely significant phenomena of the human spirit.

The conflict between republican virtue and the law of the heart, on the one hand, and Machiavellian politics, on the other, was central to Schiller's political plays. Hegel recognized that the heroes of *Fiesco* and *Don Carlos*, who struggle for political liberty, are more substantial heroes than the merely sincere Ferdinand. They are not absorbed in their own hearts. Their objects are noble and universal. Both Fiesco and Posa are men of virtue who sacrifice their lives to a great cause, the liberation of mankind from political and religious tyranny.[50] Each one is, moreover, not only chal-

49. B402–3; H274–5.   50. *Philosophy of Fine Art*, I, 261–3.

lenged by a despotic villain, but also by friends and lovers who cling to the law of the heart. The tension between private goodness and republican virtue is a vital aspect of these dramas. Friendship and love have claims here just as powerful as political idealism and courage. That the spectator is left to choose sides and, indeed, to determine the meaning of the characters' actions for himself, is part of the enduring interest of these plays.

In Schiller's dramas the full complexity of the struggle reveals itself, because the champion of republican politics is confronted with two adversaries, the evil despot and the loving, pure soul. By adopting a sequential pattern of analysis Hegel simplified matters considerably. The law of the heart has been left behind and the classical utopian faces only the ambitious men of the world, the new 'princes.' The moral tension is thus also greatly reduced. Moreover, the adversary of Hegel's man of virtue is not a bigoted despot such as Philip II of Spain, but any Machiavellian politician willing to use whatever weapons are available to serve his ambitions. In the *Phenomenology* Hegel is concerned only with a Don Quixote who behaves, not like a feudal knight, but like a talkative pseudo-Plutarchian hero of the civil life. The outcome of his opposition to the 'course of the world,' that is, to modern actuality, is, therefore, a foregone conclusion. It never amounts to more than ludicrous feints of endless rhetoric against political necessity. Hegel's play lacks both the humane sympathy of Cervantes and the moral seriousness of Schiller.

Hegel's man of virtue, emerging from the self-infatuation of the heart, sees individuality as the evil to be crushed, both within himself and in the world around him. Personal ends and ambitions must be eliminated in the single-minded pursuit of the public good. The modern world in which individuals assert their interests must be forced to return to the disciplined self-denial of a civic ethos. The man of virtue does not see that, though the modern politician is concerned only with his own designs, the forces of society ('the course of the world') control and integrate him. History puts him into his place, whatever he may think. His individuality is severely limited by collective pressures. The man of virtue, however, who wants to impose his dreams on the world, even though he is determined to repress his individuality, remains self-willed.[51] His self-sacrifice is just an assertion of selfhood. Of course, the man of virtue does not recognize this. He denies that his is a personal utopia. On the contrary, virtue is inherent in society and has simply been prevented from emerging.[52] Mankind has been misguided and the man of virtue simply has to summon the misled to their real, inherent powers and capacities for political virtue. That, at least, is what he 'believes,' since there is not a shred of evidence of a dormant civic consciousness beneath the cloak of actuality. It is the self-delusion of the man of virtue to treat his opinions, not as personal, but as a reflection of society's real, even if hidden, values. He lives in the illusion that he has triumphed over the principle of individuality that seems to dominate everyone in contemporary society except himself.

How does the man of virtue act against 'the course of the world'? As soon as he tries to actualize his intentions the inner contradictions of his attitude become manifest. In this he is doomed to share the experience of his predecessor, the man of feeling. If he enters the political arena to fight for his ideals he will cease to be virtuous. He will have to adopt weapons adapted to his age and its conditions. Moreover, he will have to assert himself as an individual fighting with and against others. If he does that he is transformed into just another participant in 'the course of the world,' and not a pure knight of virtue.[53] That is what happened to Fiesco and temporarily to Posa. The former accepts the Dukedom of Genoa to rule it well. The latter decides to turn to Philip II when he realizes that Don Carlos is useless to his schemes for liberating the Netherlands. If, however, the man of virtue decides to preserve his republican purity at all costs and to keep talking while he waits for the world to follow its 'inherent' civic mind, nothing at all will happen. The world can well afford to ignore its babbling antagonist. He is after all only a fantasy Cato, not even a real Jacobin. No more than the man of feeling can this self-sacrificing individualist tolerate the real demands of action. He does not really want

51. B407–8; H279.   52. B404–5, 408–9; H276, 279–80.
53. B405–6; H276.

to bring his dream into actuality. He merely wants to enjoy the perfection of his own virtue. He enters the 'duel' with no other end than to keep his sword perfectly clean and shining.[54]

Self-contradiction is not the only cause of the feebleness of the man of virtue. He is, above all, mistaken in thinking of himself as somehow outside of and above 'the course of the world.' To think of oneself as a being apart from society is the very definition of the subjective consciousness. That is why the man of virtue for all his self-repression is the cousin of the hedonist and the beautiful soul. But however much he may try to struggle against history, it will still engulf him. His failures, but also his successes, depend entirely upon his adaptability. If he insists on rhetoric he will achieve nothing.[55] If he really comes to grips with 'the course of the world,' he will discover that there are a great many possibilities for doing good, for improvement and for reform. To see this, however, he must give up the fancy that he is struggling against an enemy.[56] 'The course of the world' is not a territory to be conquered, but the realm of possible action. Conservation and innovation, not selfishness and self-sacrifice, are the real issues in history. The world process can, however, easily ignore or silently destroy the 'tethered knight of virtue.' [57] Everything is absorbed by the totality of men interacting to create a social pattern that has neither an inner core nor an outer shell, or an inherent and an apparent character. It is all of a piece and one can understand it and act within it, or one may refuse to recognize it and accomplish nothing. To remain 'outside' is an imaginary escape which amounts to opting for a purely rhetorical stance. It is talkative passivity, not active nobility. And that is also part of history.

The super-noble pose is merely a rhetorical one. The man of virtue never intended seriously to do anything but talk. He is not defeated by the unscrupulous machinations of the worldly, but by himself. In antiquity civic mores had their place within the context of a free people. Then public virtue was a matter of concrete ends pursued by effective political communities. The modern utopist does not find himself in such circumstances. Now republican virtue, pulled out of its

54. B409–10; H280–1.   55. B407–8; H278–9.   56. B406–7; H278.
57. B408; H278.

historical setting, is a mere abstraction, and those who devote themselves to utopias really do not mean to go beyond verbal lamentations. 'The vacuousness of this rhetorical eloquence in conflict with the world's process' is not exposed for what it is only because it now appeals to the cultivated taste of the modern age. But like all fashions it soon bores people and is quickly forgotten.[58]

The utopian consciousness is mistaken in believing that beneath the conflict of interests there is a public spirit waiting to be awakened by it. However, Machiavellian politicians are also in error. They suffer from a misapplied cynicism. The world process does not reflect their views. It is not as bad as it looks. When the knight of virtue awakens from his dreams he sees that the world is not just 'a perversion of goodness.' The so-called realist who claims that men always act selfishly is, in his own way, also ignorant. He does not understand what action really is.[59] The process of interacting, self-oriented wills is more than a sum of self-seeking individuals. History encompasses the actors, selfish and unselfish, to achieve collective ends. Individual acts abstracted from the social whole are indeed expressions of personal interests and purposes, but looked at historically, they are constituent elements in the development of a social whole. 'The way of the world' embraces both the dreamer and the realist, each one of whom can see only his own part of the whole.[60]

Hegel sneered at political rhetoric, especially the virtuous sort, to the end of his days. He had far less to say about those, men like Philip II, against whom it was directed. That does not mean that Hegel preferred them to the Posas of this world. But his silence was ambiguous, if not dishonest, even if it does not amount to a praise of tyranny. What Hegel seems to be suggesting is that the liberation of the Netherlands could not be achieved by men such as the fine-phrased Posa, but only by the notoriously silent William of Orange. Verbosity is to be taken as proof of political incompetence and inactivity. The man of virtue is clearly both. He is neither a Jacobin, nor a Napoleon. His civic ardor never goes beyond his eternal talk. It was Hegel's bitter farewell to the old dream of classical republicanism. He could never forget

58. B409–10; H280–1.   59. B411; H281–2.   60. B411–12; H282.

nor forgive the passivity of the German friends of the French Revolution. With endless rhetorical enthusiasm, these re-publicans did nothing. The French, whatever their sins, had at least acted heroically, had dared all, first for the republic and then for empire. The Germans had just stood by, docilely from beginning to end, as history simply rolled over them.[61] They had done nothing and, indeed, had not even understood their own situation. They could not perhaps be expected to make a revolution, but they might have entered into the Napoleonic order actively and intelligently. Napo-leon is never mentioned in the *Phenomenology*, but the successful efforts of that 'individuality' that acts for its own ends, but achieves universal ones, may plausibly describe that hero of political action.[62] The contrast between him and his civic-minded opponents could well have inspired Hegel's con-tempt for the latter. Why we must celebrate the success of Napoleon is less clear. To be sure great men make the world go around, but why should anyone admire them so uncriti-cally? Hegel never really answered that question. He wor-shipped success without fully knowing it. The pains of failure and defeat were, in fact, his real topic. He had shown vividly how dangerous and shattering it is for individuals to indulge in dreams doomed to failure. Hegel was surely right there. But it is a completely individualistic argument against individualism. He is, in fact, urging us to abandon subjectivity because it can do us no good.

Actors in search of purpose

The man of virtue learns that futility awaits individualists who pit themselves against society. He discovers to his cost that he cannot bring his civic dreams to life. There are no 'laws of nature' to be uncovered beneath the social world which he has been assaulting verbally. It is all a creation of his own imagination. The world is not solidly out there. Like the cognitive understanding of the primary cycle of con-sciousness, the virtuous mind sees that it has projected its own categories upon the world. There was no alien order out

61. *Lectures on the History of Philosophy*, III, 390–1.
62. B411–12; H281–2.

there. That was all a part of the self, as that self is part of the world. The virtuous talker is an individualist in an atomistic world. Practical reason, like its theoretical partner, reacts to this experience by turning inward. The vanishing external world ceases to be a field of action, just as it no longer was a source of knowledge.[63] Both know that they need self-knowledge, and each is certain only that ego = ego. Like its predecessors the self-consciousness born out of modern rationalism remains in bondage to the idea of independence. Having given up his efforts to halt the course of the world, the man of virtue resorts to the most extreme form of self-concentration. Since he insists on this isolation, his actions become obscure to himself, for without communication he cannot learn to know himself and his activity, not even his real errors.

This abandonment of the world in favor of a voyage inward is the path of Fichte's absolute ego, which recognizes nothing but itself.[64] In Fichte's view all we know is the creation of the ego's own activity. In response to its own expansive needs the ego invents the non-ego. Once the ego has posited the non-ego it yearns to be again at one with its own invention and a circular process of self-division and re-integration is set in motion. The activity of the ego in the first instance is thus one of creative imagination which projects an 'external' world, or non-ego, to which it reacts and upon which it acts.[65] This solipsism was a desperate effort to over-

---

63. B410–12, 209–12; H280–2, 126–8. See above, ch. 1.   64. B414–16; H283–5.
65. Thus Fichte: 'The ultimate ground of all reality for the ego . . . is an original interaction between the ego and some sort of something [*irgendein etwas*] of which nothing can be said except that it must be wholly opposed to the ego.' *Grundlage der Gesamten Wissenschaftslehre, Fichte's Werke*, ed. F. Medicus (Leipzig, 1911), I, 471 (my translations).
    'The science of knowledge is such that . . . its basic ideas are brought forth in everyone who considers them by the creative imagination itself. It cannot be otherwise . . . once the whole business of the human spirit rises out of the imagination.' *Ibid.*, 476.
    'Our world is absolutely nothing but the Non Ego, is posited solely to explain the limitedness of the Ego, and hence receives all its determinations only through opposition to the Ego.' *The Science of Ethics*, trans. by A. E. Kroeger (New York, 1897), 71.
    'All interest is mediated through the interest I have in myself and is only a modification of this self-interest. Whence arises this interest in myself? Simply from an impulse . . . [the] impulse craving harmony between my original Ego . . . The impulse manifests itself through a yearning.' *Ibid.*, 151.

come the Kantian gap between mind and the objective natural order. As Hegel remarked, not unjustly, Fichte meant to grasp certainty by giving up the very possibility of true knowledge.[66] That was an unphilosophical escape from learning by an ego that had declared itself incapable of communicating. It is not, however, an ego that goes to sleep. It yearns for action. In gratifying this impulse the Fichtean ego makes only one demand upon itself: it must remain entirely independent. Though it feels a need to connect itself to something, it will not do so at the expense of its total self-sufficiency. To move it must therefore take a leap into faith. Knowledge is impossible, so the ego invents a conscience, a will to good deeds, for itself. That suffices for action. 'We act not because we know, but we know because we act.' Will is everything, for the end of reason is 'pure activity, absolutely by itself alone.' [67] Neither purpose nor outcome matter. Action is its own reward for the ego that must remain at all costs alone. Like the lilies in the field the human self is simply there to be accepted or rejected, but utterly incapable of interacting with other people. A hedonist might well blush at such egoism. Hegel's reaction was predictable.

In a relatively generous mood Hegel was ready to admit that Fichte had not meant to promote capriciousness and false originality.[68] He had however invited such an interpretation by his overblown prose, and generally Hegel chose to see him at his worst. Hegel never chose to show that the absolute ego also exists in a specific social world, which plays its part in this, as in any state of self-consciousness. The Roman Empire is, for example, a constant presence in Hegel's discussion of Stoicism or the 'unhappy consciousness.' But modern self-consciousness appears to be moving in a disjointed way within a vacuum. Hegel was, of course, describing the self-perceptions of people wholly given to introspection. However, even fanatical self-contemplation is not as lunatic as to dispense wholly with an intelligible environ-

66. *Lectures on the History of Philosophy,* III, 485–6.
67. *The Vocation of Man,* trans. and ed. by R. M. Chisholm (New York, 1956), 84–6, 88–91, 98, 124. G. A. Kelly, *Idealism, Politics and History,* 191, 207.
68. *Philosophy of Right,* 258 (addition to s. 140).

ment. Fichte did not ignore his and Hegel's world. It was a world Hegel knew very well and was quite capable of describing with all the force of his formidable intelligence. However, whenever he spoke of his contemporaries he seemed to be afraid of softening the bite of his satire and of moderating his contempt by introducing considerations that might be regarded as excuses. But it also has the effect of making the pages devoted to the isolated self-consciousness unduly abstract and obscure.[69] Circumstances can serve as extenuations, so Hegel chose to ignore them, but at some cost to his readers.

What then does the absolute ego do? In Hegel's view the self that turns wholly inward does nothing but play with itself. It labors only to translate itself from invisibilty to visibility. This activity 'alters nothing, opposes nothing.'[70] The condition in which the ego places itself is 'a spiritual animal kingdom.' For it has no aim other than to maintain itself in its 'original nature.' Like an animal, such a being uses and impinges upon the environment only to sustain itself. Neither it nor its habitat are changed. The self treats its surroundings as a means to its survival as a self-defined purposeless being.[71] The notion of such an 'original nature' bears a strong resemblance to Rousseau's man in the state of nature. This virtual imbecile is perfectly content to remain alone, moved by nothing but a healthy self-love, with nothing but immediate self-gratification on his mind. He neither speaks nor works. Above all he does not suffer from the anxious compulsion to compare himself to other men, or to live up to any standards of conduct.[72] Rousseau had discovered this basic man, in part at least, through a process of introspective self-analysis, but he thought that what he found in himself was man's original pre-social nature. Hegel knew

69. Interpretations of the section that Hegel entitled 'The Spiritual Animal Kingdom' have varied widely, more so than of most sections of the *Phenomenology*. There is no denying that it is obscure and that much guess-work is inevitable. My interpretation relies heavily on passages in several later works of Hegel in which he discusses Kant, Fichte and Schlegel and is thus perhaps less intuitive than others, but that is not a perfect guarantee of accuracy.

70. B415–16; H284–5.   71. B419–20; H285–6.

72. *Discourse on the Origins of Inequality Among Men,* passim.

such a state of mind to be characteristic of highly civilized people, such as modern Europeans and ancient Romans. For him the 'spiritual animal kingdom' was composed of self-centered egotists.[73] The very thought of an 'original nature' which was wholly self-contained was the illusion of such people. Not only is man as man a speaking animal, but he is also, ineluctably, a producer. And to produce, no less than to speak, is to communicate and to inter-act with other men. To forget the primacy of work is the perpetual idiocy of the independent consciousness. It undid the master and his servant and it comes to shake 'natural man' profoundly.

The Fichtean ego is an internalization of Rousseau's isolate. When it acts, it is, like the latter, rudely expelled from its calm 'animal kingdom.' Hegel begins his account of this experience with a perfectly accurate description of Fichte's original version of the absolute ego. It must act, though it is determined to remain as self-absorbed as ever.[74] It is, as Fichte put it, stimulated by 'a something.' In fact, it does not really matter what it is that the ego initially senses, for it cannot be set in motion by anything other than self-induced impulses, or have any aims that are not wholly centered on itself. In order to act it must conceive of some end, and this it calls being 'interested' in something. Interest, however, as Kant had already noted, does not refer to the object that is said to arouse it. It only implies 'the satisfaction which we combine with the representation of the existence of an object.'[75] It is wholly subjective, describing a personal state of mind which has no bearing on reality as something given and calling to us. As such it is also random and arbitrary, since any 'something' at all can arouse the interest of the ego.[76] The 'interest' that the ego feels is merely an internalization of something seen or felt, and impels no departure from pure self-absorption. The ego does face a certain predicament, since, if it is to have a purpose for acting, it would be drawn away from itself. For purpose is something external to the self. That might involve some circularity. The ego must not act with a purpose, but without one

73. *Philosophy of Religion*, II, 319–20.   74. B420–1; H285–6.
75. *Critique of Judgment*, trans. by J. H. Bernard (New York, 1951), 38.
76. B421–2; H287.

it cannot move. Happily that vague interest does function as a pseudo-purpose and allows the ego to move without having to go beyond self-expression. The activity of the isolated ego must be a pure self-exhibition. It can display itself with more or less talent, and more or less effectively, but nothing can occur here except revealing the inner self to the world at large. Work can have no other function for this self.[77] There is no judgment of quality that the ego will accept. Since it does not even recognize, much less try to meet, common standards, it refuses to judge or be judged in such terms. The productions and actions of people who have no other end in mind than the self-expression of their inmost nature cannot be called good or bad, only accurate or inaccurate. If your poem is a perfect picture of your soul it must be praised as a success, presumably, even if your soul is utterly commonplace. Only 'the self-expression of individuality' is involved here.[78] It is all very satisfactory for such a person, for he can indeed only have 'a sense of joy in himself' when he considers how well he has transferred himself from pure inner possibility to outward expression in word and deed.[79] Self-expression would seem to be its own reward.

There is, however, a real difficulty here. For doing and producing do have consequences. The active ego cannot abdicate quite so easily. In spite of itself it has created something. A product of some kind has come into being, even though that was not the real end of the exercise. The artifact now has a life of its own. The creator thought of it as purely an expression of his own ego, a response to his inner urges, but now it escapes his grasp. Other people notice his actions and works, and they may find it all very interesting. Their egos are now stimulated and they appropriate his creation and make it the vehicle of their self-expression. It is now their 'original constitution' that is served by his work. The original actor feels deprived.[80] And he can see the gap between being and acting. The original self remains unaltered, but its works now appear transitory and fleeting, and they do not even remain his own.[81] In his frustration he de-

77. B423; H288–9.   78. B423–4; H289.   79. B425–6; H290.
80. B426–7; H290–1.   81. B427–8; H291–2.

cides to give up the notion of an 'empty ego.' He chooses to ascribe a public aim to his actions and to invest them with an inherent validity apart from fleeting fancy and self-expression. The non-ego, although it is the work of the self, is now to have an objective value. This is still the work of personal consciousness, but one that does recognize that there is a realm of given norms that is binding upon itself and on all other active egos.[82]

The actor arrives at this stage of consciousness by reconsidering his experiences as a worker. He had begun by thinking that his artifact was a mirror of his own 'original nature,' which somehow fled from him when it was completed. The work seemed to be entirely transitory. However, the product has not really vanished. It exists in actuality, in the public domain of all other conscious beings. Only the original self that it was meant to express has gone. The actor now recognizes that this identification of his ego with his work was fleeting and unreal. Other aspects of working in fact turn out to be more enduring. Purpose, choosing appropriate means and calculating possibilities were not just projections of the ego, not only inventions designed to get the ego moving. They were part of a continuing process of exchange between the active self and the actuality to which this and all other actors contribute.[83] At last this egoist abandons his total self-absorption and accepts the fusion of the self with the world in general. He does it in a deeply perverse way, however. In giving up his imaginary 'original nature' he turns to the opposite extreme. The purpose and value of work are now to be found wholly apart from the worker. They are inherent in the artifacts themselves. Since this worker does not understand that actuality is social interaction, he looks to the objects produced to give meaning to his activity.

The honest worker is one who subordinates himself to his job. He cares only for his work, not for his own satisfactions, whatever these may be. Such also is what Hegel called 'the honest consciousness.' It is the mentality of men wholly immersed in the 'matter at hand' (*die Sache selbst*). The German word *Sache* means thing, cause, action, case, matter, affair, business, concern, event, fact and circumstance, and all

82. B430; H294.   83. B429-30; H293-4.

of these are implied in Hegel's use of the word.[84] The 'honest consciousness' is convinced that activity is self-justified as long as it is done wholly for the sake of the 'matter at hand.' This pseudo-Platonic impulse leads to the idealism of work as an end in itself. The pure, abstracted, wholly impersonal 'matter at hand' is both the aim of human exertion and the source of all its worth. To be sure, the pure 'matter at hand' is not a 'thing,' out there. It is not a bafflement to the understanding. It is known as the product of human judgments. However, it is treated as an aim divorced from any specific individual at work, it hovers above him, a general term capable of being the predicate of any activity at all.[85] As such it is a convenient shelter for minds that are quite evasive, for all their vaunted 'honesty' and devotion to the job to be done. Whether the worker be a shoemaker, a scientist, a politician or a poet, he can always claim that whatever he does is just done for the sake of his craft, not for himself. However, in order to act at all he must make 'the matter at hand' his *own* conscious concern, *his* 'matter at hand,' his work. He thus has a highly personal 'matter' which is his real work, and a 'public' one, to be displayed to others. The latter is the impersonal, pure 'matter at hand,' which is said to exist entirely for its own sake. The public which expects such subordination to given tasks deserves to be deceived. For by insisting that there is a pure 'matter at hand' to which the 'honest' worker should devote himself entirely, this public disguises its own contribution to that abstract yoke. It is these others who impose this illusion of 'the matter at hand.' It is not just 'there.' The general dishonesty consists in having two attitudes to all work, one private and effective, the other public and submissive. We cannot act without involving our individuality in our tasks and to deny that or to demand such a denial is dishonest.[86] It is a deception that arises from ignorance about the real, social purposes of

84. B430; H294. Baillie's translation is unfortunate here. He uses several phrases for 'die Sache selbst,' without indicating that he is always translating the same three words. He thus uses 'matter at hand,' 'fact itself,' 'objectified intent,' 'bare fact' interchangeably. I have chosen 'matter at hand' as the most accurate rendering. It is *not* adequate, but it is close and one must remain consistent, even if it sounds awkward.
85. B430–2; H294–6.   86. B434–5; H297–8.

working. Self-consciousness might have reached self-knowledge through work, but it failed to do so. The spirit of independence is preserved under the deceptive blanket of a submission to the 'matter at hand.' One may remain quite alone in one's work as long as it is treated as a self-evident end in itself.

The 'honest consciousness' is also marked by a great respect for matters of facts. Facts, Vico had already noted, are, as the Latin origin of the word makes clear, things done. They are not just data, but something 'done or performed' as the *O.E.D.* says. They are not valid apart from human consciousness and human activity. That is why we can know them, according to Vico. They are mental artifacts.[87] Facts depend upon general acknowledgment for their validity. Once they are perceived as such, everyone is expected to accept their impersonal and binding force. In sticking to these mental artifacts the 'honest consciousness' knows that it is being truthful. To neglect the facts is, after all, to lie. But these 'honest' persons do not know, or shy away from, the real sources of facticity. They are, in short, not yet anywhere near an awareness of the inter-subjectivity in which facts engage them.

The blindness of the 'honest consciousness' as well as its dissemblances are particularly clear in those 'matters at hand' which are not facts or material products, but social 'causes.' The 'honest consciousness' accepts not only 'matters' of work and fact, as self-evidently self-justifying, but also many a 'good cause.' Art for art's sake, liberty as an end in itself, national autonomy as a sacred trust or justice for its own value, are all self-justifying social causes in this sense. The 'honest consciousness' that adheres to these is less truthful, perhaps, than sincere. The causes which it takes up have just come along. He finds them at hand. It is his own concern that gives this kind of idealist his satisfaction and is meant publicly to show his worth. The purity of his disinterested participation in a cause, which he personally recognizes to be true and good, renders his actions valuable in his own eyes. Just as keeping to the facts is honest, so, he claims, is his ad-

87. *Oeuvres Choisies*, I, 228–33, 243–4, 281. For a more complete discussion of these matters, see *The Logic of Hegel*, ss. 147–9.

herence to causes. He does not make them, he commits himself to them. Though it is, after all, only *his* attitude to *his* cause that matters to him, yet he takes credit in public for contributing to the work at hand, even if he does very little for it.

In actuality these causes are just like the 'interest' that stimulated this ego to action in the first place. The attitude of the 'honest' man is that of an aesthetic spectator who, as Kant put it, takes 'a disinterested satisfaction' in objects of beauty. He 'demands' subjectively that others agree with him in such 'disinterested' judgments, since he imputes universal validity to them.[88] This spectator's attitude need not be limited to the realm of the beautiful. Hegel saw that aestheticism was expansive and could become a pseudo-morality. To him it was, moreover, bound to be a totally superficial attitude which remained subjective, a mere mask for self-expression. The 'honesty' or 'disinterestedness' is merely a pretense, an outward show of respect for objective purposes.[89] It is really because it is his 'own' cause that the 'honest' participant cares about it and imputes values to it. His activity is only a reflection of his self-absorption. He does not want to justify a cause, or to act effectively at all. He is like the spectator who uses art to display his good taste. Causes are a foil to demonstrate his 'honesty.' It remains a matter of the self playing with itself.[90]

Until the 'honest' consciousness learns to say 'we,' to see that what matters about 'causes' is not the display of disinterested appreciation, but joining others in a common pursuit, he is deceiving himself and everyone else. Unless he means others to 'recognize' the general worth of his cause, he is merely exhibiting his own generosity and good sense. He has not risen above the egoism that enjoys being stimulated by 'something' of 'interest.'[91] That is why actualizing causes is no more a part of his design than the law of the heart was ever meant to be put to work. He does not really care to make '*his*' causes acceptable to other men. He avoids 'exposing of what is one's own in a universal element, where it comes to

88. *Critique of Judgment,* 45, 47–8. Nietzsche was not so far from Hegel when he complained that Kant saw art wholly from the view of the spectator, not the creator. *Genealogy of Morals,* III, s. 6.
89. B433; H297.   90. B434–5; H297–8.   91. B436; H298–9.

be, and has to be, "the matter at hand" for everyone.'[92] He
only discovers the falseness of his position when other men
take him seriously and call upon him to justify himself and
his views so that they can accept or reject them. At that point
he discovers that it is only as a member of society, as a man
among others that his actions, work, facts and causes have
any real significance. Then he may at last stop playing with
'causes' and begin to judge them according to shared social
standards.[93]

The playful unmasking of the duplicity of the 'honest' consciousness is also a serious discussion of aesthetic theory. Kant
had peopled the world of art with two distinct human types,
the creative genius and the reflective critic. Genius is a pure
force of nature that produces beautiful artifacts. As an expression of nature it is purposeless and ultimately strange,
even to the man who is the vehicle of this aesthetic bounty.
The consumer of beautiful things is the disinterested judge.
He judges his own responses to art. Judgment is the faculty
which organizes particular experiences by containing them
under some non-objective universal. In this case particular
works of art are judged to be or not to be beautiful, that is,
universally pleasing. The rules of taste, in terms of which we
make these judgments, are wholly subjective in origin, but
they are not arbitrary. Good taste not only calls for universal
assent; it also has a real claim to it. For it represents the
aesthetic views of common sense at its best, the appreciations
of the most cultivated and refined persons in society. Even
the genius must add taste to originality and imagination, if
his work is to communicate beauty to his most discriminating
audience. For even if beauty has no inherent purpose, art has
responsibilities. The final end of this pleasure is educative.
Art certainly cannot make us moral, but it can influence our
disposition favorably, so that we might become more capable
of being moral. Culture is not goodness, but it helps.[94]

The difficulty that Hegel saw in this theory was its failure
to unite the work of art and the spectator. The judge and the
creator of beauty were not in touch with each other. If taste
is a subjective feeling, it can have no bearing on the genius

92. B437; H299–300.   93. B437–8; H300–1.
94. *Critique of Judgment*, 15, 48–54, 120–64, 200–2.

as the creative force of nature. He simply is. If genius is a force of nature it can only pour out its creations, but it cannot speak to any public, however well-bred. Only conscious beings can communicate. The division between genius and audience had repercussions. The romantics took genius to be all that mattered. Neo-classicism, to which Kant obviously adhered, made taste with its moral implications supreme. For the neo-classical critic the probable, the typical, the comprehensible and the decent were the standards art had to satisfy. That really left no room for the creative imagination of the genius. Given the subjective origin of these rules, the perpetual quarrels among critics were moreover not as insignificant as Kant had thought. They did seem to show that these guides to art were merely imposing their own preferences upon others. They were deceiving the artist by demanding his submission to 'rules' that are of their making, rather than inherent in art as such. He in turn deceived them if he said that he was governed by the 'laws' of taste in his creative activity. It was only as *his* taste and *his* rules that they bound him.

If the romantic genius was really a force of nature he could indulge in every sort of irresponsibility. He could then quite fairly claim that once he had expressed the natural force within him, the product was of no further concern to him. The work of art now had a life of its own. Art exists for art's sake, as flowers exist in nature. It did not exist for other people and had no end apart from its simple existence. Critics might at most announce the existence of a poem, for example, but that was the limit of their function. If they were moved by the impression the poem made upon them, they could recreate it, that is, become poets ignited by a poem. There might thus be a mysterious chain of poems, but not a poet and his public. Hegel did not think that art was analogous to an effusion of nature, but a highly self-conscious activity. The genius was a self-conscious worker, developing a project, not the direct voice of nature. He could not therefore walk away from his creations as if they were not an enduring part of him. Having produced an artifact, he remains responsible for it to other men with whom he had communicated through his art. He cannot object to critics. The latter may not convert criticism into creation either and may not claim credit for it. They must accept their more modest position. They must learn to exist as neither co-creators, nor as judges imposing sentence demanded by an impersonal law of taste. Instead of two disparate figures, audience – critic, and creator are all part of a single process of aesthetic communication.[95]

Clearly like Kant, Hegel favored the neo-classical over the romantic, the social over the subjective theory. He had indeed come to see a real threat in the excesses of artistic genius. He particularly despised the romantic interpreters of Fichte's theory of the creative ego, most notably Friedrich von Schlegel's notion of an ironic ego. Here the ego is that of the artist who uses his imagination to make and destroy illusions while he hovers ironically above his own material and his audience. Self-expression in this romantic view is not just the sole possible work of the ego, but a show of its artistic power and glory. What had begun as a theory of knowledge was transformed into a public vaunting of artistic irresponsibility and of self-exhibition. Genius was now the name of a specific form of supremacy over other men: the ability to manipulate them by the imposing and withdrawing of illusions. In Fichte's case purposeless self-creation was a response to the limits of human consciousness, but Schlegel paraded it as a positive virtue, an attitude of superiority to less-inspired men. Hegel's reaction to these opinions, so prevalent among his contemporaries, was explosive. Few philosophers have ever taken such pains to excoriate a literary critic.[96] His reasons for doing so were the same ones that led him to concern himself so energetically with Jacobi. Among all forms of subjective morality, irony and the law of the heart were the only ones to be overtly irrational and inherently contemptuous of mankind. In Hegel's mind, quite rightly, irrationalism and the rejection of general, shared human values went hand in hand.

Irony exists to protect the self against community and the burdens of purposive action. Because it can make every ob-

---

95. B435–8; H298–301.
96. E.g., *Philosophy of Right*, 101–3 (s. 140); *Lectures on the History of Philosophy*, III, 506–8, 510.

jective reality nought and vain, Hegel assumed that eventually it must feel its own vanity and emptiness.[97] That is far from obvious. Personal futility which knows no better outlet than to display its frivolity by hovering above its creations and misleading or baffling an audience has found in literature apparently inexhaustible possibilities. The irony which Hegel denounced so vehemently was not, as he often implied, the personal invention of Schlegel. The romantic movement was not an idle intellectual fashion, a precious contempt for audiences and the fleeing of sensitive souls from exposure to other men. Irony did not disappear when Schlegel turned to religion.[98] On the contrary, there has been no overcoming of what is the most permanent, the most common of modern intellectual and aesthetic attitudes. In fact Hegel knew, and often discussed, the conditions that had reduced authors to playing unintelligible games. There was, after all, no public to address. To create and withdraw illusions may not be noble, but it may be normal behavior for artists in the world of independence.

Every German dramatist of any note since the century before Hegel's own had already known that there was no public for the stage in Germany.[99] In fact, there was no public of any sort, either political or intellectual. It had been the hope of Lessing, among others, that dramatic art might create a public for itself and, beyond that, a general public consciousness. Nothing came of that aspiration and Hegel was saddled with the thankless task of reviewing a century of disappointment. That may account for some of his dislike for a literature that had simply given up the effort to find an audience.

97. *Philosophy of Mind,* 571; *Philosophy of Fine Art,* I, 87–93, 217.
98. That Schlegel was a far more serious critic and theorist of literature than Hegel would admit is not irrelevant here. Indeed, he understood much that Hegel also recognized about modern literature, most notably the loss of living mythologies and of a sense of objective aesthetic values. One cannot help suspecting that Hegel really resented Schlegel's argument that modern subjective art was superior to that of Greek antiquity. When Schlegel finally turned to Roman Catholicism, Hegel could, of course, claim that the earlier bravado had been shallow and that such a conversion only proved Schlegel's original lack of soundness. For a more balanced view of Schlegel as a critic, see René Welleck, *A History of Modern Criticism: 1750–1950* (New Haven, 1955), II, 5–35, 301–2.
99. W. H. Bruford, *Theatre, Drama and Audience in Goethe's Germany* (London, 1950).

Not that Hegel wanted dramatists to cater to or to reflect the prevailing tastes of audiences. Lessing was for him the example of true genius. He had been able to hold as well as elevate his public. The 'sentimental irony' of Schlegel and his imitators was utterly incapable of such an achievement. Indeed, it did not even attempt to speak for and to a public, since it was just 'a manner of talking against people.' Nevertheless irony was not just a personal defect of wayward authors. Hegel knew that the trouble was a good deal more serious than that. The French, he was to remark bitterly at a later time, were simply better off than the Germans. They had an educated public to inspire and to respond to dramatic works.[100] And without an audience art is incomplete. In the absence of a public why should authors strive to rise above vulgarity and subjectivity? Irony does not seem all that inappropriate a reply to the circumstances.

Indeed Hegel went on to lament that modern life not only destroyed the public, but also offered no material to the dramatic imagination. The division of labor, the perfection of social institutions, the impersonality of daily life, the supremacy of the critical intelligence, all these combined to make dramatic art impossible. They offered 'no content, no form . . . identical directly with the inmost soul of the dramatist.' He really had no choice but to receive his truth and ends wholly from his purely personal perceptions.[101]

Hegel was already quite aware of all this when he wrote the *Phenomenology*. His discussion of the spiritual world of Greek art makes it perfectly clear how remote a real community of artists and their public was from anything that has existed since that distant time. Unlike Kant, he did not think that 'common sense' could set the purposes of art. Nature, moreover, did not, by acting through genius, create art. Self-consciousness is no force of nature and without it men do not create works of beauty. Finally he did not think that the refined members of society could be expected to set effective standards of taste. Only religion could achieve that and then only a religion that combined sensuous feeling with spiritual aspirations. Only the religion of Hellas, the religion of art,

100. *Philosophy of Fine Art*, IV, 277; *Philosophy of Right*, 101 (s. 140).
101. *Philosophy of Fine Art*, IV, 271; I, 84–6.

could give rise to the human awareness that created sculpture, lyric poetry and drama as a part of cults and rituals and as an integral aspect of a culture shared and made by each and all.[102] Nothing could be more remote from Hegel's own world and that is why he was convinced that art was dead.[103]

Common sense is not only no substitute for religion, it is not even a genuinely social consciousness. It has moral pretensions but these are entirely hollow. To be sure, Kant's 'healthy common sense' makes social virtue its sole object, but it looks wholly to the ego and its own self-generated categories for its rules.[104] According to Kant, the best kind of 'common sense' must be unprejudiced, enlightened, enlarged and consecutive. That is, it is independent, adopts a universal, rather than personal, viewpoint and, above all, is consistent.[105] That is the self-defined rational self. In its legislative activity it is therefore entirely formal, and like its earlier manifestation, Stoic natural law, empty and dogmatic. Each autonomous law-giver can, in principle, devise universal rules of conduct. That is how this 'common' self rules taste and is now extended to society. Like all of Kant's moral theory this was, in Hegel's view, 'the autocracy of the subjective.' [106]

To be sure, reason as law-giver does not look upon itself as wholly individual. As common sense it has a social awareness and takes itself to have communal ends, whether these be moral or aesthetic, a matter of conduct or of taste. However, though it knows its business to be social, the only voice that speaks to it is its own. The rules of common sense are intuitions that speak to it directly in the same way that 'the matter at hand' is just given to the 'honest' consciousness. Both are just 'data.' Every reasonable person simply knows right from wrong when he sees them. It is self-evident, inherent in nature and reason, an instant certainty that cannot be doubted.[107] That is the illusion of the self-legislating ego. As

102. B709–49; H490–520.   103. *Philosophy of Fine Art*, I, 141–3.
104. B437–8; H300–1.   105. *Critique of Judgment*, 136–7.
106. *Lectures on the History of Philosophy*, III, 477.
107. B440–2, 245–6; H301–2, 153–4. For Hegel's general contempt for Cicero and modern, especially Scottish, 'common sense' philosophy, see *Lectures on the History of Philosophy*, I, 92–3; II, 257–76; III, 361–3, 375–9. See also above, ch. 2.

Bentham had noticed in observing the Americans, 'all measures seemed self-evident to them because they were in agreement about them.' [108] Once specific occasions, arguments, choices and obstacles emerge, self-evidence evaporates. Common sense does not know that, because it thinks of reasoning as a matter of elementary arithmetic, and as Hegel was quick to observe, it is just as tautological. Two plus two is four, and you ought to do what you ought to do. You ought to give a man his due, but due is only what you ought to give him. It is certain, edifying and convincing, since both sides of the equation are identical. It is a pointless exercise since actual duties can only be determined by far more specific and flexible standards. To illustrate his point, Hegel chose to dissect one of the most commonly accepted adages. 'Everyone ought to speak the truth.' That implies a hidden condition: 'If one knows the truth.' That is unhappily something we may not be able to achieve. If our ability to speak the truth depends on circumstances beyond our control, then we can hardly call speaking the truth an unconditional duty. At best it amounts to saying that 'we ought to know.' That is irreducible, to be sure, but since we cannot know what it is that we ought to know until we already know it, that is a perfectly meaningless demand.[109] Clearly we need more than mere self-evidence.

Another celebrated command runs: 'Love thy neighbor as thyself.' That is the rule reason imposes upon us in our relations to other people. Now love is not only a lively emotion, it is also notoriously blind. Yet reason surely intends us to love intelligently, so that we will really benefit those whom we ought to love. Who, unhappily, really knows what is good for another person? Unintelligent love is only a cause of disaster. Foresight and much realism are needed here, and who possesses these powers? It is not something any individual person has at his command. 'Intelligent, veritable well-doing is . . . in its richest and most important form the intelligent, universal action of the state.' One individual, compared to the collective intelligence of a whole community, is 'trifling' and 'hardly worth talking about,' when one comes to consider what is genuinely best for his neighbor.[110]

108. *Introduction to the Principles of Morals and Legislation* (New York, 1948), 335–6.   109. B442–3; H303–4.   110. B443–4; H304–5.

Few passages in the *Phenomenology* tell us more about Hegel's political philosophy. The state is the necessary surrogate for our feeble reason. Individual reason cannot predict, or remember, or survey enough to benefit its neighbor intelligently. It cannot legislate the duties of love or of honesty. That is simply beyond its scope. We must rely on established social rules to guide us. If we attempt to set down general law independently of these, we only come up with commands that amount to no more than an endless series of 'ought to be.' It is never a solid social rule. To be specific, to have a content a law must be something more than self-evidently consistent. It must have a bearing on a unique situation and direct people in their actual relationships to each other. A universal content is no content at all. It may be an admonition to be rational, but nothing more. As such, reason can set criteria for judging actual laws, but not create, much less enforce, working rules of conduct. The only criterion reason can apply is, moreover, a logical one. It tests existing social laws for their consistency.[111] That is all that a universal standard can do.

Kant had indeed argued that to be consistent was the highest task of all philosophy.[112] Hegel thought this consistency to be too formal to serve even as an instrument of effective social criticism. It looks at social conventions without concern for their context and history and examines them as if they were bare commands merely to see whether they are self-contradictory. All such tests can do is to insist on tautologies and that is not a very useful procedure. Conditions do matter a good deal to anyone who is faced with making a decision or defending his actions, but such considerations are beneath reason. It only asks whether the maxim upon which one acts is completely self-consistent and subject to no possible exceptions. Everything depends on definitions. If there is to be private property then indeed it follows that I am entitled to my property. That is no great surprise, since property is merely that to which one is entitled, that being its definition. The real question is, however, whether there should be pri-

111. B444–5, 289; H305–6, 189–90.
112. *Critique of Practical Reason and Other Writings on Moral Philosophy,*
     trans. by L. W. Beck (Chicago, 1949), 135.

vate property at all. If we argue that there should be no such institution, then I am just as consistently *not* entitled to anything. Private property, the absence of property, no less than the community of property are all internally self-consistent, though clearly not compatible with each other.[113] If one gets more specific there is less certainty. It is possible to argue, as Kant had, that all objects that can serve human ends ought to do so and that this gives the first possessor a *prima facie* claim.[114] One can assume just as easily, however, that the enduring needs of *all* men, not the individual's claim or the actual possessor of a thing, are to be served and should determine proprietorship. If need justifies property then perhaps only a communistic system can distribute goods among its members in accordance with need as the only standard. That would probably contradict the egalitarian principles of such a society. For actual needs tend to vary from one person to another. Moreover, fairness would have to be given up altogether. Its criterion is always some sort of merit, some desert other than basic need. That does not mean that private property is the answer to the inconsistencies of a communistic system of distribution. Private property can also be shown to be inconsistent. Kant had also claimed that private property is that which society has assigned to one individual, to the exclusion of all other claimants. In that case, it is not the proprietor himself who excludes them, but society as a whole, which has agreed to this system of property. Society includes him in a legal system which grants absolute rights to individuals to own certain things. That is not consistent with the idea of private property as a primary right to claim possessions. Rights, for which property is here only another name, are then social creations. If expressed in general rules they can be made generally applicable. That says nothing about their content or consequences. The test of rationality is, in short, no standard at all. It can justify everything that is put into the form of a general rule, since consistency is all that

113. B446–7; H306–7.
114. Unless otherwise stated, all Hegel's references to Kant's theory of property are aimed at Part I of *The Metaphysics of Ethics* (*Die Metaphysik der Sitten*). It is most readily available, even though in very abbreviated form, as *The Metaphysical Elements of Justice*, trans. by John Ladd (Indianapolis, 1965), 51–67.

is required, but it can also be reduced to nonsense when placed next to competing but equally general rules.[115]

As a parting shot Hegel chose to demonstrate that Kant's test of universal consistency was of no use to ordinary men, even though it was meant to be available to even the meanest intelligence. That was so because we only have particular and specific obligations which cannot be universalized into general, timeless and unconditional duties. To illustrate this point Hegel took an example that Kant had originally used for his purposes: why should one repay deposits? To say that I ought to repay money deposited with me because otherwise the security of depositions in general would be destroyed did not seem to Hegel to make much sense. Like all tests which ask whether a rule is self-consistent, it fails to investigate the social bearing of the law. Why should there be deposits at all? I can simply say that I reject the idea of deposits. I then redefine the debt and call it my property, rather than a deposit. If I do that I can quite consistently claim it as my very own and refuse to return it. If *my* reason is the final test of what is rightfully mine and thine I can always legislate in a manner most convenient to myself. An ethical citizen cannot do that because his social education, his civic sense, prevents him from entering into such devious private speculations. The imperative to be consistent may not encourage such thoughts, but it certainly renders them logically possible.[116] This, in fact, is simply the way independent men are likely to think.

To make Kant the teacher of immorality and egotism is something of a conjuring trick and Hegel had to resort to considerable distortion to accomplish this feat. One only has to compare Kant's writings to these imputations to see how far apart they are. To be sure Kant held benevolence and above all truthfulness in high regard. He also offered far more plausible defenses of these virtues than Hegel was ready to admit. The obligation to tell the truth merely means that one ought not to lie, that is, not to say what one *knows* to be untrue. Ignorance is not lying, but since we are not totally ignorant we are often quite capable of lying. That one ought to speak the truth does not therefore mean that one ought to know. It only means one ought not to lie when one does

115. B448–9; H307–8.   116. B452–3; H311–12.

know what is true. To lie is not consistent with man's dignity as a rational and free being. Nor can lying be a universal law; one would still have to prove that, in truth, one is lying.[117] Benevolence is counselled as a matter of self-education, to overcome one's natural inclination to be indifferent or hostile to other people. It does not call for specific feelings of love, but for the cultivation of a disposition. That is a duty, and consistent if we are to strive for goodness. It has nothing to do with the mindless and maudlin sort of love that Hegel ridiculed and for which Kant had no use at all.[118]

Turning to Kant's theory of property one finds, first of all, a defense of the right of ownership in general, and then of private property. Like all claims, possession must be consistent with the universal law of external freedom and only sets the conditions for possible proprietorship. Only the consent of society as a whole can turn mere possession into legal right, or genuine property. Without that it is only a presumptive right. The point of the whole discussion is to give the right to possess objects a moral basis, which Hegel never examined and which contains those principles to which legal rules must conform. Consistency is not here a mere formula, but the obvious test for deciding whether a specific claim, in this case to things, conforms to the demands of the basic norm: that no one shall exercise any rights that are not compatible with the enjoyment of like rights by all others. As for the relatively minor issues of deposits, Kant certainly did think it irrational to pocket deposits. However, deposits were for him merely an example to illustrate the universal necessity for trust among men if there was to be any security of property at all. To destroy trust is to injure fatally the necessary conditions for the safety of my property no less than anyone else's. The pursuit of a dishonesty, simply because one can on occasion get away with it, is thus self-defeating. It threatens the fundamental understanding which renders not just deposits but any effective rights viable. Nor is the categorical imperative as a test ridiculous. If the maxims upon which one's acts are

117. *The Metaphysical Principles of Virtue* (Part II of *Metaphysik der Sitten*), trans. by James Ellington (Indianapolis, 1964), 80–1, 90–3; *Critique of Practical Reason*, 154.
118. *Principles of Virtue*, 52–3, 60–1, 112–18; *Critique of Practical Reason*, 189.

based cannot be made into universally acceptable rules, they are not rational. Stealing as a universal law makes not only theft impossible, since no one owns anything if everyone ought to steal, but it renders the thief's goods as insecure as those of his victims.[119] Such a rule is, on its face, ridiculous and inconsistent, and to see this vindicates reason. Finally Hegel might have mentioned, as he in fact never did, the third formulation of the categorical imperative. The command never to treat men as *mere* means is *not* just a formula or a test and it *does* impose quite specific duties on each one of us.

Hegel surely knew all this quite well. Why then did he present such a disjointed and arbitrary version of moral rationalism in general, and of Kant especially? Why did he treat Kant so derisively? It is not difficult to see what he wanted to show: how easily dissociated reason can be misused to twist social norms hither and thither without being self-contradictory and how little it could tell us about our daily duties. This accomplished, even if in a rather irresponsible way, it was easy to see how far such ratiocination was from any truly ethical consciousness. Rules generated by the independent individual reason are always apart from and opposed to social usage. The ego is here merely imposing itself on others in a capricious and possibly tyrannical way. As soon as one recognizes that, one must give up autonomous legislating and testing and return to the 'spiritual substance,' that is, to convention and the laws that actually prevail. Where, however, are we to find an ethical order to which we can go home? Not in the world of the French Revolution. Hegel had nowhere to go but to the past. He recalled the polis. Though we need not imitate her in *believing* in a higher law, we must at least look to Antigone's perfect certainty that laws simply 'are.' No need to ask about their origins. Who can know how they came to be? The question itself is an implied form of testing. All that the citizen of an ethical policy needs to know is that the laws are *his* and everyone else's.[120] We, however, do not live in such a polity and Hegel could only evoke a contrast. That is not an argument, only a shock.

119. *Critique of Practical Reason*, 138; *Foundations of the Metaphysics of Morals, ibid.*, 80–3.   120. B450–2; H310–11.

Practical reason, like its mate, observation, ends in abrupt disarray. The latter found its end in the absurdities of phrenology, the former in capricious self-will. Complete and utter scepticism might be the only available response to these twin failures of rationality. That had certainly been a recurrent reaction in the past to analogous experiences. Hegel was determined to avoid that pitfall. His turn to recollection, to an historical consciousness, was an alternative to the helplessness of the sceptic. The latter stands paralyzed before the door of knowledge. Hegel meant to move on. The memory of the past evokes both the freedom of an ethical people and the painful journey away from it to the present, but in either case the mind is raised from its self-concentration to a public awareness. Even if most of the public world of Europe has been an anarchic spectacle, the journey into its history is a journey away from subjectivity. To think historically is to learn that even the dissociated self is a cultural phenomenon, no less the creator and creation of a society, than the ethos of Antigone.[121] Through recollection each mind comes to know itself as part of a greater world. All the modes of consciousness so far considered were mere particles clipped off that historical whole. They were, in their erroneous independence, unaware of themselves as parts of social life 'actually existent.' To regain a public consciousness a sense of the unity of spiritual experiences is the first step that an individual mind can take toward knowing itself as more than a mere self-reflection.[122] To remember the political past is to move outside the confines of the immediate ego and to restructure it by a long process of learning. It is to become at one gradually with the experiences of both the 'happy people' and all those unhappy ones which brought Europe to the French Revolution.

121. B457–8; H313–14.   122. B459–60; H314–15.

CHAPTER FOUR

THE LIFE CYCLE OF A CULTURE

A people is not a random assemblage of human beings. It is composed of individuals whose lives are shaped by the same beliefs and rules of conduct and linked by language and work. They share an ethos, or to use Hegel's word, a spirit. This is not 'absolute spirit,' but the spirit of a culture, the 'ethical substance' of a given time and place. It is, in fact, Montesquieu's 'ésprit général,' that ensemble of habits, religious beliefs, manners, values, convictions and, above all, principles of laws and government which constitute the traditions and define the purposes of men with a common past and present. Hegel not only frequently expressed his admiration for Montesquieu, but he followed him in recognizing politics as the heart and directing force of a people.[1] Like Montesquieu's other disciple Rousseau, he also knew that 'everything depends on politics.' Political consciousness was for Hegel the ego of 'the individual who is a world,' of a people considered as a single historical whole with its own mind.

Montesquieu found that each regime had a specific self-consciousness which moved and ordered the whole polity. Hegel concentrated on that far more than on the specifics of

---

1. Hegel always spoke of Montesquieu's 'immortal work' from his earliest to his last years with utmost admiration; e.g., 'Über die Wissenschaftliche Behandlungsarten des Naturrechts,' *Hegel's Schriften zur Politik und Rechtsphilosophie,* ed. Georg Lasson (Leipzig, 1913), 411; *Philosophy of Right,* 16, 161, 177–8 (ss. 3, 261, 273). This is in contrast to the relatively apolitical theories of Herder which he never mentioned. I am grateful to my friend Harvey C. Mansfield, Jr for discussing these passages with me; even though we are not entirely in agreement, he was very helpful.

political constitutions, which were so central to Montesquieu's theory. He accepted Montesquieu's classification of the various regimes, but he was far less interested in their institutional arrangements than in their thinking. Just as lord and servant were states of mind and not legal or economic conditions, so the Athenian family was not a sociological unit but a 'spiritual mass.' And the *ancien régime* is seen as a tense mixture of hostile psychic phenomena. For unlike Montesquieu Hegel brought a post-Revolutionary mind to bear on politics. Montesquieu was, like the ancients, deeply aware of the tendency of all institutions to degenerate, but he did not expect the *ancien régime* to go up in flames. He therefore was just as interested in the enduring and self-preserving, as in the decadent aspects of any political order. Hegel was obsessed by the germs of anarchy and dissolution at work. Death was busy everywhere. Montesquieu knew all about change and corruption, but he also understood continuity. Hegel did not. He concentrated on political consciousness rather than on institutions, precisely because social change and destruction are the work of spiritual conflict, while organizations and institutions are the manifestations of permanence. Hegel's pictures of the two great polities, the Greek and the *ancien régime,* show traces of Montesquieu's models at every turn, but they are really quite different. Each polity is seen in a state of steady movement toward its own extinction, without any consideration of what else happened on the way. Hegel seemed not to notice the energies that allow a people to nourish its spirit and to survive. 'Spirit' is the story of how Europe's two great cultures disintegrated.

For Hegel spirit or the collective consciousness of a people when it is regarded statically is 'ethical substance,' the rules of grammar, of law, of custom that are just 'there,' unchanging and self-sufficient. The individual is called simply to conform to them. 'Ethical substance' is the sum of the many rules that govern a people. That is how it looks to the individual also. By learning the rules he receives his second nature through *Bildung.* That word means education, character formation, and also the high culture of a civilization. The individual rises to universality and leaves his mere natural self behind, by assimilating these 'givens' and absorbing them into his own personality. Looked at dynamically, as 'ethical actuality,' spirit is a process by which the individual members not only become educated, but through the words and work of each and all give effect to their cultural inheritance and alter it. They are altered as they change their world and vice versa. That also is *Bildung*. In Hegel's usage, *Bildung* is thus what anthropologists now call culture, the process by which individuals are integrated into a given society and perpetuate it. However, he also used it to speak of the most perfect manifestations of a culture, which both express its spirit and educate future generations. To know what Greece was one must read Thucydides, Sophocles and Plato. They *are* the Greek spirit, they are both its voice and its teachers. As they draw us out of our familiar narrowness, they are our *Bildung* or culture also. This, the height of spirit, as the explicit life of a people or of an entire culture such as Europe, is an active project. It is 'for itself'—self-aware. It is also the daily deed and word of every member. They give it a will, a voice and development, while they, as parts of this whole, are also its products. Ethical substance is part of an entirety, of a dynamic world.[2] Culture as an ever-moving process is surely an idea that expresses a deep sense of the instability of social norms, and it is less suited to the study of organized behavior and institutions than of the shifts and turns of beliefs and attitudes. That was what Hegel meant to discuss and he had found an adequate scaffolding for the narrative that was to follow: the tale of decline and fall.

Hegel not only had to cope with the experience of the French Revolution, but also with its intellectual heir, Kant and the philosophy of moral autonomy. In response to this extreme expression of dissociation he developed a theory of culture which treats individual reason as radically limited by the collective spirit. As he had often done before he used Kant's theory of knowledge to undermine the latter's moral philosophy. Culture must be treated, Hegel argued, as a category of the human mind equivalent to causality, for example. We cannot organize experience without the thoughts and words we possess as members of a given culture. We cannot

2. B89–90, 458–61, 514–16; H27, 314–16, 347–8. *Vernunft in der Geschichte,* 65, 114–15, 122–3, 177.

reason at all in fact until the time and age are ripe for humanity to do so. Our understanding, especially our education, is entirely dependent upon the culture in which the individual understanding is exercised. Cultural knowledge is not what it was for Montesquieu, organized information, but knowledge of the limits of the individual's intellectual powers. Culture, as a category, must now be added to the projections that the mind makes to render experience intelligible. That strikes deeply at the pretensions of practical reason. Self-consciousness now must include the notion of culture as an integral part of the ego and as the very principle of its development. The autonomy of the rational self is severely challenged. For practical reason had meant to legislate for each and all in accordance with its own independent demands. Reason imputes rationality to society because the free agent, standing outside its confines, can order his social experiences, assign his duties in society, entirely in terms of his own legislative reason. Society is subject to individual, not to collective cultural norms of rationality. Such an outlook simply ignores historicity. The social character of self-consciousness is forgotten. That is because practical reason denies that 'the ethical substance,' the norms of a people, *is* reason. It not only *has* reason, but possesses rationality itself. Culture generates the very thoughts that individuals consider their own and that they, in turn, eventually bring to bear upon society. It is a dynamic process in which individuals express, interpret and contribute to the cultural whole of which each is an inescapable part. Indeed every specific type of thinking is but a splinter from that whole. If one analyzes individual ways of thinking, as Hegel had just done, one is abstracting from the cultural world. Consciousness, self-consciousness and reason are all members of 'spirit.' They are only imperfectly known if one does not see them as phenomena of a cultural mind, parts of 'the individual which is a world.' [3] That is why Hegel had to turn to 'spirit' at this point in his book.

Such reflections were wholly foreign to Montesquieu who, though he did not aspire to omniscience, did not doubt the capacity of the rational individual understanding to order the mass of information about mankind available to it. One

3. B475–80; H313–15.

had to resign oneself to the limits of the possible, to be moderate, but that did not impugn in any way the inherently universal scope of observing reason nor the powers of the explanatory understanding. The limits were all in a world of unreasonable actuality, not in reason itself. Hegel, however, had to see philosophy itself, his own and that of all his greatest predecessors, as necessarily limited. All rational powers are of their time and place. That made knowledge dependent upon the historical moment. No one can rise beyond the possibilities of his own time. Hegel was, at best, intellectually fortunate to be living in an age of death and transition.[4] It permitted him to look back, fifteen years after its outbreak, to the French Revolution and see it as the end and fulfillment of a culture. It had left a political vacuum, a perfect vantage point from which to reconstruct a now entirely finished world. It was the best time for recollection, the historical equivalent of being at the end of time. Out of the various disparate experiences the dead culture could be relived as a tragic drama in which its representative figures, embodying its vital attitudes, are the chief actors. There are, indeed, two tragedies, that of Athens and that of the *ancien régime*. Each found its completion in its own destruction. Hegel's view was thus tragic, while Montesquieu's was not.

In retrospect the dénouement of a tragedy is clear. But the movement toward that final moment need not be presented as a simple single-file march from starting point to finishing line. Hegel's drama was certainly not a mindless recital of who said what in chonological sequence, nor a chain of intellectual causes and effects. Because of the intimate relation between effective causality and the attribution of responsibility, there is always a strong moral urge to show who produced a given outcome and who was, thus, to blame. However, Hegel was perfectly serious in his resolve to avoid reducing philosophy to edification. He did not propose to give out grades for good and evil notions. His whole design was to show the whole quest for certain knowledge as a single, ordered whole, composed of interrelated spiritual phenomena.

---

4. *Lectures on the History of Philosophy*, I, 51–5; III, 545–54; B75; H15–16. See especially, *Philosophy of Right*, 11: 'It is just as absurd to fancy that a philosophy can transcend its contemporary world as it is to fancy that an individual can overleap his own age, jump over Rhodes.' ('Preface.')

The end of a culture is thus not 'caused' by this or that specific ideological configuration or preceding state of mind. Its dissolution is the working out of its principle to its maturity and death. All its experiences on the way are movements to a single moment: the end of a 'world,' be it Athens or the *ancien régime*. Each is recognizable as a whole, an organic development of spiritual forms, and all are parts of the greater process of world history.

In order to render the ethos of a dead culture intelligible in retrospect Hegel avoided the use of metaphors drawn from any extraneous realms of experience. There is, again, an obvious moral motive for speaking of states of mind in terms drawn from the most common experiences of all mankind: physical motion, pain and labor. The consequence of such evocations is to confuse consciously expressed thoughts and purposive speech with non-conscious and uncommunicated experiences. Often enough, moreover, it also adopts an imagery that makes thought and language appear like shadows of something 'behind' or 'under' them, that is somehow felt to be more real, because it seems more tangible. Hegel tried to deal with the phenomena of the human spirit in their own terms. Our spiritual past is *res dicta*. That is its whole substance, and Hegel recognized the spoken word, language, communication, as a primary spiritual phenomenon, with its own characteristics and development patterns. The rationality of their perpetual change was to be found in an immanent teleology. Hegel saw spiritual history as a development in which original psychic dispositions gradually unfold all their possibilities. Their aim is full explicitness and this gives form to this entire process. It is not a unilinear progress. On the contrary, much that is good and beautiful is lost – art, happiness and freedom, in the case of Athens. At the end there is only intellectual gain, as philosophical self-consciousness is enhanced.

Changes in collective self-consciousness are never quiet or painless. The actors in this historical drama are moved by intense passions. A culture that ends in the French Revolution is not lethargic. Hegel compared its warring elements, public and private, to water and fire. The air is the unchanging idea of 'good' and 'bad,' which each warring group absorbs and makes its own. As water and fire they consume, but are in turn consumed by the earth, the culture which both want to possess, and which embraces both. They rise from it and return to it, the 'knot' that ties all.[5] The course of European history is always like that, a violent interplay of elemental spiritual passions. Each culture, each 'earth' is the departing point and purpose of its warring members, but though they animate it, they also destroy it. Hegel's drama is all struggle and destruction. The duel was his first and enduring model of men seeking self-knowledge. In each culture there are several duels. In post-ethical society there is the unending feud between the individual and society, for men no longer think of themselves as political animals. The battle between the family and public authority, between private wealth and public service, is endemic. Most decisive of all is the struggle between the divine and the human law, faith and unbelief. That war unbalanced the ancient city and it destroyed the *ancien régime*. When Oedipus imagines that he is omniscient because he has all human knowledge, fate proves his ignorance. When he and his audience learn that fate is character, that is his own ego, the conflict remains. The moral and social law are now at odds within each psyche and in society itself. The self-conscious ego is not apart from its culture and Socrates is the heir of Oedipus. Socrates' death cannot conceal the social disarray that his life proclaimed. Philosophy and comedy preside over the disintegration of the beautiful city.[6] The *ancien régime*, divided between a harsh secular culture and an escapist religion, suffers the same experience only more violently. The protracted tension between Catholicism and its enemies comes to a head in the French Revolution. But the cycle of both cultures follows the same stages even if the content of experience is quite different in the two. Comedy laughs, but philosophy alone is left to contemplate the ruins and to recreate the past as an act of synthetic remembering.

Honor and wealth on the road to revolution

European culture is not the immediate successor of the Greek polis. Rome lies between the two. It is both a unique moment

5. B518–19; H353–4.   6. B462–3, 510–12; H317–18, 348–9.

in history and a transition between two worlds. Its importance for the rise of Christianity cannot be over-emphasized,
but that is not the full extent of its continuing vitality.
The individualism of those who know themselves to be
opposed to their world was born here and it lives on in unaltered and unabated form. For Rome was not destroyed in a
day. Not only did Hegel think his own age much like that
of the Roman emperors, but he knew very well that Roman
political ways had endured. Above all, its legal system still
dominated Europe's civil life.[7] Law and justice were not
bonds that tied men together in Rome. In Athens justice expressed the ethos of a people and every law was inspired by
it. Law and government drew the citizens together in peace
and in war.[8] In Rome law is atomizing. There are no longer
citizens, but legal persons, bearers of legally guaranteed
rights. The Roman is his property. As such he is a being of
chance, the creature of law. Scepticism is his appropriate
mentality, since he really is dependent and independent at
the same time, with no stable self. Anyone can, after all, be,
and then cease to be, a proprietor. It is not a full description
of any human being. It encompasses neither a full individual
nor a complete citizen. For it isolates the owner, whose proprietorship is exclusive. The Roman thus sees himself as a
person apart from the city.[9]

The only form of government that can hold such people
together and even represent their spirit is imperial rule. The
emperors guarantee the security of legal status but they also
express a generalized contempt for human life. The gladia-
torial stadium is their model of the world. A mania for destruction is the real spirit of this government. Its lord and
master presides over the death of classical culture and of all
the various peoples of the ancient world. Yet the victims do
make a discovery. They learn that they are free, that they
have an individual ego, a life apart from this general destruction. This ego is an exile, a stranger in this world, which is
only a transient vale of tears for men. However, quite in
spite of itself, the stranger creates a culture out of this very
sense of estrangement.[10] The spirit in self-estrangement, the

7. B750–2; H521–3. See above, ch. 3.   8. B473–4, 480–1; H323–4, 329–30.
9. B502–4; H343–5.   10. B504–6; H345–6.

rejecting of this-worldly life permeates the entire culture of the *ancien régime*. The European order is not governed by 'the will and self' of a people.[11] Political life is disclaimed as a crude realm from which the spirit seeks to escape. Since it is defined as worthless, at most something to be endured, it is in fact without spiritual value. Men make their world. The constitution of a state is determined by the religion of a people.[12] Christianity devalues culture, and so that culture is an impoverished scramble for wealth and power. 'Good' is self-relinquishment, the flight to a selfless beyond. 'Bad' is self-preservation and social activity. However, though the Christian may yearn to leave this world, he in fact cannot escape it. He can only structure it, as indeed he does, when he imposes his standards of 'good' and 'bad' on it. It is his culture and though he cannot openly acknowledge it, he maintains an unaccepted 'household arrangement' with a culture that he despises. He is, as such, a stranger to himself and to the world he has created. Christian culture has evidently reachèd a depth of self-illusion so dense that Plato's cave resembles a solarium in comparison.

It is in a sense paradoxical to speak of culture of self-estranged people. Without civic consciousness, rejecting the world, are not Christians culture-free? They are not. By treating some kinds of conduct, especially self-relinquishment, as 'good' and its opposites, worldliness and self-absorption, as 'bad,' they create a culture in the world they deny. When the Athenian in his piety speaks of himself as a father or a son, he is never merely this particular man, but knows himself to be an Athenian father or an Athenian son. He is immediately raised to a universal consciousness.[13] In the European order that sort of coherence no longer prevails, but even by just speaking a language men of necessity generalize their ego. With their words and work they do rise above pure particularity and also have to come down from the 'beyond.' Moreover, even the 'good,' self-renouncing Christian must attend to his survival. That is why in due course the Enlightenment can force faith to recognize its cultural activity

11. B511; H348.
12. *Lectures on the Philosophy of Religion*, II, 298; *Vernunft in der Geschichte*, 129. See below for what Hegel meant by religion.
13. B468–70; H320–3.

and destroy all its pretensions in the process. It makes Christianity face up to what Oedipus had to learn: that religion is the expression of a human consciousness and the reflection of human experiences. Christianity begins in the misery of Rome, but the 'unhappy consciousness' perpetuates not only its own condition of being estranged, but a world that invites alienation. It deprives society of ethical possibilities by creating a culture that corresponds to its own self-divided consciousness.[14] That also proves to be a weakness, for the Enlightenment can readily show that the human world is more than a desert to be traversed by pilgrims, and that faith had implicitly recognized that all along by building its house on earth. Faith is doubly estranged for it could neither reach the 'beyond' for which it yearned, nor accept the here and now, in which it was doomed to live.

The secular culture of Europe, its family life and political institutions, lacks the 'indwelling spirit' of antiquity. It suffers from a lack of spiritual dignity, since its religion rejects it. Nevertheless, Hegel used the word *Bildung* to describe it. Was he just mocking it? It is quite possible. He certainly intended to show the distance that separated the ideal pretensions of the *ancien régime* from its actuality. Not the least of its claims was that it preserved the spirit of classical antiquity and educated its youth accordingly. That certainly was an illusion. In spite of all that, Hegel did insist that this world did raise, as any education does, its unformed individual members to a higher and more general level of consciousness. As he was to say often, learning the classics is the best means to rise from being a mere specimen of humanity to a genuine individual.[15] Moreover, Hegel was very far from despising the high culture of Europe. It is the task of the individual, even in a very imperfect society, to absorb its best ideals and through his actions and words to give them life, however faulty.[16] Individuality is not a natural expression of a unique personality, as so many romantics thought, but something moulded by culture. It receives as much as it gives back. An education that tries to follow Rousseau's *Emile* by withdraw-

14. B510–11, 514–15; H348–9; 350–1.
15. 'On Classical Studies,' *Early Theological Writings*, 321–30.
16. B514–17; H350–3.

ing children from common life is, in any case, bound to fail, Hegel wrote later. No success can be expected from efforts to run away from the world. The power of the world is too great for that. It reaches everyone. It is by becoming a citizen of a good state that we come into our right.[17] Rousseau had, of course, also known that quite well. And Hegel knew that the *ancien régime* was not a good state, which also was Rousseau's main point. In speaking of its *Bildung* he meant to show that *any* society educates its members. And that to be cultured, especially in the sense of absorbing a 'high culture' was infinitely better than to remain a mere brute. Nevertheless, in view of his contempt for the society and values of the *ancien régime* and its failure to develop a social ethos, the title *Bildung* is ambiguous, if not openly sarcastic – except when it refers to Europe's literary culture.

The world educates us whether we run to a 'beyond' or hide in 'nature.' It is inescapable. Nevertheless the yearning to leave the world moulds a culture. Europeans feed and are fed by unethical association. They are independent men unaware of their social character, even those among them who accept their political obligations. Nobody recognizes himself as part of a greater whole. Pure culture, the republic of letters, can and does flourish in this world, but it is the only republic that prospers here. Instead of a happy people, this is a society composed of rebels and priests, all of them frustrated as they suffer various kinds of unsatisfied longing. It is all a mass of conflicts and contradictions. And this is due to 'that thing unknown among the ancients' as Montesquieu had said. Europeans are the victims of 'the contradictions between the obligations imposed by religion and the world.' [18] Three educations haunt them, those of their teachers (the Church), their fathers (the kin), and the world. The latter, as Hegel agreed, always proved the strongest. In any case, real civic virtue is not one of the lessons taught or required by the *ancien régime* as a 'world.' Honor is its real ideal.

Though the experiences of Europe's public consciousness are all lamentable, Hegel described them with much verve and even a touch of black humor. It is much the most lively

17. *Philosophy of Right,* 261 (addition to s. 153).
18. *De l'Esprit des Lois,* IV, 2.

section of the book. It is also very inventive and elusive. For Hegel contrived to make a picture of an age that was a mosaic of literary memories. Only the epic of master and servant can rival it. Indeed, that earlier encounter foreshadows later conflicts among opposed forms of consciousness. The antagonists who dominate the *ancien régime* are the feudal state-servant and economic man. Since it is the very definition of culture that some conduct be 'good' and its opposite 'bad,' one of these must be the former, the other the latter. 'Like' and 'unlike,' the two poles of a rigid logic, dominate collective thought. The life cycle of a culture thus is bound to be a process by which these two and the social groups, 'the spiritual masses' identified with them, exchange places. When what was once thought to be 'good' is regarded as 'bad' and vice versa, a culture is dead. When individuality replaced communal custom the polis had died. In the *ancien régime* originally aristocratic notions of state service are 'good' and wealth is 'evil.' When that is reversed, the *ancien régime* has reached its final hour. Its military aristocrats define themselves as selfless state-servants. That is their image of themselves and that is their cultural ideal, the 'good.' Wealth, although it seems passive, also has its cultural functions and voice. As production wealth creates, through the division of labor and the market, a network of exchanges and communications. Wealth is, moreover, not just production, but also the necessary means for generosity, independence and magnificence. Economic man has his own social activities and social ideals, though these appear hostile to the state. For those who choose the life of wealth it is the 'good.' However, it is not initially they, but the military aristocracy, their opposites, who decide what is 'good' and 'bad' in this culture.[19] And the military professes to loathe wealth. 'Like' and 'unlike' know no middle term, no way out of their hostility.

The imperishable model for those who, hating wealth, devote themselves to state service is Plato's *Republic*. Whether this is a cultural archetype, or whether it is only a part of their classical education, it inspires the illusions of this aristocracy. In any case, its members think of themselves as Platonic guardians who have relinquished all individuality and

19. B519–20; H354–5.

all greed for the sake of the state they serve. At the core of this devotion there is a tension; for this state service is merely a step toward personal self-perfection. The destruction of individuality is in the philosophic guardian incomplete. In the persons of their vastly inferior feudal imitators egoism is barely concealed. The *Republic* has always had its critics. Aristotle had already noted that nobody is happy and nobody can find self-fulfillment in the community of the guardians. Such a program of state service cannot meet the demands of those who seek to develop their whole individuality within society. They reject it in favor of wealth and a life of liberality and magnificence. An Aristotelian nobleman serves culture by expansive self-display.[20] He knows that a culture needs both government and wealth, and he appreciates both. That is too complex, too difficult for most men, Hegel noted. They make their judgments syllogistically, 'good' is the opposite of 'bad.' State service is the opposite of wealth. State service is 'good,' therefore wealth must be evil, or vice versa.[21] 'Like' and 'unlike,' a rigid dichotomy, rules their thinking. It is a way of judging that is ready-made for perpetual social and psychic conflict. For no man is simply good or bad, like or unlike, equal and unequal. In his heart the state-servant loves riches. Historically he is a timocratic man. The man of wealth, for his part, secretly longs for political prestige. In effect he is an oligarch. In time both are forced to recognize their own pretensions, to become self-conscious. They begin by seeing only their opposite in each other. They also end that way – in a simple reversal of labels of good and bad. That is the actualization of the dualistic logic of 'like' and 'unlike.'

The timocrat does not have to confront his illusions until a centralized monarchic state arises. When through his words and works he actualizes his overt self-consciousness he is forced to recognize the distance between his self-image and his actual, objectified ego. That, after all, is the experience of every state of consciousness, personal or public. Politics is talking and by constantly proclaiming his submission to state authority, by insisting on the state as the public good, the aristo-

20. *Politics*, II, 1261a–1266a; *Nicomachean Ethics*, IV, 1120a–1125b.
21. B525–6; H358–9.

crat makes it effective. He makes the idea of state authority into a social fact. Authority is translated into power.[22] A state cannot remain a mere object of passive reverence. If it is recognized as the supreme common good, it must have the ability to act and to demand services as its due, and so it does. An institution corresponding to the words of those who say that the state is the public good must appear to give words their explicit effect.[23] The cost of absolute monarchy to the aristocrats is great. They are now *made* to render service and lose their independence, which had been their real, though unspoken 'good.' Language has undone them. The monarch needs and uses them, but he also requires wealth, and honors it and anything else he pleases. He can make unequals equal, eliminate distinctions, reduce like and unlike to identity. He is indeed the supremely independent individual and like the Roman Emperor before him crystallizes the real, if not the admitted spirit, of his subjects: independence at any cost. The economic man, who is also self-centered, has much to gain from this redefining monarchy. He is no longer 'bad.' The monarchy does not despise him or force him to suppress his individuality, and so he discovers his own pride, asserts himself as the 'good' man and a new cultural ideal. Now timocrat and oligarch, like and unlike, equal and unequal, come to blows and the chaos of democracy is at hand. Nothing now has its appointed place. The old predicates no longer attach themselves to their usual subjects. Everything is mixed up. Molière and Beaumarchais are there ready to perform the functions of Aristophanes. Only 'pure culture,' the republic of letters, unattached to either power or wealth remains intact, and mocking wit reveals the whole truth about this culture.[24]

Hegel's account of this development is intricate, a constant movement back and forth between what this culture claims to be and what in actuality it is. And he goes over it all more than once. Thus, while the core of aristocratic culture, the belief that state-service is 'good,' appears on the surface to be entirely appropriate to men who are ready to give up their lives in the performance of their military duty, it is inherently discordant. If philosophic self-perfection gave even the

22. B529–30; H361–2.   23. B531; H363.   24. B531–48; H363–76.

ideal Platonic guardian a self-centered impulse, personal 'honor' in fact is all that defines the ends of feudal state service. Fundamentally the European aristocracy was, therefore, anarchic in its impulses and in its innermost cultural ideal. The 'haughty vassal' only served the state because that was the source of his 'honor.' He did not submit to the state authority. He only offered his 'counsel.' He served himself and his own idea of the state.[25]

Economic man is incapable of engendering a cultural ethos because he rejects the public realm. He does not wish to universalize himself. In this he is clearly inferior to aristocratic man, who does embody a specific political ideal. The world of wealth is culturally impotent because it does not require any specific sort of public education. Anyone can somehow or other become wealthy. It does not demand a specific style of conduct, or the subjection of oneself to public values. Wealth is purely instrumental. It provides power and it is the basis of all independence, but it cannot inspire educative norms.[26] Nevertheless wealth creates social bonds. As an individual, economic man may only work to enrich himself, but the results of his labors benefit society as a whole. Moreover, though he may not realize it, he is part of a cooperative network, the general economy, and, as such he is an eminently social being.[27] However, by turning away from the state he dooms himself to a position of cultural inferiority.

Aristocratic man is both dishonest and mistaken in his contempt for wealth. Not only does he secretly yearn for the wealth he despises, but he is blind to the self-less contribution, the communal function, of economic activity.[28] The man of wealth also tends to be one-sided in his views. He appreciates his own realm of activity and calls it 'good,' but sees the state as only an oppressor, an alien constraining force. He recognizes the repressive, but not the educative functions of political culture. For him it is all negative.[29] Neither one of these two opponents has any sense of society as a whole, each one cares only for his own independence. If the aristocrat were a true nobleman he would have a perfect sense of

25. B527–8; H360–1.   26. B538–9; H367.   27. B520; H355.
28. B525; H359.   29. B522–3; H357.

the whole and of his place in it. He would know the state not as a means to an end, but as 'the truth,' the aim and source of all social virtue.[30] This is an inclusive consciousness which sees wealth as a part of the whole. This would be 'the heroism of service' realized, and a genuine source of state authority.[31] Such nobility does not mark the European aristocracy. It defines itself by rejecting its opposite. The man of wealth and the aristocrat both have a negative self-consciousness that expresses their mutual hostility. Each is the conscious denial of the hated other. Both are exclusive, self-protecting and self-absorbed. Although the aristocrat claims that state service, especially in its military form, is his educative ideal, he obeys the 'authoritative power of the state' with 'secret malice,' he 'hates the ruler' and sees government as a chain. He is 'ever ready to burst out in rebellion.'[32] As long as his power is not curbed the emergence of the state as an independent institution is impossible. In the feudal scheme there is no real place for self-conscious state power.[33] There are only nobles meeting in 'counsel,' freely offering their advice, but no real 'governmental control.' All 'the clap-trap about what is universally the best,' and the service to the common good and so on, is just so much verbiage which serves as 'a substitute for action to bring it about.'[34] Even when the aristocracy is ready to die in its military function, its members do so with considerable inner reserve. In spite of their overt pretensions, they do not really sacrifice their individuality to the state.[35] They die for 'honor.'

The contribution of Montesquieu to these pages of the *Phenomenology* is evidently considerable. Hegel's debt to Montesquieu's discussion of honor as the principle, the living spirit, of feudal monarchy, is clear on every page. Since, unlike Hegel, Montesquieu did not yet have to account for the dissolution of the *ancien régime,* he was far less concerned with the anarchic tendencies of honor. Hegel saw it as a perpetual rebellion. That is a great difference between them, and one that also colors their respective views of the function of commerce in the *ancien régime.* Montesquieu had been willing to grant Plato's complaint that commerce destroys the

---

30. B524–5, 526–8; H358–61.   31. B527; H360.   32. B525; H359.
33. B527–8; H360–1.   34. B528–9; H361.   35. B529; H361–2.

'purest morals,' but like Hegel, he was quite ready to settle
for less than personal perfection. It was enough that commerce bring peace, that it reform the manners of the barbarians and widen men's horizons. It was 'the cure for the most
destructive prejudices.' [36] The pursuit of wealth was a thoroughly stabilizing force in political society. Montesquieu believed that there had even been a general decrease in Machiavellism, and an end to *coups d'état* since the demands of commercial life had been recognized.[37] Hegel's hindsight was
less placid. He agreed with all that Montesquieu had said on
behalf of the social value of economic activity, but he also
saw its political feebleness. The response of the aristocracy to
the claims of wealth had been one of destructive fury. The
noblemen had not been tamed, and the rise of commercial
attitudes had only helped to enflame their always abundant
anger and pride. Economic man can do nothing to alter or
pacify them. There is no reconciliation at all.

The next step in the development of European culture is
the transformation of feudal lords into courtiers. For Hegel,
as for Montesquieu, this marks the dissolution of the aristocratic ethos. However, Hegel's account of this process of
spiritual disintegration is quite different. Montesquieu saw
the court as the arena of a despot, Hegel as the incubator of a
revolution. Indeed it is one of his most original compositions.
The inner struggle between the feudal principle of honor
and the classical principle of state service becomes overt.
What had been implicit becomes explicit. The contradiction
within aristocratic culture becomes an open confrontation in
which both sides must speak. Now speech in general, political
discourse especially, is inherently communal, generalizing as
it forces the speaker to submit himself to a common standard.
The speaker becomes a social being, an actor in the polity. In
speaking, even if only to defend his claims, the aristocrat performs a public act and obeys the rules of the general order.
"[It] is the power of utterance, *qua* utterance, which, just in
speaking, performs what has to be performed.' [38] The aristocrat loses his supreme autonomy in expressing himself in
words. Words generalize his particularity. In short, he liter-
ally talks himself to political death.

36. *L'Esprit*, XX, 1, 6.   37. *Ibid.*, XXI, 20.   38. B530; H362–3.

The authority inherent in a shared language is not the only spiritual force that works against the spirit of feudal autonomy. In the course of this verbal combat between honor and state authority, the 'spiritual substance,' the social ethos, emerges as an independent value within the public consciousness. Both of the extreme sides acknowledge the primacy of this ethos, at least verbally.[39] The two conflicting sides of the aristocratic mind are united in their professed devotion to the public good, but only one really means it. Eventually honor is forced to an awareness of its own falseness and partiality, and so to defeat. The claim to self-sufficiency and honor must give way to the self-proclaimed aristocratic ideal of obedience to the public good, to the state. The aristocratic psyche is split by its inner contradictions. The call to state service, however, remains an empty aspiration, as long as there is no state with an identifiable will and power of decision to be served. For Europe's aristocratic political culture had nothing comparable to the government of the classical city. The general good is just a rhetorical abstraction, even for those who define themselves as its servants. Nevertheless, the spoken commitment to serve the public order inherently favors the emergence of a unitary sovereign state. The real beneficiary of the process is the unlimited monarch, the one noble who actualizes state authority. It is now effective power. For the monarch gives a voice and a personality to the empty notion of state authority, but he does so in a deeply unethical way. For he is the product of the the aristocratic spirit in decay, not of a revived civic ethos.

The real creator of the unlimited monarchy is again language. 'The silent heroism of service turns into the language of flattery.'[40] The aristocrat makes himself into a courtier, and, as such, he identifies the state with the person of the prince. It is the language of flattery that 'puts one individual self-consciousness at its pinnacle.' For by addressing him as they do and by choosing to stand around his throne as ornaments, the courtiers make kings men apart from the rest of humanity. Flattery and its culture turn the phrase 'l'Etat c'est Moi' into an actuality, and not a fantasy. The Sun King is the expression of that lack of public solidarity inherent in

39. B531–2; H363–4.   40. B533; H364.

aristocratic individualism. In him the power of the state and honor are now united.[41] He is the embodiment of all the aspirations of this culture, its wealth and its power. And yet, he is nothing but a particular self-centered, isolated individual. Hegel did not repeat Montesquieu's marvellous litany of invectives against courtiers, but he also recognized the cultural unity of courtly manners and royal despotism. Honor had become servility.

The aristocrat does not sacrifice his independence without a return. In exchange for his flattery he receives political power from the king. He becomes the active agent of the royal state.[42] The monarch now demands that he render service. He makes state power work. Aristocratic self-respect is, however, completely eroded. That happens not because the aristocrat is now a servant of the state; he had fancied that role all along. His identity collapses because he is now the hired and paid servant of the state. He is now just another wealth-seeker, in no way different from the 'base,' despised economic man. In terms of his own values he is now simply ignoble. Since he had defined himself as the very opposite of the man of wealth, he can see his new situation as nothing other than the triumph of the 'bad.' His nobility is now only a title, at the disposal of the monarch, a meaningless legal privilege, a mere name. The honor that he still receives as a gift from the monarch has no value under such circumstances. The monarch can bestow honor on whomever he pleases. It also has a price now. The aristocrat's state of mind, in short, is one of 'thoroughgoing discordance.'[43] The rebellious impulses, which had never been far from the surface, burst forth painfully, for they are now mixed with profound self-contempt. The aristocratic consciousness revolts against its situation in a frenzy of rage.[44]

Economic man for his part now realizes that he need no longer be quite so subservient to the aristocracy. He knows that wealth gives independence and that the monarchy needs and honors it. Indeed there is no reason why he should not display some arrogance toward the men of rank, since he has more of what they both want: money. Many a nobleman is,

41. B533–4; H365–6.   42. B534–5; H366.   43. B535; H366.
44. B536–8; H367–9.

in fact, hopelessly in debt to him. He therefore imagines that in feeding these aristocrats the differences between him and them have been eliminated. And he fails to see the hot rage in the heart of his clients. One thinks at once of M. Jourdain. He may still cringe before the count, but he does try to seduce the marquise during the supper he offers them. His family's contempt for his antics shows a pride in their station that is not unmixed with disdain for the courtiers. The count accepts the hospitality of the *Bourgeois Gentilhomme* only in order to fleece him, but it is an infuriating humiliation for him to be the guest of M. Jourdain. His honor is hardly restored by gulling his host. That is particularly evident in the peculiar 'baseness' of the flattery which he heaps upon the wealthy bourgeois. The latter is in any case also a victim of the decay of aristocratic values. Wealth cannot create social standards, and although the old values inhibited him, their lapse does him no good. M. Jourdain and his like cannot count on the honor of counts. The latter no longer observe their social obligations. An 'abyss' of arbitrariness threatens both the aristocrat and the bourgeois.[45] Decadence, in short, engulfs political and economic man together.

The language of flattery is only a very crude and partial expression of the prevailing spirit. The perfected speech of a culture that 'plays the game of self-dissolution with itself' is that of wit, of 'ésprit.'[46] For nothing now means what it had once meant. What formerly was called good, is now said to be bad, while what had been bad, is now 'the highest form of free consciousness.' Everything is upside down, and appearance and reality bear no resemblance to each other. Every moment judges every other, and everyone feels free to criticize as he pleases. No distinctions remain.

The master is an incompetent wretch who depends entirely on his clever, capable – and contemptuous – servant. In the world of *Figaro* and of *Jacques the Fatalist* the valet is master, whatever the titles may say. 'Nobility is base and repudiated,' while the most ignoble persons now have the 'most highly developed form of free self-consciousness.'[47] Figaro may be a servant, but we admire him just as surely as we despise and laugh at the count, his master. Such a spiritual situ-

45. B539–40; H369–70.   46. B542–3; H372–3.   47. B542; H373.

ation can only give rise to mockery. The congealed sneer on the face of that prince of professional spongers, Rameau's Nephew, mirrors the complete and perfect truth about this culture. And Diderot speaks for 'pure' culture, for the 're-public of letters,' freed from the constraints of the social institutions of wealth and power.[48] The spirit of liberated individuals, fully aware of themselves as men without determinate relationships, has now come into its own.

Hegel saw very clearly that the helter-skelter utterances of Diderot's mad musician were not really incoherent, and that his jeers expressed an unusually penetrating vision. It was Diderot's own. For, as Hegel noticed, the defender of good, sound morals is reduced to monosyllables. Where the Nephew scorns military duty, social responsibility, public esteem, friendship and family as illusions and 'vanity,' the 'I' of the dialogue is silenced. 'I' can only produce specific examples of moral conduct to contradict the Nephew's account of general selfishness and anarchism. The feebleness of the good soul's replies is just there: he has nothing to offer but isolated instances of virtue. It is the shameless bohemian who has truth, candor and frankness at his disposal. For he is the voice of the nihilistic spirit. And nihilism is the truth and final aim of Europe's aristocratic culture, now at its very end and pinnacle. For only now has the spirit of complete unfettered individualism, which was implicit in aristocratic *Bildung* all along, come fully into its own.

A Diogenes (Rousseau) might choose to retreat into solitude in the face of so much amoral egotism. However, that is only another form of selfishness, a vanity no less vain and self-oriented than the sociability of the degenerate Nephew. To escape from society is only another way of expressing the spirit of all-pervasive disintegration. Certainly a whole society cannot be expected to return to a primitive condition. Rousseau's demand is, however, not without significance. For it is really not a call to go back to nature, but to rise to a higher level of social consciousness.[49] And the Nephew also, in scorning himself, his own greed and vanity, no less than the universal scramble for wealth and power, has transcended the culture he so faithfully represents. In the midst of vanity

48. B541; H371.   49. B545–6; H374.

and meaningless usages he comes to know the real aim of individuality: to seek one's own values. *Aude sapere!* [50]

The man who sees the *ancien régime* as it really is, in that act, rises above it. He always was beyond the 'good' and 'bad' of that society. It was only a scene of vanity in which wealth and power alone counted. Its religion had always looked upon the world as worthless and by half-turning away from it had ensured that it be so. This culture actualizes, acts out, its own conception of itself. It is an empty vanity fair, because it always took itself to be no more than that. That was its true intention. It is Diderot who recognizes the torn and broken condition of this world and who by rejecting it and its self-image moves beyond it. The nihilism of the Nephew is an end and a beginning. It is the task of philosophy, of Hegel's book, to begin again. [51]

Belief and unbelief on the road to revolution

The culture of the *ancien régime* is both the source and creation of Christianity as an established religion. This is a religion that is as self-divided and discordant as the culture of which it is a part. For this is the spirit in self-estrangement, at home neither in the world which it despises, nor in the longed-for 'beyond,' which it cannot reach. Religion in general is 'pure consciousness,' the way a people thinks. It is all the ideas of a people. Ultimately 'pure consciousness' is thinking about thought, philosophy. That, however, is only something *we,* who look back upon the past, know. The

50. B546–8; H374–6. Philosophy must begin now where the Nephew left off. *The Logic of Hegel,* s. 19.

51. Hegel's immediate appreciation of Diderot's masterpiece does him much honor. The work first appeared in Goethe's translation in 1805, just as Hegel was preparing the *Phänomenologie.* According to Goethe, absolutely nobody in Germany would read Diderot's work, because the spirit of fervid nationalism made them hostile to everything French. Clearly Goethe had at least one distinguished reader, and Diderot a perceptive admirer, in Hegel, who never wavered in his admiration for France and for French literary culture. It may be worth noting that he did not follow Goethe's interpretation of the dialogue. Goethe saw it as a psychological portrait of a well-known Parisian character, Hegel as the picture of a general spiritual phenomenon. These two approaches remain the two main lines of interpretation even now. See Goethe, *Nachträgliches zu Rameau's Neffe, Werke,* 45, I (Weimar, 1900), pp. 221–38.

pious of all earlier ages believed that they were thinking about something posited, about objects that had an existence apart from human consciousness. This 'other' is simply cultural experience structured into pictorial images and then raised by the imagination to a super-mundane sphere.[52] Because of this incompleteness, 'pure consciousness' is doomed to a condition of self-estrangement. Christianity is indeed not alone in its inability to accept its cultural character. All religions tend not only to be unaware of, but even hostile to the political order. Unlike all other types of morality, religion divorces its standards of good and evil from their real life in the human spirit, and imputes them to another higher being, 'beyond.' [53]

The Christian believer who imitates the self-sacrificing figure of Jesus thinks of Christ as both within his own spirit and as a distant goal to be reached. *We* know that this belief is the articulation of the collective spirit of a culture and an age. *He,* however, sees his efforts as a struggle to free himself from the shackles of both nature and society. That is a recurrent attitude of religious thought. The clan worship of the ethical people was a belief in the divine law of the nether world, which, as Antigone showed, stood in opposition to the human, civil order. The unhappy consciousness thinks of nothing but escape from the intolerable world of imperial Rome. Both beliefs reflect what they oppose. The nether world of Antigone is a projection of the ethical family. The beyond of the unhappy consciousness is a haven for the atomized victims of cultural destruction who have lost their homes on earth. Christianity is similarly merely a *belief*.[54] It believes in a realm 'beyond,' that is simply the opposite of the actual.

Belief is, however, not the only aspect of 'pure consciousness.' There is also the mystic's desire for immediate and complete union with the divine spirit. This is 'pure insight' which knows that its ego is universal spirit, that the divine spirit is already manifest in the human soul. All that remains to be done is to clear the mind of all extraneous content, especially of all culture-ridden belief. In acting, pure insight therefore has no other aim than to destroy belief. It has no content of its own. It is pure denial, the will to be free of

52. B549; H376.   53. B550; H376–7.   54. B550–1; H377–8.

everything that stands between the ego and its perfect spiritual self-realization. Pure insight does not concern itself with a beyond that is merely the actual world idealized. It knows that it *is* spirit here and now already. It only has to liberate itself from what it knows to be false: belief.[55]

We who look back upon this discordant state of 'pure consciousness' know that these tensions are necessary stages of the development of the human mind. They are already contained in the three persons of the Trinity. First there was God as the sovereign ruler of the universe. He next realizes himself in the person of a human being, who lives and dies, sacrificing himself. Finally there is a return to the original unity, but as a single holy spirit which is both divine and human. It is the spirit of humanity.[56] The Christian believer is arrested at the second stage of this movement. He holds fast to Christ whom he longs to imitate. Through prayer and self-sacrifice he also tries to redeem this wicked world. He acts within culture, structures it and tries to save it, even as he longs for escape from this tormenting world.[57] Pure insight also acts within the realm of culture. For it is not merely private mysticism struggling against the intrusions of a faith that is not ready to go beyond imagery to pure spirituality. It must also try to universalize itself, to appeal to humanity as a whole. It therefore calls on all men to shake off a confining religion to liberate the holy spirit within each. The purpose of pure insight is now to persuade decadent Europe to free itself from the accidents of society and nature, and to cease being 'a herd of self-conscious animals.' Each one is to perfect himself by becoming what each potentially already is: rational.[58]

Hegel did not really explain how the mystic's personal passion for self-purification and perfect spirituality suddenly becomes rationalism. The latter was of course the real historical foe of traditional religion, but its descent from 'pure insight' is not at all self-evident. How did we get there? Hegel's account of the turning of pure insight from the self to the public, from spirit to reason, was not, in fact, fanciful. It was not a contrivance but a perfectly accurate summary of Lessing's

55. B551–4; H378–80.   56. B554–5; H380–1.   57. B555–6; H381.
58. B557–8; H382–3.

theology. Lessing had argued that revealed religion was only a step in the spiritual education of mankind. A third age was dawning in which the holy spirit as universal human reason would transcend both the Old and the New Testaments. Matured mankind would then have reached its moral destiny.[59] Hegel admired Lessing intensely and had no reason to doubt that his readers would recognize his allusion to him at once. He was not writing the history of religion, but offering the best and latest theological interpretation of its meaning. Lessing was indeed the glory of the German Enlightenment that had looked to the purification of religion, not to its destruction. The French Enlightenment did, however, wage a duel to the death against the ancestral faith, and it was to this 'perversion' of pure insight that Hegel now turned.

The real, the French Enlightenment is perfectly certain that belief is 'a tissue of superstitious prejudices and errors,' a deception by a selfish priesthood and the support of despots. The task of the Enlightenment is simply to do away with these powers of darkness.[60] To that end it addresses itself directly to their victims, the naive, natural consciousness of the general public. In the course of this effort rationalism acquires a content. It now is not *pure* insight. It is no longer, as it originally was, a mere denial. It now affirms whatever faith rejects and reviles whatever faith treasures. It does not seek to transform the human mind. It does not have to, since all it has to do is simply wipe away belief. It finds its task quite simple. In fact, it spreads like an epidemic. Opinion is, after all, fluid, and the uncritical mind shakes off Christianity like an outworn skin, and reverts to a natural state of unbelief.

Hegel noticed, with some spite, that the strategy with which the Enlightenment had undermined Christianity was just like the clever machinations that the Nephew had ascribed to Jesuit missionaries abroad.[61] And in fact some of the *philosophes* had also been surprised by their own successes. When d'Alembert saw how quickly the Jesuits had

59. Gotthold Lessing, 'The Education of the Human Race' and 'The Christianity of Reason,' *Lessing's Theological Writings*, ed. and trans. by Henry Chadwick (Stanford, 1956), 81–101.
60. B561–3; H385–6.   61. B563–5; H386–8.

been dispersed he wondered why anyone had ever feared them so.[62] As for the similarity between the tactics of Jesuits and *philosophes,* Rousseau had already noticed it with bitter contempt.[63] Hegel also noted that 'pure' insight when it enters into a power struggle with faith becomes just like its enemy: a new creed. But it is wholly dependent for its system of beliefs on the faith of its opponent. It simply says 'no' to every 'yes' of the latter. Pure insight, however, simply ignores its own newly acquired credal character. The Enlightenment is, in short, 'not very enlightened about its own nature.' [64] That is entirely due to its failure to see what Lessing had taught, that faith is a necessary step in mankind's spiritual development, not a foe to be vanquished and banished from the public mind. The Enlightenment, however, condemns itself to becoming just like belief rather than a new, more comprehensive consciousness. As belief and unbelief accuse each other of malice, slander and lying, they become increasingly alike. The Enlightenment which has long ceased to be 'pure' acquires ideas and beliefs.[65] We have here in short a reversal not unlike that experienced by aristocratic and economic man. 'Like' and 'unlike' change places.

In its war against faith the Enlightenment makes four attacks. Its first accusation against faith is that God is a creation of the believer's own consciousness, not vice versa. Faith knows that of course. It knows that God is its own consciousness, but it also feels trust in its unity with God. In obedience and in religious communion faith finds itself continually reassured that its consciousness is not erroneous, that God *is,* and that its trust is not misguided. Even though it is only through these acts that it produces God in its own spirit, it does not doubt God's presence.[66] The second accusation is that faith is a deception and delusion foisted by priests upon the people. That is a foolish accusation, since belief springs from the deepest recesses of each human mind. One cannot impose an alien faith upon people. They believe what they must. Indeed if the first accusation, that God is the invention

62. *Sur la Destruction des Jésuites en France, Oeuvres Complètes d'Alembert* (Geneva, 1967), II, 48–9.
63. *Rousseau Juge de Jean-Jacques, Oeuvres Complètes* (Paris, 1959), I, 967–8.
64. B582; H401.   65. B565–7; H388–90.   66. B567–9; H390–2.

of the believing consciousness, be true, then the latter has obviously not been tricked into faith. At worst faith is self-deception, but that precludes being duped by a conspiracy of priests and tyrants. If faith is certainty of one's own self, then the idea of delusion is clearly baseless.[67] This charge was of course politically the most effective. It was the Enlightenment's most successful move in winning the public over to its side.

The third accusation really follows from the second: faith is a primitive worship of sticks and stones. It thinks of spirit pictorially, it treasures idols and relics, addresses prayers to persons and ascribes magical power to bread and wine. This is also no news to faith. It knows a mere object when it sees one, but these particular things are symbols for it. Faith does not hold them to be divine, but only signs on the path to God. The Bible, the Enlightenment goes on to say, is not an historically reliable book. Whether it reports miracles or natural events, it is not credible as an historical document. The Bible is, however, not a work of history at all for faith, but revelation and inspiration. It is not a newspaper reporting the events of the day, but the Word that unites the believer with God. If faith starts to justify the Bible by rational historical explanations it has already become infected by the Enlightenment. That had of course happened. In Germany Michelis' rationalist and historical interpretations of the Bible were very influential. Hegel had been the pupil of some of the less inspired followers of that great Hebraist and translator. It was evidently a very dispiriting experience for him.[68]

The final accusation against faith is that its self-sacrifice and asceticism are foolish. The welcome news from the Enlightenment is that one should enjoy one's food as well as every other earthly pleasure. To deny oneself these may show one's independence of these things, but what is to be gained thereby? It is with this, the first directly moral thrust in its duel against faith that rationalism reveals what it has become in the course of this long battle: pure worldliness. This is not the first time that the social implications of an argument

67. B569–70; H392–3.
68. B570–3; H393–5. H. S. Harris, *Hegel's Development* (Oxford, 1972) for an account of Hegel's student years.

reveal the whole character of a philosophy. The Platonic upside-down world and behaviorism expose the real structure of idealism and of observing reason, respectively, in just the same way. Now the Enlightenment comes forward with a program of its own. It is no longer just the denial of belief. Now it is an overt invitation to the joys of gluttony, lust, luxury, and avarice. What began as mere anti-Christianity has now become a positive proposition. When private pleasure is generalized into a new moral theory it is utilitarianism. That is to replace the old religion.[69]

The Enlightenment may have an easy time as long as it is only dealing with the cruder forms of superstition. Hegel, however, is also reminding us indirectly of other, more significant moments in this intellectual struggle, most notably Voltaire's encounter with Pascal. After all, more than any other writer, Voltaire brought 'human right' to bear against faith. And that, Hegel thought, was the heart of the matter.[70] Pascal's religion was already a response to rationalism, especially to Montaigne's scepticism. 'The unknowable absolute Being,' as Hegel noted, is a God who has been subjected to rationalist interrogation.[71] And Pascal's God was not only hidden from human discernment, he was also presented to the calculating intelligence as a safe bet. It is as much one's first interest as it is one's first duty to care about one's immortality. If there is a life after death, one is the gainer in having chosen faith. If there is none, one has lost nothing. It is a self-serving wager.[72] And this, as Hegel repeated with considerable emphasis, is one of the reminders that reason brings to faith. It forces the self-sacrificing believer to remember that he is, after all, pursuing his own end, and his personal interests, in adhering to the program of eternal salvation. It was one of the many ways in which reason makes faith understand itself.

The other reminder that reason serves on faith is also evident in Pascal. It is that faith is not reason, but its opposite, folly. And indeed, Pascal did reaffirm Tertullian's 'credo quia absurdum' without flinching.[73] To Voltaire, this pro-

---

69. B574–5; H395–6.   70. B581–8; H400–6.   71. B512; H349–50.
72. *Pensées, Oeuvres Complètes*, ed. by Jacques Chevalier (Paris, 1954), s. 335, s. 451.   73. *Ibid.*, s. 588.

vided the opening for a new attack. First of all Pascal's bet
was not in his eyes a very good one. For to renounce the
pleasures of the earth was not to lose nothing. And if there
is no eternal bliss, it is senseless to pursue a contemplative or
ascetic life.[74] Instead we ought to seek our own well-being
and comfort, and those of our fellow men – here and now.[75]
Secondly, the obscurity of faith was no recommendation in
Voltaire's eyes. Absurdity and incomprehensibility bore more
resemblance to lies than to the truth, he remarked. The roads
to understanding can be found around us, not in desperate
obscurity.[76] To such reasoning self-sacrifice is not merely
'purposeless as well as wrong'; it is also devious. For these
demonstrative gestures do not prove a selfless desire to shake
off worldly entanglements.[77] In this, Hegel thought the Enlightenment wrong. He did not share the Voltairean suspicion that this was really an 'impure intention,' that is, just
another, and a self-interested, way of ordering the actual
world, rather than a real effort to escape from it.[78] Nevertheless, the accusation again reminds faith of what it is. It forces
the faithful to recognize that they have been living a double
existence, one uncritically submissive to the 'beyond' and another 'in the world of sense' where they have been speaking
and acting in the manner of that world. Until the Enlightenment shakes it, faith simply 'manages to conduct a household
of its own' in each one of these spheres. When it is asked to
account for its worldly conduct, it has no answer to offer to
the Enlightenment and to the latter's gospel of utility.[79] For
utility is the truth of its terrestial existence also.

'Religion exhaustively summed up in the conception of
profitableness – all this is for belief utterly and simply revolting.' [80] Nevertheless, this truth of the Enlightenment,
even if it be only a human one, is beyond rejection, because
in their earthly dealings the faithful, like all human beings,
perform utilitarian calculations. Whatever religion, 'sentimentality' and 'speculation' may manage to say against it,
utility is the truth of the historical world.[81] Even the belief

74. *Lettres Philosophiques*, ed. by Gustave Lanson and A. M. Rousseau
(Paris, 1964), II, 205–7.   75. *Ibid.*, II, 196–7.
76. *Ibid.*, II, 202, 213, 187–8.   77. B585–7; H404–5.
78. B574–5; H395–6.   79. B581–2, 587–8; H401, 405–6.   80. B580; H400.
81. B594–5; H411.

in salvation is after all a calculation of eternal utility. Moreover, neither faith which is a projection of individual consciousness, nor any other spiritual phenomenon, can be
divorced from the living self that thinks and acts and shares
the historical experiences of other men.[82]

For faith this attack on every one of its motives, and the
constant need to justify itself in purely human terms, is a
disaster. It cannot withstand this assault on its integrity. Although, in principle, faith should recognize its true character,
once it has been freed from superstition, its trusting spirit is
too deeply shaken. It cannot be simple, unreflective belief
any longer, now that it has been compelled to defend itself
rationally. To offer explanations and justifications is not the
way of faith. All that is left is a deep emptiness, sheer yearning; and this 'stain of unsatisfied longing' is a blot on the Enlightenment.[83] Religion is left to languish as pure feeling
while thought concentrates on 'pure thinghood.' That is
inherently an unstable and volatile spiritual situation. The
Enlightenment hopes that the idea of utility, with its immediate appeal to natural reason, will replace all traditional
attitudes. And to a very large extent the principle of utility
does become the law of the world. Utility can and does provide a coherent picture of the world. It can order all sense
experiences in a hierarchy in which each thing exists for the
sake of something else, as a means. Human pleasures are the
apex of this hierarchy. The way to judge experiences is,
therefore, not to ask whether they are good or bad, but only
whether they are useful or useless.[84] Whatever pleases men is
most useful of all. Even moderation is but a way of en-
hancing pleasure. The pursuit of self-interest is the road to
a greater sum of pleasure for all, to the common good. Everything, in short, finds its place in this vision of interlocking
pleasures. No reader of Mandeville's *The Fable of the Bees*
will suspect Hegel of imagining things. Indeed, he may well
have been thinking of that very popular hymn to the utility
of vice, which only said crudely what Voltaire implied more
intelligently. Everything and everyone is mutually of service
to the pleasure principle, which God may well have initially
created, but which now runs its independent course, easily

82. B583; H402.   83. B588–91; H406–7.   84. B594–5; H411.

known to each and all of us.[85] This is the Enlightenment's alluring substitute for the traditional religion of Europe.

This truth of the Enlightenment is not as stable as it appears at first. Utility covers a deep fissure in the Enlightenment. The Cartesian identification of thought and its objects falls apart. The deistic Enlightenment has a God, 'a supreme being,' that does not interfere with this world, but guarantees the rationality of man as a thinker. This is now the ultimate intellectual arbiter between the useful and the useless. The materialist Enlightenment sees a universe of matter in which man is only another particle, whose pains and pleasures are the reactions of a machine in motion.[86] Since both look to utility, their conflict does not emerge until the Revolution when they collide and collapse. Then the man who is free to decide what is and is not useful disposes of the man who is a thing that may or may not please and be pleased. In that encounter the Enlightenment comes to know 'the fruit of its deeds.' [87] Until that bloodbath, however, both agree on the truth of utility and all seems well as 'heaven is transplanted to the earth below.' [88]

That return from the 'beyond' is only a very partial victory. It does not bring the divided spirit back to unity. The struggle between dependence and independence continues here below. Moreover, if 'good' and 'bad' can play their duel as 'water' and 'fire' only between 'air' and 'earth,' then the collapse of heaven may leave no space for them. The hour of moral immobility may have come. Hegel was hardly charitable to the Enlightenment in these pages. He did not accuse it of plotting the French Revolution. That emerged out of the inflammable materials of a decadent culture as a whole. What did so obviously infuriate him was the failure of the French Revolution, which the limitations of the Enlightenment foreshadowed. The descent from the 'beyond' was not a return to an ethical polity. The truth of the Enlightenment, the idea of utility, was an invitation to an orgy of individual independence. It had liberated men from superstition, but only to plunge them into a greater anarchy. It was merely the penultimate stage in the disintegration of

85. B579–80; H399–400.   86. B591–4; H408–11.
87. B595–6, 604–5; H411–12, 418–19.   88. B597–8; H413.

a culture that had always been anarchic. In later years when Hegel no longer mourned for the lost moment, he became much kinder to the men of the Enlightenment. He praised their noble devotion to the cause of rationalism. They were not to blame for the Revolution. That was the fault of a slavish religion and an unreformable regime. There was no Burkean nostalgia at all. Hegel thought that the *ancien régime* had been just as horrible as the Enlightenment had said it was.[89] It deserved to be destroyed. In the *Phenomenology* however, Hegel was still shaken by the failure of the Revolution to do more than that. He could not forgive the Enlightenment for having merely destroyed superstition without ushering in a true polity.

The French Revolution

The turn toward revolution begins when the idea of utility proves less stable than the Enlightenment had thought. Men might agree about utility as a predicate, but not as the end of human action. Each mind suddenly discovers that it has its own ideas about what is useful. Moreover, the mind that decides what is useful or useless does not choose to look upon itself as a part of the web of utility. The ego assigns utility to others, but not to itself. In fact, it discovers its complete and unfettered freedom in making these decisions about utility. It now knows itself to be entirely its own master, free to make all choices in terms of its own ideas of pleasure. This emancipated self is certainly not prepared to let a priest represent it before God or to determine what is right and wrong. Everything seems possible, for there are no social barriers left. Social ranks, classes, and powers are all gone. Nothing can resist the will that is aware of nothing but itself.[90] In the context of a nihilistic culture and of unsatisfied 'yearning,' this new independence proves explosive. The febrile mixture of longing and cultural disintegration can only encourage the sense of total liberation. That is why this

89. *Lectures on the History of Philosophy*, III, 379–402; *Philosophy of Mind*, s. 552. For a just appraisal of Hegel's lack of religious belief and his enduring debt to the spirit of the Enlightenment, see Walter Kaufmann, 'The Young Hegel and Religion,' in Alisdair MacIntyre, ed., *Hegel*, 61–99.
90. B599–602; H414–16.

is a spiritual change unlike any other. In this 'purely metaphysical,' asocial state, the individual is thrown back entirely
upon his own psychic resources, his own will.[91] It is a state of
void in which there is only self-awareness. Nothing else is
real any longer. That is a 'new mode of conscious life –
absolute freedom.' [92]

The only tension that remains is between the particular
and general will. The individual does not generalize his will
by rising to an established and shared public consciousness.
He insists that his personal will is general, simply because
he is part of the people which is said to be sovereign. Since
he is called to act on behalf of all, his subjective will *is* the
general will, or at least so he thinks. As a part of the sovereign, these individual wills might have adopted a free
constitution. That would have been an enduring political
achievement. However, the freedom of each will would have
been curtailed. It would have cheated those who fought in
order to be able to lay down the law directly, who wanted to
be perpetual legislators.[93] Their ardor is really the dynamism
of pure insight at work still. The latter has accomplished its
task. No obstacle now hinders it. It has cleared the mind of
all traditional cultural deposits. The ego is now liberated,
and pure liberty is its sole principle of action. However, there
are hindrances in the external world. There are other wills
which can only be removed by killing. Every government,
every law, every opposed will is an intolerable barrier to a
liberty that will endure no limits. So all must go. Liberty has
no task except death.[94] That transforms it. Terror changes
the man of 'absolute' liberty into pure matter. Each ego now
sees itself threatened as mere material to be consumed by
the lord and master, death, whom it enthroned in its hour
of 'absolute' liberty. From having been a perfectly autonomous master, the revolutionary has now become the utterly
instrumental servant. Mortal fear teaches him again to
accept discipline. He is reunited with society, 'the substantial
reality.' [95]

Hegel was not inventing anything when he saw revolutionary rage emerging from the dissolution of the idea of

91. B512; H350.   92. B599; H414.   93. B602–4; H416–18.
94. B604–6; H417–19.   95. B606–7; H419–20.

utility. That was the actual course of conflict. It begins when usefulness ceases to be a mere description and becomes an aspiration, an aim to be pursued.[96] The arrangements of this world are never sufficiently useful, they must always seem to require effort to be made more truly so. Utility turns out to be a call for action. Hegel was nothing if not perceptive. In the early phase of the Revolution the notion of social utility certainly did inspire many people with profoundly religious hopes and expectations for social regeneration. It was the master idea of a Barnave no less than of a Robespierre. Every institution, every law, every proposal was justified in terms of social utility. Even the rights of man, which to us might seem to be limited by the demands of social utility, were not seen as anything but an expression of individual interests that contributed to the greater good of the whole. Siéyès explained them in just such a way.[97] Clearly Hegel had followed the debates of those years carefully. For he saw not only the overwhelming impact of the ideology of social utility, but also its crusading dynamism. He also knew why it proved so corrosive. For who defines the useful? All revolutionaries appealed to it, but each one had his own idea of what and who was really useful. There is no longer any God to settle the quarrel. The 'empty *être suprême*' now 'hovers there merely as an exhalation of stale gas.' [98] It guarantees nothing.

What remains is an anarchy of wills, which Hegel imputed to Rousseau's teachings. Each individual not only decides for himself what is useful for him but also what is generally useful. Each will regards itself as a perfect expression of the general will, which alone is valid, but which cannot be found except in the perfect union of all wills. That precludes compromise and submission. Indeed, the two seem identical now. For each one speaks for all, not only for himself. To accept the decision of another person is, thus, to betray the general will, of which one's own is an inseparable and surely perfect part. Unless all agree, there is no general will; for each one regards his own will as the correct general will.

---

96. B599–600; H414–15.
97. These remarks owe much to Jean Belin, *La Logique d'Une Idée Force: L'Idée d'Utilité Sociale Pendant La Révolution Française (1789–1792)* (Paris, 1939).   98. B602; H416.

Since agreement is impossible, given the multiplicity of actual wills, only anarchy is conceivable. Anything else is a limitation upon one's will. For this consciousness 'the world is absolutely its own will and this will is [general] will.' [99]

No power is able to offer any resistance to anarchic liberty. Tacit consent through representation is clearly unacceptable. This is 'a mere symbol of willing.' The 'concrete actual will' of 'each and every personality' must do, and do consciously, anything that is done on behalf of all. Nothing less than complete direct democracy is acceptable. All must participate. The individual will that is the general will can only 'realize itself in a work which is a work of the whole.' [100] Now 'its purpose is universal purpose, its language universal law, its work universal achievement.' [101]

The will is, however, subjective for all these pretensions, and each individual sees that. For him the general laws of the state are thus just the assertions of the individual, subjective will of another person. And each individual must be a little sovereign. If the revolutionaries had settled down to their original design for constitutional government in a pluralistic order, they might have created a differentiated, but free society. However, in *any* order, even in a free one, each person must play a determinate role which inhibits his autonomy and denies, in practice, the universality of his consciousness.[102] That had in essence been Condorcet's objection to the constitution of the United States. It was based, he complained, on the theory of balanced powers and the identity of interests, rather than on the equality of political rights.[103] The 'idea of submission to self-imposed laws' would still be a cheating of a self-consciousness that wants to achieve a general, not a particular task. Only actual legislating, and not by proxy, will do.[104] However, even legislation, as a perpetual activity, fails. For any decision, any deed, puts an 'individual consciousness in the forefront.' At most each participant has only a small share in the act. Then someone must execute it, and that is an imposition. Law excludes someone eventually, and so ceases to be universal.

99. B600; H415.   100. B601; H415.   101. B601–2; H416.
102. B603; H417.
103. *Esquisse d'un Tableau Historique des Progrès de l'Esprit Humain,*
    Oeuvres (Paris, 1847), VI, 198–202.   104. B603–4; H417.

The only possible action of completely universal participation is 'negative action.' 'It is merely the rage and fury of destruction.' [105] Rousseau had, of course, recognized the difficulty clearly enough, though not its possible implications. Any government must of necessity be a departure from equality, and so from the general will. Anarchy being impossible 'among men as they are,' he decided, with profound resignation, that the political corruption of the general will was inevitable.[106] Hegel, unlike some subsequent interpreters of the *Social Contract,* recognized its egalitarian character fully, though he ignored Rousseau's pessimism. The general will was not an external instrument of domination, but a justification of an unrealizable democracy. What Rousseau held to be impossible proved to be so in actuality. However, the possibilities of negation were still hidden from even Rousseau's political imagination, while Hegel had ample opportunity to observe them.

The only possible public activity which excludes no one is the act of rebellion. All can join in turning against any actual, or suspected, usurpers of the general will, and that means any potential government. No government can claim to be more than a mere faction, since all are necessarily exclusive. No government is general. That had been Rousseau's point all along. And there is no external standard according to which the legitimacy or illegitimacy of any government, or of its opponents, can be measured except the general will, which in actuality is the will of all those in revolt. To be either government or organized opposition must therefore be a crime against the general will. Without political stability there can be no laws, and so no judgments based on law. Suspicion is tantamount to guilt, intention equivalent to the commission of crime. In all cases there is only one available response: to remove the obstacle to the reign of the general will. Death becomes the real lord and master, and killing the most casual and obvious political act.[107] The state of absolute liberty is now recognized for what it is, exactly what Hobbes had said it was, a condition of universal fear of

105. B604; H418.
106. See the author's *Men and Citizens* (Cambridge, 1969), 204–12.
107. B606–7; H419–20.

violent death. The individuals who come to this realization 'submit to negation and distinction once more, arrange themselves under the spheres' again and return to their specific functions and places.[108] The Revolution is over. It achieved absolutely nothing. It was the occasion of 'no universal works of language,' no laws, and 'no deeds and works of active freedom.' [109] It is all notably reminiscent of that Corcyraean revolution which Thucydides had made the paradigm of those upheavals in which 'death rages in every shape.' [110]

Out of this tumult and horror 'the ethical world and the real world of spiritual culture' would have arisen. That is, a return to the Greek polis might have occurred. 'But that is not the form the final result assumed.' The Jacobins had dissipated the classical republican aspiration, perhaps forever. Hegel did not say that such a rejuvenation had simply been impossible. He said only that it did not come about. Instead, after the *ancien régime* was destroyed, nothing substantial was left in the world of culture, only 'disaster and ruin,' 'nothing that gives a filling.' [111] These quiet remarks carry a burden of deep regret. This was for Hegel the real failure of the Revolution. Hellas was not reborn. Europe *might* have been refreshed and returned to its origins, to the source of all its spiritual creativity, but it was not. Democracy did not reach its true form in the ethical state of a free people. Everything was dissipated in a war of all against all, in the terror of unrestrained liberty. When that passed, all hope and all spirit had been exhausted.

If the fear of the lord death had turned self-consciousness back to its origins and forced it to reconsider its entire journey from antiquity to the present, a new ethical society might have emerged. The rejuvenated spirit would have re-created the ancient 'interpenetration' of the will and society. Ethical knowledge would finally have replaced the struggle of independent and incoherent wills. That is not what happened. Instead the terror turned men's minds away from politics altogether. Political self-assertion is no longer mistaken for freedom. The personal subjective will is abandoned in favor of the universal rational will, which alone is truly

108. B607; H420.   109. B602–3; H416–17.
110. *The Peloponnesian War*, III, s. 81.   111. B607–8; H420–1.

autonomous. That is a step toward moral knowledge, but not toward political freedom or ethical action. Europe just looked away, or to be exact, it took to 'the moral outlook.' [112] Beyond that, however, the end of the old culture presented speculative philosophy with a great opportunity. One could now retrospectively know the whole history of knowing. It is not exactly an occasion for rejoicing, for this feat of remembrance takes place on the field of skulls.[113]

112. B608–10; H421–2.   113. B807–8; H563–5.

CHAPTER FIVE

BEYOND MORALITY: A LAST BRIEF ACT

The age of hypocrisy

The French Revolution has brought Europe's flawed public culture to an end. It is succeeded by the era of moralism, or to be exact, of hypocrisy. The reigning thought of the Revolution was unrestricted individual independence and it survived its political disasters, though in an altered form. It is internalized as pure moral freedom, as Kantian moral autonomy and it has no immediate political implications. Indeed, it is both a response to and a perpetuation of a political vacuum. This is the extremity of the independent consciousness that began its career in the ashes of the Greek city. Beyond it is the door to self-knowledge. The answer to the question 'What am I?' awaits us when 'we' have passed through the experiences of the 'moral point of view.' It teaches us that man as man is free to determine his moral existence and what duty is. For all its faults and weaknesses it recognizes what neither ancient ethics nor Christianity could know: that the individual ego is not just a part of a city or a religious community but of humanity as a whole. That had been implicit in the heroic consciousness and in monotheism, but it can only now become explicit self-consciousness. 'We' who have traversed all the experiences that prevented the emergence of this knowledge are now ready for the last step. In spite of all its terrible tendency to self-edification and hypocrisy, the moral ego breaks down the local and particular barriers to self-knowledge. After the spirit of a people and of a faith are spent, the ego finds its place and knows itself.

The age of 'the moral point of view' is not a glorious one. It is the expression of both less and more than Kant's moral philosophy. It is less because it reflects only its psychological and social infirmities, more because it is the culmination of the attitudes that really had Socrates as their author. This autonomous self that is its own master, or practical reason imposing itself upon the world, is not 'character,' only knowledge. We are again reminded of how far we are from Antigone.[1] Indeed, if this outlook creates any recognizable human type it is the hypocrite. And it expresses itself not only in a hypocritical personality but in a veritable culture of hypocrisy. We are, in short, in Hegel's and our own era. Kant and Fichte are not accused of being hypocritical, of course, or even of having produced this lamentable world. Hegel does not even name them here. However, by cleverly stringing together very familiar and telling passages from their writings, he meant to show that they had provided the age with its reigning opinions. We are therefore not exactly faced with Hegel's great predecessors, but with general attitudes which they supported and structured for their contemporaries. They were the true voices of this culture and as such above it. Though Hegel was never effusive in the tributes to Kant that honesty seemed to wring from him, he never treated Kant with the contempt he visited upon the great man's self-appointed disciples.[2] He never doubted the intellectual necessity of Kant's philosophy or its immense importance as a phenomenon of the human spirit. It was also the spirit of post-Revolutionary Europe. That was philosophically its weakest side, but culturally the most important. Like the revolutionaries, moralism makes an excessive demand for complete individual autonomy. Autonomy and the awareness of autonomy 'is its substance, its purpose and its sole and only content.'[3] Duty is no chain on autonomy, for duty consists entirely of self-imposed rules freely accepted by the sovereign individual. He is a 'world within' himself.[4]

1. B613–14; H423–4; see above, ch. 3, and B485–6; H332.
2. B107–8; H41. For Hegel's praise of Kant, see e.g., B609–10; H421–2; *Philosophy of Right*, 28, 89–90, 253 (ss. 15, 135, addition to s. 133).
3. B614; H424.   4. B615; H424–5.

This awareness is all that concerns him as a moral being. Nature plays no part in this moral order. Pleasure and passion have been banished, as have all other natural or instinctual motives for action. That is why the crisis of actualization has an even more devastating character in Kantian moralism than in the case of all the other brands of subjective morality. Moralism does not just fail the test of actualizing its principles, it cannot even try to meet it. Hegel had illuminated with cruel efficiency the occasions on which the men of pleasure, of the heart and of virtue disintegrate. The awful psychological tensions that their philosophical contradictions create at the moment of action simply shatter them. Kantian moralism never acts at all. Passivity, indeed paralysis, is built into this state of mind. For to act at all requires some expectation of happiness and the use of one's body and emotions. That suffices to render all action morally faulty, unfree and tainted by impure motives and the laws of physical causality. The man who says he acts as a Kantian moral man is a hypocrite. Kantian moralism is fit at most for judging, not acting. The insuperable cleavage between moral freedom and the laws of nature permit no other possibility.[5] For '[any] event occurring in time [as change] . . . [is] necessary under the laws of nature while at the same time its opposite is to be represented as possible through freedom under moral law.' [6] Hegel virtually wrote his whole criticism of moralism around this sentence from Kant's *Religion Within the Limits of Reason Alone*.

To demonstrate what he took to be the massive defects of Kantian moralism, Hegel not only disregarded the vital *Foundations of the Metaphysics of Morals* entirely, he also shrewdly chose to consider *Religion Within the Limits of Reason Alone*. Perhaps Hegel thought this relatively accessible work to have a greater impact upon the thinking public. He also may have judged it to express the Kantian outlook more perfectly, since unlike the *Foundations,* but like the *Second Critique,* it emphasized the subjective necessity of faith in God. He was, after all, not offering an analysis of

5. B615–16; H425–6.
6. Kant, *Religion Within the Limits of Reason Alone,* trans. by T. M. Greene and H. H. Hudson (New York, 1960), 46.

Kant's philosophy, but a bird's-eye view of Kantian moralism as a quite general state of mind. Hegel was certainly not impartial in his selection, but there is much in that work to make morality seem a pursuit of internal self-perfection and a striving for a 'beyond' that precludes achievement. When he charged that this was a morality that was merely 'an absolute task or problem' and 'an everlasting ought to be, which never *is*,' Hegel was on fairly solid ground.[7] First of all, Kant thought that human evil was simply 'inextirpable by human powers.'[8] Yet morality postulates that it must be *possible* to overcome it, so that we remain obliged to keep trying. The best we can achieve is to 'progress endlessly by continuing from bad to better.'[9] This moral growth is the gradual ascendancy won by moral maxims over sensuous nature. It is an effort to alter our motives. Reform cannot come from just improving our behavior, but only through transforming our inner 'cast of mind.'[10] Our inner state is what matters since any act that arises from any motive other than the commands of the moral law is worthless. Anything else is a pursuit of self-love or of some desire for happiness, and this is the essence of evil. Unlike the Stoics Kant did not regard all our inclinations as inherently bad. Some are quite neutral. Morality does not demand their destruction, but only their consistent subordination to its laws.[11] The great and insuperable obstacle to this end is our desire for happiness. Yet we need not despair. If we were truly moral we would be worthy of happiness, and discover that nature and moral duty were at one – at some infinitely remote point.[12] That is, however, only an act of rational faith.

Hegel began his assault upon moralism with Schiller's old complaint about Kant. The divorce of moral reason from happiness would reduce us all to a monkish and miserable condition.[13] Mankind simply cannot renounce happiness and, added Hegel, the remote hope of some eventual harmony between duty and happiness is at best a mere 'postulate.' It has to be made since duty must act, must impose

---

7. B620, 289; H428–9, 189–90.   8. *Religion Within the Limits*, 31–2.
9. *Ibid.*, 46.   10. *Ibid.*, 43–4.   11. *Ibid.*, 50–2.   12. *Ibid.*, 41–2.
13. See above, ch. 3.

itself upon nature. And without some incentive to our
psychological and physical nature we cannot move. Moral
action is therefore always self-defeating. Its end is to liberate
the moral will from the necessities of nature, but to act at
all we depend upon our natural inclinations and sensibility.[14] Morality thus becomes an interminable task, a struggle against nature that can never be won. As an undertaking
it cannot advance, and the actualization of duty is indefinitely
postponed. In fact, if morality is just a battle, then it cannot
even contemplate its own victory. For if it were to accomplish its task, if the moral will were finally to crush inclination, morality would have become superfluous. It would now
have no work to do at all.[15] However, there really can be no
moral improvement, since the basic tension cannot abate.
Morality is just striving without any result.

'The contradiction involved in an undertaking that at
once ought to remain an undertaking and yet ought to be
carried out' is a recurrent one.[16] It appears again when pure
duty is confronted with our many actual duties. These are
all contaminated by the circumstances, causes, and conflicts
of the natural and social world. To perform any one duty
means that one has abandoned 'pure duty,' yet that is all one
ought to follow. Action, performing duties, is however what
morality demands. To actually do any one of one's duties is,
therefore, to fail to act upon 'pure' duty. In sum, 'there is
no morally complete self-consciousness' and therefore 'there
is no actual existence which is moral.' [17]

There was one element in Kant's moral theory that Hegel
hated even more than its passivity: its vestigial Christianity
and craving for a 'beyond.' For Kant the one being for whom
morality and pure duty are not a task but an accomplish-
ment was not man but a Holy Legislator. To Hegel this
seemed a mere device, invented to render moral action more
plausible but less honest. Moralistic man invents a Holy
Legislator to reassure us all that there is a Being who guarantees the ultimate harmony of duty and happiness. He is the
one Being in whom the two are at one, the personification of
the rational faith in the unity of nature and reason. Now

14. B616–19, 638–9; H425–8, 442–3.   15. B619–20, 632–5; H428–9, 436–9.
16. B620; H428–9.   17. B621–4, 626, 637–40; H429–31, 433, 441–3.

Hegel not only hated this vestigial Christianity, he also took it to be hypocritical. Although *Religion Within the Limits* opens with a ringing affirmation that man does not need 'another Being over him to apprehend his duty nor of an incentive other than the law itself for him to do his duty,' the importance of just such a Being grows considerably in the course of the work.[18] For it emerges that though morality is neither derived from religious faith, nor obedience to the commands of God, it does 'ineluctably' lead us to religion. It 'extends itself to the idea of a powerful moral Lawgiver, outside of mankind, for whose will that is the final end (of creation) which at the same time can and ought to be man's final end.' [19] Moreover, morality cannot be achieved by individuals, but only by an entire community or mankind as a whole, living in a wholly uncoercive, loving 'ethical commonwealth' for which this Lawgiver alone legislates.[20] Since we know that we are obliged to work for this end that is our duty, we would despair if we could not believe in a moral ruler of the world without whom we could not reach this end. For if we strive to do our duty we may finally receive an incomprehensible 'grace' which will erase the inevitable faults of even our best acts. In short, the harmony between nature and morality, happiness and duty, subjective and universal reason is all guaranteed and depends on a Holy Legislator. We *must* believe in this harmony. It is the promise Kant had made Schiller: that the man who does his duty for duty's sake will find happiness as well.[21]

We 'must' believe in all this, of course, only if we begin with an extreme dualism in which inner and outer in man and in nature, morality and nature, duty and happiness, and active and passive egos are opposed to each other.[22] Moreover, the Holy Legislator does nothing to heal these conflicts. As Hegel saw it, this figure merely provides moralistic man with an excuse for total passivity and offers him an invitation to hypocrisy. Since the Holy Legislator is admittedly the projection of the moralistic mind, it is fraudulent of the

18. *Religion Within the Limits*, 3.
19. *Ibid.*, 5–6; *Critique of Practical Reason*, 119, 189–90, 227–34, 246–9.
20. *Religion Within the Limits*, 90–1.   21. *Ibid.*, 18–19.
22. *The Logic of Hegel*, s. 60.

latter to claim that it knows less than its own creation. If the
Holy Legislator can harmonize morality and nature so can
the mind that devised this Being.[23] However, it is the explicit
function of that Holy Legislator to exist only in the 'beyond.'
'Because the universally best ought to be carried out, nothing
good is done.' [24] If moralistic man does nothing he is, however, failing altogether, for the very purpose of morality is to
act. To reduce morality to a mere thought, to utter passivity,
is pure hypocrisy. The more moralistic man, therefore, rails
against the hypocrisy of those who claim that their natural
acts are moral, the more he reminds us of his own hypocrisy,
that of not acting at all.[25]

It is, in fact, not hypocritical to recognize that moral autonomy is an aim and not an actuality. And to hope for its
possibility does not mean shifting the responsibility for
morality on to a Holy Legislator. Given Kant's well-known
loathing for hypocrisy and pious self-deception, it was a mean
blow.[26] It was not, however, capable of striking Kant. After
all every single one of Hegel's criticisms of Kantian morality
rests on just those limitations upon the possible, in morals as
in knowledge, that Kant had himself explicitly brought
forward.[27] But Hegel was concerned less with Kant directly
than with that deepest folly of a culture which sets too high
a value on inner purity and self-perfection. That is why even
those who try to do without a Holy Legislator remain self-
imprisoned. Kantian moralism, in Hegel's account, was thus
only a step toward an even more extreme state of eccen-
tricity. The next stage of moralism is a reaction against the
contradictions and uncertainties of the law of pure duty.
Fichte's idea of conscience is a deliberate rejection of all that
wavering and self-torment. It is 'simply spirit consciously
assured or "certain" of itself, spirit which acts directly in the
light of this assurance.' [28] No shifting back and forth between

23. B623–7, 635–9; H431–4, 439–42.   24. B631; H436.
25. B639–41; H442–4.
26. *Religion Within the Limits,* 37–8, 168, 176–7, 186.
27. The one sentence of Kant that Hegel seems never to have read closes the
Foundations of the Metaphysics of Morals: 'And so we do not indeed
comprehend the practical unconditional necessity of the moral imperative;
yet we do comprehend its incomprehensibility which is all that can be
fairly demanded of a philosophy which in its principles strives to reach
the limits of human reason.' *Loc. cit.,* 117.   28. B641; H444.

self-legislation and the Holy Legislator and no vain search for universality torment this consciousness. The voice of conscience is infallible. If one likes playing with words as much as Hegel did one cannot fail to notice that con-science is not just any sort of moral intuition, but that it means 'with knowledge' and, in German, certainty as well. In Fichte's version of the categorical imperative this aspect of conscience is certainly evident.

'Conscience is the root of all truth and whatever is opposed to conscience is false.' [29] Nothing could be more uncomplicated. No need to worry about consequences and circumstances which are, after all, not within our control. For conscience knows what is right instantly and certainly. There is also no mention here of matching one's maxims against a universal standard. This is not practical reason, after all, but just individual, inner, self-assured conscience. It is the eternal 'Here I stand.' 'Act always in accordance with your best conviction of your duty, or act according to your conscience.' [30] One would expect nothing less from the absolute ego in its moral phase. There is no occasion here for indecision or for dissimulation.[31] Nor is there any difficulty with happiness. Certainty is invariably accompanied by a happy feeling of inner harmony.[32] This is evidently subjectivity at its most extreme, but to Fichte it implied no indifference to others. The conscience does not only seek agreement, but feels a duty to convince other people of its own rightness. In cases of conflict between conscientious people each one has an obligation to work for harmony, if at all possible. One must persuade others. This must, of course, be a matter of reasonable discourse only, since one has a primary duty to respect the conscience of others.[33] Duty in practice consists entirely of knowing one's own mind and sharing one's convictions with others.[34] Since personal conviction is all that matters conscience is not troubled by pure and mixed duties.[35] Duty is a simple inner command, and one simply has to translate that inner voice into action. One speaks out boldly and announces one's convictions so that

29. Fichte, *The Vocation of Man*, p. 90.
30. Fichte, *The Science of Ethics*, 164. 31. *Ibid.*, 174. 32. *Ibid.*, 178–9.
33. *Ibid.*, 245–6. 34. *Ibid.*, 262. 35. B645–6; H446–7.

others may recognize them. This is the absolute ego in its loquacious phase. However, this endless verbosity is no isolated occurrence; it is accepted social usage. Conscience is a social fact and an objective, socially sanctioned form of conduct. Conscience does not have to chase after causes in the manner of the 'honest consciousness.' It knows that it is its own cause and that others expect it to be followed.[36]

Certainty is not a proof of truth, and the omniscience of conscience is the ultimate illusion of autonomous man. Nevertheless, it is an ineluctable part of man. To be human means to have a conscience. Hegel was not inclined to deny that altogether. In later works he was both to affirm the worth of individual conscience and its compatibility with social ethics. Personal conscience is somehow 'holy' and gives the individual 'his infinite value.' [37] It is always 'a sacrilege' to violate this inner realm.[38] Finally conscience is an active force; it moves men to act. There is no perpetual crisis of actualization here. The self of conscience knows what must be done and does it, or at least says it. It is 'for the first time in moral experience, moral action as action.' [39] However, Hegel's 'true' conscience is quite different from either Fichte's or the Protestant version of conscience. It is highly socialized. It certainly does not imply the supremacy of private conviction and it is not a menace to society. In its 'pure' form, however, it expresses and encourages the spirit of a society that is always on the verge of dissolution. It is this sort of conscience only that Hegel describes in the *Phenomenology*. It is a conscience that is its own law and accepts nothing that stands in its way. 'It is now the law that exists for the sake of the self and not the law for the sake of which the self exists.' [40] Personal self-expression can bear neither the universal moral law nor the local law of a community.

In this uninhibited condition conscience not only finds action easy, it also finds a justification for everything that it does. If it finds itself in conflict with law or convention it rejoices, for it sees proof of the depth of its convictions in

36. B646–52; H447–51.   37. *Vernunft in der Geschichte*, 63.
38. *Philosophy of Right*, 91, 137, 272 (s. 137, 213 with additions).
39. B647; H447–8.   40. B649; H449.

these moments of discord.[41] Since Fichte thought that promoting the re-education and progress of mankind were the primary end of conscience such conflict is only to be expected.[42] All that matters is that one express one's convictions to convince others of one's moral perfection. However, if conformity to social rules is no proof of conscientiousness how is one to gain the respect of others? How are they to know whether the claims of conscience are genuine or mere selfishness? 'Conscience, then, in its majestic sublimity above any specific law and every content of duty, puts whatever content it pleases into its knowledge and willing. It is moral genius and originality . . . it is divine creative power . . . "service of God," for its action is the contemplation of this its own proper divinity.'[43]

The truth from within is now the sole judge in all its own cases. Conflict and mutual suspicion are bound to arise, and conscience as the governing principle is quite incapable of resolving them.[44] Even if it does resort to some universal rules of conduct to justify its judgments there is infinite room for arbitrariness. And conscience never hesitates to assert itself. It knows. What gives it that knowledge, however, is personal caprice, opinion, preference and interest.[45] When conscience acts it can and usually does 'attach its feeling of conscientiousness to any content.'[46] That means it can call anything it chooses good and right, which means, in practice, that it sanctifies the purest selfishness.

In the actual world a man may regard it as his duty to increase his property for the sake of his family. Other people may see only greed there. Another man may feel that he has a duty to preserve his life. Others may see only cowardice in that. Who is to judge? When each conscience is free to know, decide and state what its duties are, there is no choice but to assent to any expressed declaration of duty.[47] One might, to be sure, suggest to conscience that it would be best to do what is generally known to be good for all, rather than to pursue a self-set path. That is, however, a solution that con-

41. B654–7; H453–6.   42. *Vocation of Man*, 100–18.   43. B663; H460.
44. B653–4; H452–3.
45. B654–5; H453–4. See also the entire section dealing with Socrates in *Lectures on the History of Philosophy*, I, 384–448.   46. B654; H453.
47. Fichte, *Science of Ethics*, 315–17; B654–5; H453–4.

science will never accept. For the general good is not its own truth, but a standard set by law and social custom and right. The validity of these does not derive directly from the individual's own knowledge and convictions. They are externally imposed limitations which conscience in its freedom and self-sufficiency cannot endure.[48] That is also why conscience though it wants to be accepted by others will not make any compromises for the sake of harmony. That would be a concession to the general good and it would also require conscience to engage in calculations about the consequences of deeds. Compromises express a concern with the results of what one does and predictions about its effects on other people. Such concessions to the world of probabilities and circumstances are wholly repulsive to conscience. It knows what to do, and the worth of that knowledge is just that it is its own. It cannot allow itself to be hampered with weighing duties and considering outcomes.[49] Each conscience is free to 'bind or to loose.'[50] In that way all are equal. Each one holds to the purity of his motives no matter what he does. Each one is, however, free to doubt the motives of all others. Everyone must analyze and estimate the 'real' motives of other men in terms of what they know, their own conscience. Knowing themselves so well they are likely to see nothing but low motives in others also.[51] The conscientious are suspicious, as well they might be.

The only way out of this impasse is mutual persuasion. Conscience regards this as its chief duty. After all self-declaration is how it manifests itself. An act is dutiful because the agent says that his conscience tells him so. Self-oriented as this language of conviction is, it is not the language of nihilism and scorn uttered by *Rameau's Nephew*. The conscientious do not suffer from self-contempt. On the contrary they speak out to display their own perfection.[52] That is how conviction realizes itself. When we speak we not only express ourselves we also present ourselves to others and learn to see ourselves as they see us. We become intelligible to ourselves in the act of making ourselves intelligible to others.[53] The

---

48. B655–6; H454–5.   49. B656–7; H455.   50. B658; H456.
51. B659–60; H457.   52. B659–60; H457.
53. B660–3, 340–2; H458–60; 229–31.

language of ethical men is that of law and convention. Pure
moralism is reduced to silence in its purity and inactivity.
Kantian moralism is at least not talkative. The language of
conscience is that of self-worship, but it need not remain
solitary. Conscience that must speak can always find some
mutual admiration society whose members accept each other's
professions of good intentions and purity of purpose and this
gives much pleasure to all. They share 'the glorious privilege
of knowing and expressing, of fostering and cherishing, a
state altogether admirable.' The ironist here clearly is Hegel,
and not for the last time.[54]

Hegel was very much aware of how satisfying these associations of the high-minded can be, but he could not yet guess
how effectively they reinforce the self-assurance of their members and how secure a basis they offer for every conceivable
bit of moralistic casuistry. He was more impressed by their
instability, and to be sure, the tendency of moralizing parties
and sects to disintegrate is proverbial. We are back with the
dynamics of sectarianism that afflicted the law of the heart.
The truly self-nourishing conscience, the 'beautiful soul' is
too tender to endure any society for long. It must flee inward. Communities of 'beautiful souls' do not last. Their
essential egotism soon reveals itself and they degenerate into
the vanity of irony and hypocrisy.[55] The specific character
and content of the language of private conviction is such that
it can never bind men together. The paradox of language is
that though we share it, it is capable of reducing us to isolation. There are no principles or words of unity among self-
admiring consciences, even if they all approve of each other
and this way of talking. 'This general equality breaks up into
the inequality of each individual existing for himself,' because there is no way of overcoming the opposition of these
individuals to other individuals or to society in general.[56]
Each one demands that he be respected, but for what? Unless
there is a common standard, even if it be only common
humanity, to judge actions, there is no ground for respect.
The sovereignty of personal conviction renders such a yard-

54. B664; H460–1; *Philosophy of Right*, 101–3 (s. 140); *Lectures on the
History of Philosophy*, III, 506–8, 510.   55. B663–7; H460–3.
56. B667; H463.

stick impossible. Its language is therefore just an act of self-assertion. Assurances of inner righteousness, without any references to actions, are not automatically convincing. Not deeds, only inner states are offered up to be recognized. Here duty *is* merely a matter of words. It is a situation that has only two possibilities, evil or hypocrisy. Evil is honest and declares, 'I do as I like.' Hypocrisy behaves the same ways but proclaims loudly, 'I act out of deep, inner conviction.' Evil expects to be condemned. Hypocrisy insists on admiration. That is how conscience becomes simple selfishness.[57]

Like many intellectuals Hegel could excuse evil, but hypocrisy revolted him. Evil can be explained. Hypocrisy must be unmasked.[58] He agreed with Pascal that the undisguised sinner is only partially evil. He avoids, but does not tarnish goodness. He does not confuse good with evil, he merely turns his back upon the former. Hypocrisy, on the other hand, soils goodness by exploiting it to cover up evil. It is an injury to and an abuse of the very idea of the good.[59] In the *Phenomenology* Hegel only hinted at his loathing for hypocrisy, but in the *Philosophy of Right* he gave free rein to his feelings, and they were intense. One can hardly blame him. For he realized that in the modern age hypocrisy had not merely altered in extent, but in character. It had become a total environment, not just a common failing. In an earlier age La Rochefoucauld could still laugh at hypocrisy as 'the compliment vice pays virtue,' but he was only dealing with the naive hypocrisy of a Tartuffe. Molière's hero, after all, just pretends to be more pious than other people in order to cover up his wicked schemes. Tartuffe's hypocrisy was merely one form of unctuous fraud among many others. Modern hypocrisy, if it resembles anything known to the past, is most like the Probabilism of the Jesuits which Pascal had hated so deeply. This was the obnoxious proposition that any apparently immoral behavior could be excused if some orthodox authority could be found anywhere that would seem to permit it. And some legitimate Christian authority always could be discovered, with a little effort, to provide some sort of justification. Modern hypocrisy dispenses with

57. *Philosophy of Mind*, s. 571; *Philosophy of Right*, 90 (s. 135).
58. B668–9; H464–5.   59. *Philosophy of Right*, 94–5 (s. 140).

this reliance on authority. If it is possible, and it always is, to claim that one is following one's own conscience, one's actions must be judged to be dutiful. There is, moreover, an internalized Machiavellism here that covers even the most criminal actions. The maxim that the end justifies the means is applied here to justify any sort of crime as long as it can be said to promote some noble personal ideal. In short, men of 'deep convictions' may get away with murder.[60] Their lives are wicked, but their hearts are pure.

Conscience is utterly incapable of curing the moral disease that it generates. The more it rails against hypocrisy, the more it encourages the vice. For what can conscience do but demand an ever more complete reliance on its own supremacy and inwardness? Yet it is this very appeal that forces one into hypocrisy.[61] The upshot is that no one is much concerned with hypocrisy any longer. It is typical of our shallow age that hypocrisy is accepted as the inherent condition of our moral life. It is not the least mark of Hegel's intelligence to have noticed this novel character of his and our world. For unlike cynics, old and new, he did not simply point to this or that example of hypocrisy. He showed that hypocrisy had become a logical and psychological necessity of moral life. When people are continually encouraged to follow nothing but the inner voice of conscience without regard to social conventions or to the consequences of their conduct, they must deceive themselves and each other. The dissociated conscience is doomed to this by its very principle which cannot admit that good actions can come from knowing and following social rules or even one's own intelligently calculated interests. These may well, in fact, inform conscience, but conscience can never admit that, and so, it lies. Moreover, the struggle for mutual recognition is under these conditions bound to be interminable. For no conscience can join another. The quest for recognition fails in the face of the rigid autocracy of each conscience. No 'we' emerges.

As in so many of Hegel's outbursts against his contemporaries there is a certain ambiguity here. If hypocrisy is indeed the spirit of the post-Revolutionary world, then hypocrites are its 'good citizens.' To excoriate them for not being 'good

60. *Ibid.*, 93–103, 256–8 (s. 140 and additions).　　61. B669–71; H465–6.

men' would make sense only if they had defied some more
universal standards of good and evil. That, in fact, is what
Hegel accused them of doing. But where are those rules and
who is to establish them? There is not even a word about the
modern state here, and the ethical city is a thing of the past.
Later, in *The Philosophy of Right,* in discussing the transition
from morality to ethics, Hegel was to say that he had treated
that subject differently in the *Phenomenology.*[62] That is
somewhat misleading, since no transition to ethics occurs in
the *Phenomenology* at all. We move directly from morality
to humanity. Indeed, neither the absence nor the presence of
a state can do much to alleviate the hypocrisy of this culture.
The language of hypocrisy is as appropriate to it as flattery
was to the court-culture of the *ancien régime.* Moralistic man,
Fichtean egoists, Jacobi's 'beautiful souls,' the sentimentalists
and the ironists, all are perfectly representative men, the best
that this world can have. For it is not a failure to obey the
state and its laws that really defines the hypocrite. 'True conscience' may well be perfectly law-abiding, but it can be just
as hypocritical as the disobedient conscience. Self-righteous
obedience is not necessarily political obligation, and it can be
just as passively self-righteous and self-exhibiting as its disobedient twin. Perhaps that is why Hegel eventually relegated
even 'true' conscience to the sphere of 'civil society' where indeed it can flourish freely though surely not without ample
scope for hypocrisy.[63]

In later years Hegel became far more concerned with hypocritical defiance of custom and law, with those who misused
conscience as a license for self-assertion against society. In the
Phenomenology he was, however, concerned with the more
profound difficulties of moralism, with its strangling inability
to act, which had made hypocrisy a social norm, rather than
an exception. However, even in his later years when he did
become preoccupied with the tension between public duty
and private conscience, Hegel knew that the flight inward
could well be the last resort of men who were superior to
their society.[64] That had clearly been the case of the Stoics

62. *Philosophy of Right,* 103 (s. 140). The polis of course was not a state at
all, just a 'people.' B731–2; H506–7.
63. *Philosophy of Right,* 87–91, 103–4, 133, 233–4 (ss. 132, 137, 141, 207, and
additions to ss. 133–7).   64. *Ibid.,* 92 (s. 138).

amidst the horrors of the Roman Empire. The tension between such individuals and the political order is not always
trivial, as it clearly was not when Socrates confronted his
judges. As the conscience of a free people, that tribunal was
the 'privileged conscience' to which even Socrates had to
yield. That also would have to be the case if the court were
the voice of 'a true State.' However, even if one accepts the
individual's claim to be the weaker one, as Socrates did, one
can do so for deeply individual reasons and with no cost to
conscience or 'daemon.' [65] As for hopelessly degenerate governments like that of the *ancien régime,* they posed no moral
questions for Hegel at all, only political ones. The great and
enduring difficulties of conscience do not, in any case, arise
out of those occasional conflicts between private duty and
public authority. It is the dynamics of inwardness that are
inherently self-destructive. Certainly, Hegel never argued
that the freedom of man as man could mean anything else
than choosing and being responsible for one's actions. That
means turning inward. The real problem is how conscience
is to be 'condensed out again.' [66] For if that does not occur
one is doomed to passivity and to the culture of hypocrisy.
That is the very epitome of the tension that began when independent man emerged from the struggle between the contemplative master and his toiling servant. It is the major
political theme of the *Phenomenology.*

How then is conscience to be 'condensed out again'? Can
the knowledge that the 'world spirit,' or history, is 'the master
and lord' of all reconcile conscience to action? [67] It does not
do so directly. Obviously, one cannot know here and now
what can only be retrospectively recreated. The future is just
another 'beyond' and the judgment of world history cannot
make our decisions for us in the present. It can however act
upon us indirectly. It teaches conscience that its certainty is
merely incomplete knowledge because it is personal and immediate, not general and comprehensive. Retrospection is
both all-inclusive and impersonal. It can therefore teach conscience moderation and resignation. Before it heaps guilt and
shame upon every action conscience must be reminded of its

65. *Lectures on the History of Philosophy,* III, 442–3.
66. *Philosophy of Right,* 255 (addition to s. 138).   67. B675; H469–70.

own limitations and of the inherent imperfection of every individual judgment. When conscience has been taught to resign itself, the will to act is liberated from the chains imposed upon it by moral perfectionism. Conscience in short is
forced to accept the demands of action, by learning to live
with error. Heroism is the ability to act in spite of human
fallibility.

Usually when Hegel spoke of heroes he had those 'world
historical' great men in mind, Alexander, Caesar, and, for a
time at least, Napoleon. To this list one must add Socrates,
the only one whose life and influence he chose to consider
seriously. These were the men who acted, whatever their
motives, to do the work of the historical moment. They were
the great revolutionaries, the waves of the future, the voice of
their age. They were more; all significantly expanded human
consciousness by tearing individuals and whole peoples out
of their immediate locality and habits and moving them
toward extended states of consciousness and so toward a universal spirit.[68] In the *Phenomenology,* however, Hegel is not
talking only of the world historical hero, but of the heroic
aspects of the human ego generally. Conscience, however, can
come to appreciate the heroism of performing imperfect
duties and with it to an acceptance of actuality only after the
final duel for recognition has been fought. It is the last river
that must be crossed, before self-consciousness can reach a
knowledge that is more than the certainties of a moralistic
culture or, indeed, of any merely partial world.

The last duel: hero and valet

When the self-declaiming conscience has finally reduced duty
to merely a matter of words, only two choices remain. Either
one admits that one's actions are egotistic and stops canting
or one limits oneself to critical examination of the motives of
those who act in an effort to remain, or at least to appear,
pure, even though passive. The man who acts knows that he
behaves selfishly, confesses his fault and says 'I am so,' as indeed he must, for we are all 'so.' In confessing his misdeeds

68. *Philosophy of Right,* 218 (s. 348); *Vernunft in der Geschichte,* 89–90, 96–
    105, 170–1.

he asks for forgiveness and reaffirms the validity of the universal law. The hypocrite, however, will resist this appeal. He refuses to admit that he has erred. By doing nothing he claims to have evaded the dangers of moral failure. He is, therefore, free to judge the motives of others, and he finds them to be low. Whatever is done is 'really nothing' but avarice, ambition or lust. Nothing can pass through the eye of his needle. Knowing his own penchant for rationalizing his conduct he clearly finds that attack is the best defense. If duty for duty's sake keeps him from doing anything at all, he can still preserve the moralistic stance by scrutinizing the deeds of others. By carefully analyzing the motives of those who act the hypocrite can easily find some selfishness lying at the root of their works.[69] This moralistic reductionism is not only mean-spirited, it is also paralyzing. Its final success would bring a reign of pure verbiage upon us all.

The man of action who is confronted by this nagging moralism defends himself by confessing. He admits that all actions involve some evil and the responsibility for evil. He expects the judging consciousness to admit its own limitations in turn. For the frankly evil man, in confessing, recognizes that there is a language that can reconcile conscience and action. It is the language of shared responsibility, not that of personal conviction or of self-cultivation. The 'beautiful soul,' however, in its hardness rejects the offer. It does not recognize that it has any fault to confess, that it is anything less than perfect in its self-absorbed passivity. It refuses to recognize the baseness of a stance that criticizes others without ever daring to act. The language of inner purity saves the hypocrite from such risks, and he rejects the invitation of the man of action who speaks of his deeds in terms of public values and social necessities. The hypocrite refuses to join the common fate and the shared language of mankind. He thinks that with this refusal he can somehow escape from the world of history and the demands of public communication. The evil man is left to cope with these and must in addition bear the moralistic censure of the hardhearted hypocrite. The latter chooses to remain above politics, above necessity, above action, above everything, in fact,

69. B671–3; H466–7.

except his perfect, private inner motives. Since no action can ever escape his judgment, this base valet knows that there are no heroes. That is because he is a valet, however, and mean, not because there really are no heroes. The man of action who confesses his faults, who says 'I am so' and dares to act, may very well be a hero. He knows that history demands this of men. It is the moral valet who does not understand that the judgment of history, that 'master and lord of every deed and over all reality,' does not judge according to moralistic rules. It does not search out motives, but actions.[70] A man is his deeds, especially looked at retrospectively.

The hero, however, is not denying the claims of conscience altogether. When he 'confesses' he is asking for reconciliation. In rejecting the fraternal hand the judging valet demonstrates the harshness and the narrowness of conscience as a form of punitive justice. His is also a most abject form of servitude. For the moralistic judge is not only a social type, he is also a manifestation of the ego. We all carry a magistrate within us. He is the passive ego in its most developed form, just as the hero is the erotic ego at its height. That is why the moralistic man whose inclinations are forever being crushed by his sense of duty 'carries his lord in himself, yet at the same time he is his own slave.' One half of him is continually judging and punishing the other and Kant's account of a bad conscience is, in its ways, just as terrible as the wrath of the Lord.[71] Unable to be at one with himself, the man of conscience is quite incapable of embracing the man who embodies all those active impulses which he denies and punishes in himself. He may in fact not even quite understand the meaning of the hero's confession. It is not a demand for justice or even for pardon. When the hero confesses, 'I am so,' he admits that his acts had been evil and by that very act submits again to the rules he had rejected. This is neither humility nor self-abasement, but a return to the communal rules. Knowing that he excommunicated himself by his acts of wrongful self-assertion he is now ready to return to human fellowship. His confession is an act of self-purification, which

70. B673–6; H467–70; *Philosophy of Right*, 84 (s. 124).
71. E.g., *Metaphysical Principles of Virtue*, 100–3; *Critique of Practical Reason*, 204.

should put his conscience to rest and signal his fitness for the world of mutual rights and obligations.[72] The past is wiped out.

Hegel was very far from proposing Christian forgiveness of sins as a remedy for the self-destructive extremity evoked by the rigors of Jewish and Kantian legalism. The stiff-necked valet who personifies the flaws of that sort of justice with all his harsh externality is not asked to love and there is no suggestion here that justice according to law is dispensable. On the contrary, justice, the rights and duties of the world, must be preserved even though we must go beyond it. The only aspect of the Christian attenuation of justice that Hegel admired was the possibility of purging oneself of guilt by acts of confession. To be sure, the hero confesses not to a deity, but to other men, and without any loss of human dignity. The meaning of the confession is similar: the sinner is reconciled to the good, but it is now a human, not a divine goodness. Above all, he is at one with himself. A personal inner rejection of our immoral acts can return us to an easy conscience. Confession is the outward sign of that inner conversion. It means that we have purged ourselves and are now back at our original position, at one with ourselves and with the demands of morality. We need not be forever haunted by the judge within us, or doomed to the eternal inner torments of insatiable remorse. For a conscience that reduces us to a sense of perpetual moral failure, unless we be ascetic supermen, can only paralyze, it cannot educate. Hegel was not Nietzsche, to be sure, and he was not summoning us to a realm beyond good and evil, but he did recognize the psychological possibility of being neither amoral nor guilt ridden.

Only when the judging consciousness recognizes its own partiality, its one-sidedness in the face of the collective life of mankind, is its hard heart broken. It also confesses, recognizes that action is not simply bad, and ceases to judge men in terms of private motives. It learns to see them as part of a public whole. With that reciprocal recognition becomes possible. The hypocrite sees that in his self-centeredness he was just like the evil man and the two are now reconciled.[73] This is not just mutual forgiveness. It is the fraternity of those who

72. B673–7; H468–71.   73. B676–9; H470–2.

know that because they are men, nothing human is alien to them. The reconciliation of conscience and action, or of the self and the world is not an act of love. Genuine fraternity is less fragile and less 'figurative' than any religious ideal. It does not wait for a beyond. It is realized as a necessity of the intellect in its life here and now.[74] It is when men fully understand that they are parts of a shared history that they come to see that the subjective 'I' is an incomplete self. In recognizing each other the man who acts and the man who judges really discover their identity as men. They recognize their common character. In 'the spiritual daylight' of the present the 'I' discovers that it is half of a 'we.' Each 'I' is a necessary part of the whole development that has brought both to this point, but now it is a genuinely new self that really knows its own history and structure.[75]

This reconciliation of the moralistic valet and the active hero is really the victory of the latter. It is the intellectual triumph of action over passivity. As such it is clearly a recurrence of that earlier combat between the contemplative master and his productive servant.[76] Now, however, the hero-master is active while the valet-servant is passive. This reversal of roles is not entirely insignificant. For the slave never succeeded in liberating himself. He forced his master to recognize their common humanity. However, the Stoicism that they shared did not affirm the primacy of productive action but the contemplative values of the master. It is a mere flight from actuality. The 'yes' that the hero wrings from the valet is a far more decisive and complete victory for the principles of work and action. The merely judging consciousness of the valet is eliminated. In making his 'confession' the hero only gives up his evil self-centeredness, but not action or the passions which inspire it. The valet gives up reflective morality, which is all that he brought to this struggle for recognition.

In the confrontation between master and slave Hegel challenged one of the most fundamental assumptions of classical thought: the superiority of theoretical over practical reason, and above all, of thought over work. In the second round, between hero and valet, he struck even more deeply, by asserting the superiority of passion over reason. For as he was

74. B793–5; H552–4.   75. B226–31; H140–3.   76. B234–46; H146–54.

to note later, 'nothing great has been and nothing great can be accomplished without passions.' Since 'impulse and passion are the very life-blood of all action,' only the dead and hypocritical inveigh against passion as such.[77] Indeed, since men are the totality of their acts and must be judged accordingly, 'The true being of a man is . . . his act, individuality is real in the deed.' It is not to be found, as both moral and descriptive psychologists claim, in something behind or underneath human action.[78] The worth of acts, above all, does not rest on the unknown and unknowable states of mind that may inspire them. All that can be safely said is that without passions, impulses and personal interests no deeds, great or small, would ever occur at all. 'The true intrinsic worth' of these feelings depends on whether the actions to which they give rise conform to the ethical demands of society, above all to prevailing law.[79] In short, what matters is the contribution that the passions make to social life, and to Hegel it seemed evident it was greater than that of reflective reason. It was thus specifically against Socrates and Kant that he argued when he claimed that '[a] passion, as for example, love, ambition, is the universal itself, as it is self-realizing not in perception, but in activity . . . [For] the individual the universal is his own interest.' [80] This is Hegel at his most radical. Not just subjectivity, rational or irrational, and not only the primacy of moral reason are at stake. The very structure of the individual psyche is here forced off the center of the philosophical stage, to be replaced by social rationality. It is the social function of passion and action that raise them above individual reason. Whatever the place of reflective reason may be in the individual soul, it does not inspire action. Moreover its divisiveness and its isolating force, as much as its passivity, render private reason socially irrational.

77. *Philosophy of Mind,* ss. 474–5. To be sure, Hume had already reduced reason to being the servant of passion, but it was not Hegel's or Kant's reason.

78. B349–50; H236–7; *Philosophy of Right,* 83–4 (s. 124). 'What the subject is, is the series of his actions.' The psychologists who forget that are all valets of the lowest kind.

79. *Philosophy of Right,* 161–2 (s. 261). 'In whatever way an individual may fulfill his duty, he must at the same time find his account therein and attain his personal interest and satisfaction.'

80. *Lectures on the History of Philosophy,* I, 413.

Fraternity does not flourish among ratiocinating men. Indeed, it is reason both moral and analytical that inspires the malicious habit of looking for the flawed motives of actions. It keeps us from our fellow men, whom we passively observe and judge. Reasoning paralyzes and dissociates men. That is the lesson of Socrates' life and of Kantian moralism. Shaking as this harsh rejection of traditional philosophic attitudes may seem, it comes as no surprise to 'us.' For Hegel had told 'us' at the outset that he did not think of philosophy as his great predecessors had conceived it. The task of philosophy was no longer one of calm contemplation, nor was it a wholly individual effort. Not only is truth a 'bacchanalian revel where not a member is sober.' [81] Philosophy cannot find its ends in the serenity of pure mathematics, syllogistic logic or the stars above us. Its real model is that other celebration of Bacchus, the tragic drama in all its turbulence. We have now come to its end.

The reconciliation between the hero and the valet is the last, the final act of the drama of the human spirit. Conscience has done its work by tearing the individual out of his time and place and made him see himself as a member of the universal order of humanity. It is, however, a passive consciousness. This is the inactive, the merely consuming, ratiocinating half of the ego. The hero's consciousness is the active erotic half. In confessing it declares its will toward unity and mutual recognition with not only the valet, but with the other part of the human ego. When the latter finally utters its 'yes' the ego is at last at one. That unity is the self-knowledge of the ego. It knows that the tension between conscience and action is permanent, that to be human is to be part of a universal whole, of mankind, but also to be individual and particular. The division and resolution of its two sides is the process of spiritual development, the unending creativity of thought as perpetual learning. To know that is to know the limits as well as the character of knowledge. It is knowing what knowing is. The self that is conscious of its own morphogenesis knows its place, has come face to face with itself as a particle of humanity. When valet and hero join in mutual tolerance they recognize their shared human-

81. B105; H39.

ity and they know that god, as the holy spirit that is their own, is in their midst.[82]

The *Phenomenology* might well have ended here. However, Hegel felt compelled to review everything he had already said about religion by treating it as the final cycle of consciousness. The main purpose of this exercise was to remind Christians, again and again, that God is dead.[83] Philosophy can now dispense with the figurative, pictorial thought of revealed religion, that treats God as something out there to be reached. In keeping with Lessing's theology Hegel again recalled that God-as-man was dead and was to be replaced by the holy spirit. That spirit is the creation of mankind's collective self-consciousness as it develops in time. In the presence of a dead culture and a collapsed faith we are ready for absolute knowledge. For we know that religion and culture are both the creations of the human spirit.[84] This knowledge is the work of retrospection. It comes at the end, when philosophy can look back upon its own completed course. It does so without any sense of triumph. History as the work of men may in some indefinite future realize the unity of humanity. For knowledge that is not a primary concern. Its business is the unity of knowledge attained by gathering the whole together in thought. That is the Golgotha of the human spirit.[85] We who have thought it all through must be consoled by the fellowship of so many great men who have preceded us and whose work we have made our own.

The cycle of religion is necessary to bring the *Phenomenology* to a close and to illuminate that spiritual pinnacle which philosophy alone now occupies. It does not, however, bring the book to a perfect completion. The closing lines of the *Phenomenology* may be moving and effective, but they should not be the last ones we read. Hegel had suggested at the outset that one ought to return to the 'Preface' after one has gone through his entire argument. It is only now that the beginning is really intelligible and, in keeping with Hegel's design, serves also as a fitting end. The circle is closed and the purpose of the whole is now evident. The process of intellec-

82. B677–9; H471–2.   83. B778–84; H543–8.   84. B796–7; H555–6.
85. B808; H564.

tual self-creation, the movement of the ego back and forth
from particularity to generality as it goes from one stage of
development to the next, is now part of the reader's own intellectual life. 'We' have come to know philosophy as the
education of mankind and so our own. Nevertheless, even if
the 'Preface' is read as a summing-up, the *Phenomenology*
comes to an end by fits and starts and a commentary on it,
such as this one, is doomed to a similar coda.

Indeed, the political argument of the *Phenomenology* ends
with the death-rattle of the *ancien régime,* the last completed,
fully known culture. The symmetry of Hegel's exposition
would have demanded that no more be said about the spirit
of peoples. The moralistic point of view is not the spirit of
any cultural whole. It reaches beyond that. That may be a
characteristic or perhaps even an aggravation of a world in
which there is no discernible public culture. Hegel had in
fact claimed that Germany was suffering from just such a
fatal condition. It had not even reached the political level
of Richelieu's monarchical state, with a central executive and
military organization. In Germany the individual tended to
be completely separated from his kind.[86] Moralism was not
likely to improve that situation. However, even though Hegel
had already put down his thoughts on the political immaturity of his countrymen, he did not mention the subject in
the *Phenomenology.* Moralism is not discussed within any
context at all. It is simply tacked on, as if it were the dominant mood of post-Revolutionary Europe. Nevertheless, the
paralysis of the moralistic man is treated not as a general state
of mind but as an idiosyncrasy. For we are assured that if he
were to give up his opposition to those laws and conventions
that are valid apart from the convictions and interests of the
individual, he would not find action so difficult.[87] We hear
nothing, however, of the culture of which these would have
to be a part. Europe settles down after the Revolution, but
in what way? Certainly Hegel was not suggesting the possibility of a return to the *ancien régime* or presenting it as any
sort of model for emulation. In fact, tacitly the absence of a
public order is accepted. Hero and valet are united in mutual
toleration as members of humanity. They are not joined by

86. 'The German Constitution,' *Hegel's Political Writings,* 215–23, 242.
87. B656; H455.

any common public purpose, enterprise or system. In dissecting moralistic man Hegel was able to have his say about Kant's and Fichte's moral theories, but he did so at some cost to the style and coherence of his masterpiece.

It was not until he came to write his *Philosophy of Right* that Hegel was able to make the call for the acceptance of the rules actually prevailing in society more than a hollow and false challenge. By then he had decided that political philosophy was possible even in the world of independent men. That juristic state (*Rechtsstaat*) could be thought of as a whole in the sense that Aristotle had considered the polis as a unity. Its various parts could then be made intelligible in terms of this cultural universe.[88] That meant not only a muting of the stark contrast between freedom and independence, but also a new, positive appreciation of the social function of legality. It also forced Hegel to give the activity of willing a constructive task within the state. It is no longer merely the self-assertion that Hegel had imputed to the revolutionaries at their anarchic worst. The law is now seen as an integrative institution and it expresses the will of independent men who are socialized in such a way that their pursuit of private ends reinforces their personal and collective adherence to public values.

The last pages of the *Philosophy of Right* tell us that the republican ethos of Rome fell victim to class war and that its isolated inhabitants were then held together only by abstract right. Civil law united them at least partially.[89] That is not the story told in the *Phenomenology*. There civil law is the agency of disintegration and only despotism keeps these egotistical proprietors together. Theirs is such a state of distraction that only scepticism can express their spiritual woes. To be sure, the legal system of modern states is more than just 'abstract' right, that is, civil or property law. That is only a partial aspect of the legal system considered as a comprehensive whole. Nevertheless, civil law does transform natural individuals from mere possessors into proprietors with guaranteed rights. They become legal persons.[90] That is no longer a term of contempt as it was in the *Phenomenology* but a

---

88. *Philosophy of Right*, 10–15, 34–5 ('Preface,' ss. 1–2, 31–2); *The Logic of Hegel*, s. 198.   89. *Philosophy of Right*, 221–2 (s. 357).
90. *Ibid.*, 37–40 (ss. 34–40).

proud title which expresses the culture of right, a public consciousness and a stage in the development of mankind. Right as a legal system is the spirit of a people at a given time and place. It is a stage in the historical development of mankind.[91] As such the legal system does not only attribute the right to own things, but also sets a pattern within which individuals may satisfy their intellectual, economic and moral ends. There are even occasions for genuinely ethical activity here. The legal systems of modern states, in short, fulfill at least some of the functions of the polis. The matter was not, as Hegel had already noted in the *Phenomenology*, a state.[92] It did not have to socialize post-Christian individualists. The juristic state does achieve that. It does so by serving a cognitive function, for it designates the spheres of socially acceptable action for each person. The law issues warrants which inform individuals of the permissible forms of social conduct. If an individual chooses to engage in any of these justified kinds of social activity he may do so.[93] It is the law, after all, that permits the use of a knife to the surgeon, but not to assassins. No one has to become a physician, but if he has a license to practice, he may use a scalpel. This issuing of licenses, for marriage no less than for economic and other social activities, is the guidance which develops modern ethical men.

This education is addressed to the ego-as-willing. In the *Phenomenology* men are socialized by work and speech. In speaking the language of his culture a man becomes intelligible to himself in the very act of making himself known to others. He re-internalizes this new 'objective,' socially restructured self and becomes a self-conscious member of a group. Ethical men speak the language of the law.[94] Independent men can do that only if they recognize that the law expresses their will. Hegel therefore now had to show that the ego-as-will also follows the path of the speaking and working ego, and that the norms of society are just as integral to it as is pure duty. Hegel upbraided Rousseau for having seen nothing but a sum of capricious private wills in the general will, but he grudgingly admitted now that Rousseau had

91. *Ibid.*, 15–16, 33–4 (ss. 3, 30).   92. B730–3; H506–7.
93. *Philosophy of Right*, 38 (s. 38).   94. B660–1; H458–9.

been right in basing the state on acts of will.[95] In the *Philosophy of Right,* the ego-as-willing is the source and the product alike of the legal system. It begins as self-expression of personal demands, but public exposure transforms it and the re-defined will is internalized as a new will, conditioned by its public experiences. This instructed will now seeks to actualize its purposes in keeping with the demands of the rules, and thereby it re-enforces these and indeed participates in their renewal and preservation. A socially educated will is a will created by law, but it is also law-creating. The will thus acquires a cultural juristic dimension, as does the ego generally. And this historical, public-, 'right'-oriented will is as much a part of the ego as is the moral will. Both are inherent in the ego-as-willing. In presenting the ego-as-willing, rather than as speaking and producing, Hegel was, of course, addressing the independent consciousness. The latter defines itself in terms of will and can accept a place within the juristic order only if it recognizes itself there. Then law ceases to be a limiting obstacle to it. The law is known now, even by moral man, as a self-imposed system of volitions. Now he also can act.[96]

The law as a system of licenses and as an expression of the individual's socialized will is liberating, for it permits the individual to act, to be effective in pursuit of his own purposes. He is transformed by recognizing the ethical realm, that is, all those actions that are both legal, desirable and good, and in keeping with his now undivided ego-as-will. Rousseau had, of course, said as much when he wrote that the social contract changes a 'narrow stupid animal' into a man.[97] Hegel refused to honor his debt to Rousseau, but that should not blind us to the fact that Rousseau's contract was not an agreement involving the exchange of objects but also a spiritual rebirth. Hegel did not stop there since this world of socialized individuals was, for him, only an historical moment. For the present, however, the system of rules allows men, who cannot overcome their independence, to will a polity.

95. In fact, Hegel knew perfectly well that Rousseau had not identified the general will with the will of all. *The Logic of Hegel,* s. 163. However, in the *Philosophy of Right* he chose to see nothing but anarchism in Rousseau. *Ibid.,* 33, 156–7 (ss. 29, 258).

96. *Ibid.,* 20–33 (ss. 4–29).   97. *Social Contract,* I, 8.

Independence is preserved, but the juristic state is sufficiently unifying to be a subject of philosophic thought, a self-contained whole.

Within that state there are even spheres of genuine freedom, of membership in ethical groups. There is the primary family, and that second family, the corporation made up of members of the same trade or profession. Here independence is partially transcended.[98] The public servants who provide for the education of the young and the welfare of the indigent can be said to exercise what amounts to moral citizenship, a new ethos.[99] The law thus creates opportunities for more than mere proprietory rights. It even arranges ethically viable forms of group life, enlarged families. That is not the freedom of real citizenship to be sure, and no reader of the *Phenomenology* will be convinced that the distance between independence and freedom has been reduced, simply because one can attribute an occasional civic experience to the members of a market society.

Until Hegel had worked out this scheme of juristic society as the integrative political order of independent men, he was in no position to sneer at the inactivity of moral men. He had no grounds for summoning them to their social duties. As long as freedom 'has been' and is not even to be thought of as 'not yet,' there was no room for anything but a choice between types of egotism. Later Hegel was to ask us simply to forget the lost world and to accept the rules such as they are. The *Phenomenology* was, however, his elegy to that world of freedom. It is the remembrance of the steps which led mankind away from experienced happiness to a vision of truth, from freedom as ethics to freedom as the knowledge of necessity. These two freedoms have nothing in common. The freedom of knowledge is not any sort of happiness and Hegel did not claim that it was. He abruptly invoked the memory of Golgotha to remind us what the end of the quest for self-knowledge implied. The *Phenomenology* ends when philosophy reaches its goal which lies beyond law, morality and religion.

98. *Philosophy of Right*, 110–19, 152–4 (ss. 158–77, 250–6).
99. *Ibid.*, 132–4, 148–50 (ss. 205–8, 239–43).

INDEX

Cambridge Studies in the History and Theory of Politics

TEXTS

LIBERTY, EQUALITY, FRATERNITY, by James Fitzjames Stephen. Edited with an introduction and notes by R. J. White

VLADIMIR AKIMOV ON THE DILEMMAS OF RUSSIAN MARXISM 1895–1903. An English edition of 'A Short History of the Social Democratic Movement in Russia' and 'The Second Congress of the Russian Social Democratic Labour Party', with an introduction and notes by Jonathan Frankel

TWO ENGLISH REPUBLICAN TRACTS: PLATO REDIVIVUS OR, A DIALOGUE CONCERNING GOVERNMENT (C. 1681), by Henry Neville, and AN ESSAY UPON THE CONSTITUTION OF THE ROMAN GOVERNMENT (C. 1699), by Walter Moyle. Edited by Caroline Robbins

J. G. HERDER ON SOCIAL AND POLITICAL CULTURE. Translated, edited and with an introduction by F. M. Barnard

THE LIMITS OF STATE ACTION, by Wilhelm von Humboldt. Edited with an introduction and notes by J .W. Burrow

KANT'S POLITICAL WRITINGS. Edited with an introduction and notes by Hans Reiss; translated by H. B. Nisbet

KARL MARX'S CRITIQUE OF HEGEL'S 'PHILOSOPHY OF RIGHT'. Edited with an introduction and notes by Joseph O'Malley; translated by Annette Jolin and Joseph O'Malley

LORD SALISBURY ON POLITICS. A SELECTION FROM HIS ARTICLES IN 'THE QUARTERLY REVIEW' 1860–1883. Edited by Paul Smith

FRANCOGALLIA, by François Hotman. Latin text edited by Ralph E. Giesey, English translation by J. H. M. Salmon

THE POLITICAL WRITINGS OF LEIBNIZ. Edited and translated by Patrick Riley

TURGOT ON PROGRESS, SOCIOLOGY AND ECONOMICS: A PHILOSOPHICAL REVIEW OF THE SUCCESSIVE ADVANCES OF THE HUMAN MIND ON UNIVERSAL HISTORY. REFLECTIONS ON THE FORMATION AND DISTRIBUTION OF WEALTH. Edited, translated and introduced by Ronald L. Meek

TEXTS CONCERNING THE REVOLT OF THE NETHERLANDS. Edited with an introduction by E. H. Kossman and A. F. Mellink

REGICIDE AND REVOLUTION: SPEECHES AT THE TRIAL OF LOUIS XVI. Edited with an introduction by Michael Walzer; translated by Marian Rothstein

GEORG WILHELM FRIEDRICH HEGEL: LECTURES ON THE PHILOSOPHY OF WORLD HISTORY: REASON IN HISTORY. Translated from the German edition of Johannes Hoffmeister by H. B. Nisbet and with an introduction by Duncan Forbes

A MACHIAVELLIAN TREATISE, by Stephen Gardiner. Edited and translated by Peter S. Donaldson

STUDIES

1867: DISRAELI, GLADSTONE AND REVOLUTION: THE PASSING OF THE SECOND REFORM BILL, by Maurice Cowling

THE CONSCIENCE OF THE STATE IN NORTH AMERICA, by E. R. Norman

THE SOCIAL AND POLITICAL THOUGHT OF KARL MARX, by Shlomo Avineri

MEN AND CITIZENS: A STUDY OF ROUSSEAU'S SOCIAL THEORY, by Judith Shklar

IDEALISM, POLITICS AND HISTORY: SOURCES OF HEGELIAN THOUGHT, by George Armstrong Kelly

THE IMPACT OF LABOUR 1920–1924: THE BEGINNING OF MODERN BRITISH POLITICS, by Maurice Cowling

ALIENATION: MARX'S CONCEPTION OF MAN IN CAPITALIST SOCIETY, by Bertell Ollman

THE POLITICS OF REFORM 1884, by Andrew Jones

HEGEL'S THEORY OF THE MODERN STATE, by Shlomo Avineri

JEAN BODIN AND THE RISE OF ABSOLUTIST THEORY, by Julian H. Franklin

THE SOCIAL PROBLEM IN THE PHILOSOPHY OF ROUSSEAU, by John Charvet

THE IMPACT OF HITLER: BRITISH POLITICS AND BRITISH POLICY 1933–1940, by Maurice Cowling